The Road to Gdansk

The Road to Gdansk
Poland and the USSR

Daniel Singer

Monthly Review Press
New York and London

Cop A

Library of Congress Cataloging in Publication Data
Singer, Daniel, 1926–
   The road to Gdansk.
   1. Government, Resistance to.   2. Russia—
Politics and government—1953–   3. Labor and
laboring classes—Poland—Political activity.
4. Dissenters.   5. Solzhenitsyn, Aleksandr
Isaevich, 1918–   I. Title.
JC328.3.S47   323.6'5'0947   80-39914
ISBN 0-85345-567-8
ISBN 0-85345-568-6 (pbk)

Monthly Review Press
62 West 14th Street, New York, N.Y. 10011
47 Red Lion Street, London WC1R 4PF

Manufactured in the United States of America

10 9 8 7 6 5 4 3 2 1

To my mother and my father

Contents

A Note from the Editors

Thirty days before the Gdansk shipyard strike erupted, we received the manuscript of Daniel Singer's book on the dissident movement in Poland and the USSR. While we were editing the manuscript, the author, whose home base is Paris, traveled to Poland and spent more than two weeks interviewing many of the principal figures in the great strike wave that followed Gdansk. This book contains his analysis of the situation leading up to the Polish crisis, and a first-hand report from the scene.

Introduction

Stalin Is Dead

> *"The unbelievers were delighted, and as for believers, there were some among them who were even more delighted than the unbelievers themselves. . . .*
>
> *What happened was that an odor of corruption began to come from the coffin, growing more and more perceptible. . . ."*
> —Dostoyevsky, The Brothers Karamazov

Readers may recall the shocked grief and revulsion of Alyosha Karamazov as he discovered that the corpse of his saintly master, Father Zossima, was stinking. The collective reaction after Stalin's death was both less sudden and more traumatic. Nearly three years elapsed after the funeral before the believers were told by Khrushchev, the official keeper of the shrine, that their demigod had not been as holy as he had been painted. But once the coffin lid was lifted, the odor began to spread. In the following quarter of a century it was to affect party members and fellow travelers, sympathizers and mere onlookers. It was to change the moral climate of politics. The shock may prove salutary in the long run, even if it has not so far. Indeed, not unsuccessful efforts have been made to present the stench of decaying Stalinism as the natural smell of socialism and in this way to discredit Marxism, revolution, or the very idea of resistance to the established order.

Macaulay once claimed that there is no spectacle more ridiculous than the British public in one of its periodic fits of morality. He obviously had not seen successive generations of leftists

cursing their former gods and damning what they had worship-
ped. Let me hasten to add that learning from past mistakes is a
virtue, passion against parties or doctrines that led one astray is
perfectly natural, and heretics are the salt of the earth. But
periodic bouts of recantation are something quite different.
Moral indignation turns into moralizing, converts give the impression of changing bandwagons rather than ideas, and people
who rebelled against a gruesome and treacherous orthodoxy in
the name of socialist principles trample those very principles to
the applause of their new sponsors.

Leaving aside these stage performers making capital out of
their conversions, genuine motives for disenchantment have not
been missing in the last twenty-five years. The illusions which
survived the Soviet invasion of Hungary were shattered when
Soviet tanks entered Prague. Hopes raised by China's Cultural
Revolution crashed with the fall of the "Gang of Four." The
atrocities of Kampuchea's Pol Pot regime, the invasion of Kampuchea by the Vietnamese, and of Vietnam by the Chinese—all
this has been too much for a single generation to swallow. And
yet it is not enough to explain the current political disarray.
After all, previous generations have been submitted to no lesser
shocks: the mass purges of the 1930s, the Nazi-Soviet Pact, the
postwar repetition throughout eastern Europe of the Moscow
trials should have strained the allegiance of the most faithful.
The basic difference is that in the meantime millions have ceased
to view the Soviet Union as a socialist model.

The discarding of mythical models and the recognition, however belated, of crimes committed in the name of socialism are
indispensable steps on the road to recovery. They should be
followed by an open and unflinching debate over the causes of
the disease and possible remedies. Despite the publicity surrounding spectacular about-faces, however, it cannot be said
that critical analysis has gone very far. The keepers of Soviet
orthodoxy and their followers, naturally enough, have refused
to see the crisis of their model. Disappointment has come from
sections of the new generation of alleged rebels. In retrospect, it
is possible to see that in chanting "Marx, Engels, Lenin, Stalin,
Mao, and Lin Piao," they were as empty and dogmatic as later,

when merely reversing the slogan, they put the blame for the gulag on Marx. These rebels were irrational in both their enthusiasm and their indignation.

By now the reader will have guessed that this book is far from trendy. Its author having hailed the French student and worker rising of 1968 as a possible portent of Marx's return to his home ground, that of advanced capitalism, does not change sides because events are moving more slowly than he would have hoped. He feels no need to bury Marx, to apologize for his convictions, or to wear a cross, any cross whatsoever. And, having twelve years ago treated Paris and Prague as part of the same struggle, he still wonders how this struggle can be resumed and linked together, despite the seemingly stiffer odds. But to think of potential action, of ends and means, of real situations, one has to give up introspection or abstract preaching for the unfashionable realm of concrete history.

The three essays herein thus not only reflect a common state of mind but express a common purpose. Stalin is dead. Whether one dates the beginning of his reign in the middle or the late 1920s, the Soviet Union has now lived longer under his successors than under Stalin himself. To explain the tragedy by the wickedness of one man, never tenable, is by now plainly absurd. On the other hand, the system linked with the man's name, shaken and apparently threatened for a decade after his death, has somehow survived. This Brezhnevian restoration raises the questions which are at the heart of this book. How solid and permanent is this new stability? What contradictions are hidden behind the apparently stable surface? When will they reach breaking point and who is likely to exploit them?

To stress the importance of the answers is to labor the obvious. The future of the other nuclear giant, dominating half of Europe and looking beyond, interests everybody. For a socialist, however, the problem has two additional dimensions. One is the reluctance to accept that the changes embodied in the October Revolution ultimately lead to a dead end. The second is more practical. To be able to present the Soviet bloc as a mighty monolith, threatening and immutable, should help our ruling classes at home. The capitalist establishments, too, are not as triumphantly safe as they look. Barely out of the sixties, with their unrest of the young generation, they were thrown at once into an economic crisis, still unfinished but having already destroyed the postwar image of modern capitalism as a guarantee for growth. True, the system has confirmed in the process its capacity for survival. Nevertheless, a Soviet bogey helps it to silence the opposition as Solzhenitsyn's message—revolution leads to the concentration camp—earlier helped to demoralize the generation of young rebels.

In the West the return of the classical capitalist crisis compels the establishment to refurbish its obsolete ideological wares of the postwar period. In eastern Europe a different kind of economic crisis puts no lesser strain on the Soviet establishment. My ambition here is not to find a definition for the Soviet system, to determine whether it is "state capitalist," or a "bureaucratically degenerated workers' state," or what-not.[1] It is to suggest that if in the first quarter-century after Stalin's death the Soviet economy was sacrificed to preserve the old political order, in the second quarter-century the political structure is likely to burst asunder under economic and social pressure. It is to show that Marx's celebrated mole has kept on digging eastward, too, that contradictions, far from vanishing, have gathered momentum, and that a socialist opposition could seize the resulting opportunities.

In addition to mood and purpose, the three essays are linked by a common focus: internal and external pressure for change. The protagonist of the first was inevitable. Even if one thinks, as I do, that Solzhenitsyn's success is due more to the collapse of the Soviet myth than the other way round, the impact of his writings in the western world is undeniable. And Solzhenitsyn is not only the moving witness and the false prophet, he is also a pure product of the Soviet regime and an illustration of what happens when the road forward is blocked. Solzhenitsyn's message looks ostentatiously to the past, his chosen constituency, the peasantry, is shrinking, yet the fact that he nevertheless finds an echo in the country strong enough to frighten the leadership is a measure of the damage wrought by Stalinism and an indication of the ideological desert into which Stalin's heirs are preaching.

Indeed, this lesson can be extended well beyond the frontiers of the Soviet Union.

Since whatever its immediate attraction, the "messianism of backwardness" cannot prevail in the Soviet Union for long, the second essay analyzes the pressure for change that has accumulated within Soviet society. Since 1968 there can be no doubt that the Soviet Union itself will be the location of the main battlefield in the Soviet bloc. The countries of eastern Europe may show the way, hasten the pace, influence the course of Russian events, but Moscow will not allow them to break radically with the established pattern. The decisive conflict will ultimately have to be fought within Soviet frontiers.

Soviet society, it will be argued, is far from frozen. The weight of rural Russia is declining. The rising working class is no longer made up of uprooted peasants thrown into town. Mass education, while transforming the workers, has also produced an army of teachers, technicians, and production engineers who do not quite know where they belong. Altogether, the various social groups, while no longer decimated by Stalin's mincing machine, have not yet acquired the cohesion to crystallize and express their interests. So far, the only obvious conflict is within the Communist Party, between the apparatchiks and the technocrats, a conflict bound to intensify as the pace of the Soviet economy slackens. The authorities in their search for higher productivity will be driven to break the existing truce, to attack directly the interests of the workers and thus lead, unwittingly, to the revival of a labor movement.

I will not attempt to specify when this will happen, on how big a scale, or even to assure that such an outcome is inevitable. Though Brezhnevism as a pattern of rule is clearly doomed, the scenarios for the succession are many. If in the following pages the accent is put on a growing and evolving labor movement in the widest sense of that term, this is due to a combination of analysis and opinion. It is, in my view, the most likely prospect and it has my preference.

But can the workers play a role in that part of the world? The third essay, on Polish workers, shows how much can be achieved within a decade. In the winter of 1970–1971 the shipwrights of

Szczecin and the women of Lodz gained for the Polish workers the right to block unwanted policies. In the summer of 1976, when the government tried again to boost consumer prices, this veto power was strikingly confirmed. The strikes and concessions they wrung in the summer of 1980 suggest that the Polish workers may be on the way to conquer the right to strike. In any case, Poland, with its mass of peasant smallholders and its mighty Catholic church, is not presented as a model: it is shown as an example of how workers could suddenly climb on the political stage all over eastern Europe.

Finally, there is the question of joint action on the two sides of the Elbe, despite the different political contexts, of which a writer is particularly conscious. To apply Marxist tools to our current predicament, to view the situation in terms of class conflicts, to refer to the social division of labor or the class roots of the withering state is now very unfashionable. To be with it and sound scientifically up-to-date one must invoke the names of Moses or Mohammed, Krishna or Christ. To swim against such an obscurantist trend, however, does not call for much courage. I run the risk of being dismissed as a dinosaur; such a risk does not compare with the ordeals facing unorthodox thinkers beyond the Elbe.[2]

A Rudolf Bahro is thrown into prison and then expelled from East Germany for expressing his views. Polish dissidents like Jacek Kuron or Adam Michnik, on their way to give a lecture in Poland's "flying university," never know whether they will be arrested or beaten up. The signatories of the Czech Charter in 1977 lie in jail and the wrath of the state spreads to their next of kin. The Soviet dissidents face the choice among the camp, psychiatric ward, or exile. And we are talking here about prominent, hence relatively protected, people. In the circumstances, the elementary duty of the western left is to fight for the rights of the east European dissidents, including the freedom to express views we do not share. Here the obligation is simple. The attitude will become more complex once we reach the higher stage of collaboration with the opposition in the Soviet bloc. Then action will be inspired not just by sympathy for the victims but also by a broad agreement with their political objectives.

Is it not far-fetched to expect some such collaboration in the not so distant future? This optimistic assumption rests upon two unmistakable trends. Firstly, the economic crisis proves that the current reactionary rule, prevailing in both the East and the West, is not as solidly entrenched as most people think. Secondly, the narrowed economic gap between the two halves of Europe means that if we were to find socialist solutions in the West, they would answer problems arising beyond the Elbe, too.

Sixty years ago the western proletariat and its political parties failed to come to the rescue of the victorious and isolated Bolsheviks. The tragic failure does not explain it all, and does not release us from the need to make a critical analysis stretching beyond Stalinism to the behavior, plans, and the very conceptions of the Bolsheviks. But the failure and the resulting isolation in a backward country have a great deal to do with the so-called primitive socialist accumulation, of which Stalin's rule was the most ruthless expression. Paradoxically, Stalinism did not have its worst reputation when it was at its cruelest, with concentration camps packed to the full. On the contrary, with its seamy side hidden, it was still a source of inspiration. It is only now that the "odor of corruption" is spreading throughout the world.

The price that we in the advanced capitalist countries have to pay for this is heavy. There is the guilt by association. There are the communist parties, which have long ceased to be instruments of revolutionary action, but have preserved the system of military command from above disguised under the title of "democratic centralism." There is also the ideological desert after half a century in which "orthodox Marxism" was the name given to the set of "dialectical" quotations made to measure for the Kremlin.[3] But whatever our price may be, it is light when compared with the burden carried on the other side of the Elbe, where it is the people's daily reality. There Marxism is perceived as the cloak concealing injustice, exploitation, and the Soviet tanks. The main message of this book is that, as the mole keeps on digging, conditions may soon be ready in the Soviet bloc for the emergence of a socialist opposition. The main obstacle lies in this identification, and it is here that we in the West would help, if we could preach by example.

To talk of potential socialist examples in the industrialized countries of western or eastern Europe sounds more Utopian today than it did, say, twelve years ago, when Paris and Prague were stirring. Yet we should not be surprised by the apparent relapse. Opportunities for radical change are exceptions, fleeting moments between long intervals, when the conservative inertia

> ". . . makes us rather bear those ills we have
> Than to fly to others that we know not of."

The hesitation is even greater when the alleged future is successfully presented as the devil about which we know only too much. Yet it is in those long intervals that contradictions build up and discontent reaches breaking point. The walls are not as solid as they look.

Finally, there is the limit of a metaphor. Socialism, despite the behavior of some of its alleged practitioners, is no religion and Stalin was no Father Zossima. Dead he certainly is, but he is also very far from buried, and it may take generations to get rid of the stench. The reason is obvious. To bury Stalinism really means to revive the idea of socialism and to begin its construction all over again, a prospect as deadly for the aged leaders of "really existing socialism" as it is for the old capitalist masters. Nowhere in these pages will it be argued that the task is easy, but if the book manages to show that this task is, by its very nature, our common job, it will have made its contribution—a handful of sand thrown onto the coffin.

One

Solzhenitsyn: The Witness and the Prophet

> *"'No, don't! Don't dig up the past! Dwell on the past and you'll lose an eye'*
> *But the proverb goes on to say: 'forget the past and you'll lose both eyes.'"*
> —Solzhenitsyn, Introduction to
> The Gulag Archipelago

> *"How could anyone possibly say that the October Revolution was in vain?"*
> Tvardovsky, in The Oak and the Calf

In literary history there can be few cases of such a sudden rise of a writer to national and then international fame. In November 1962 the 92,000 copies of the Soviet magazine *Novy Mir* were snapped up as soon as they reached the stands. The public knew, by one of those mysterious channels, that the eleventh issue of that year contained something exceptional, a short novel or long story called *One Day in the Life of Ivan Denisovich*. The author, the unknown zek Alexander Solzhenitsyn, became famous in the Soviet Union almost overnight and in the world at large within months.[1]

For millions of Russians, unfortunately, the subject matter of the book—the universe of the concentration camp—was neither strange nor abstract; it was a fact of life. Yet for the first time these Russians could recapture in a novel the mood and the quintessence of their season in hell. Foreigners, naturally, had no such intimate knowledge. On the other hand, they had every facility to read about repression in Russia, though most of them, it must be admitted, did not bother. Now *Ivan Denisovich*, through its artistic concision and power, was compelling every-body to look at the cruel past and its current implications. For both Russians and foreigners the publication of the book was also an event in yet another sense. The decision to publish such a sober indictment, a decision taken by none other than Nikita Khrushchev himself, was hailed as a significant extension of the Soviet frontier of freedom, a step on the road toward the dis-mantlement of the Stalinist heritage.

The hopes of such a smooth transition from Stalinism, carried out largely from above, have been dashed. Eighteen years later, the author of *Ivan Denisovich*, though a Nobel-prize winner, lives in exile in Vermont. In the intervening years he has pro-duced a tremendous amount to justify his sudden reputation. From his prolific pen as well as from his drawer (or more accu-rately from his secret hiding places) manuscripts have been flowing unceasingly: poems in prose, plays, short stories, three full-length novels, the monumental *Gulag* trilogy, a volume of literary memoirs, and a host of more directly political and polemical writings. Admittedly, out of this impressive output only three short stories were officially published in the Soviet Union. Solzhenitsyn's Russian readership has been limited to the restricted circles of the deliberately circulated illegal manu-scripts, the *samizdat*. Outside the Soviet bloc, by contrast, his books are sold by the million. Alexander Solzhenitsyn is now arguably the most famous living writer in the western world, subject of endless controversy, in the form of theses, studies, essays, and innumerable articles. And yet, in a curious way, he remains an ambiguous, contradictory, and controversial figure.

Paris was a good vantage point to watch this confused con-troversy. The French Communists took out of context some pas-sages in *The Gulag Archipelago* about General Vlasov and his soldiers to dismiss Solzhenitsyn as a traitor, although they could perfectly well have argued, within context, about Solzhenitsyn's reactionary outlook. However, any serious treatment would have compelled the Communist Party to deal in earnest with Sol-zhenitsyn's charges about the horror of concentration camps, their impact on political life in the Soviet Union, and the survival of Stalin's system well beyond Stalin. For the party, therefore, the cruder—and the shorter—the better. The Right, for its part, welcomed Solzhenitsyn with open arms and hailed his every work as gospel truth. After a time, some of his more awkward pronouncements—say, about the virtue of authoritarian rule when tempered by Christian beliefs—had to be played down. But his main message, namely that the revolution is the root of all evil, has been a godsend for the conservatives of the western world. Coming from a man with his talent and his experience, it is a perfect weapon for the establishment.

The two contrasting reactions were thus true to form. More puzzling was the attitude of that part of the Left unburdened with a Communist Party card. In dealing awkwardly with the subject it has given the impression of being paralyzed by a Manichean pattern. The noncommunist Left acted on the absurd assumption that to dissociate itself from Solzhenitsyn's philosophy would prevent it from attacking his torturers. It has behaved in this strange fashion as if calling a spade a spade and Solzhenitsyn a reactionary meant giving one's blessing to Brezhnev or whitewashing Stalin. This tortured mental paralysis was well illustrated when Alexander Solzhenitsyn came to Paris in the spring of 1975 for his first appearance on French television.

On the eve of his performance, Solzhenitsyn gave a press conference at his publishers. As this was at the time of the impending collapse of the puppet regime in Saigon, he lectured his bewildered audience about the victory of brute force over the values of culture and civilization. The very idea of Thieu as the defender of any values—other than those of the dollar or the piastre—was so grotesque that the journalists present at the conference, presumably out of sympathy for Solzhenitsyn, chose not to mention it in their reports.[2] Only Jean Daniel, editor of the leftist *Nouvel Observateur*, in front of the cameras the following evening dared to raise the issue and to deplore Solzhenitsyn's stand. As a result he was clubbed from Right, Left, and center, despite the fact that he had wrapped up his criticism in all sorts of regrets and had added his hope to resume a "common struggle" with Solzhenitsyn. To fight *for* Solzhenitsyn is one thing. But can a progressive, even a liberal, let alone a radical or a revolutionary, envisage a common struggle *with* the Russian preacher, now that his views, his outlook, his *Weltanschauung* have been spelt out fully? The confusion springs from the duality of Solzhenitsyn's works and struggle.

Is there anything more moving and inspiring than this victim defying the mighty and ruthless establishment, this zek emerging from eight years in the concentrationary universe and, in the dangerous circumstances of exile, getting down at once to his work and his mission? The sudden fame after *Ivan Denisovich*, even the Nobel prize, are merely means for accomplishing his task, allowing him to speak for the silent, to be the voice of the downtrodden. He does not rest on his laurels. In secrecy, permanently threatened by police spies, with only the help of a handful of fellow victims, he painstakingly gathers the corpses, the bones carried by the rivers of the Archipelago, to erect a monument that will bear witness and that nobody will be able to dismantle. Is there anything more moving than the sight of this undaunted individual refusing to yield to the threats and the corrupting power of the ruling Leviathan?

But the moving witness is also a strange preacher and a false prophet. The defender of the oppressed in the Soviet Union is the champion of the torturers in Vietnam and of the executioners in Indonesia. The most famous Russian rebel despises the western establishment because it is not, in his view, sufficiently repressive and authoritarian. In his frequent declarations on world problems he stands "to the right of Goldwater," to borrow a quip attributed to his fellow Nobel-prize winner, Henry Kissinger. Nor is Solzhenitsyn's attitude due to his sheer ignorance of the West. On his home ground, too, picking up the struggle of the Slavophiles against the westerners, he is a reactionary in the etymological sense of the term. He is hankering after an idealized, imaginary past, after a land ruled by a benevolent tsar and inhabited by happy Russian peasants—*muzhiks*—a Mother Russia without the stench, the knout, and the pogroms. And the two visions fit into a coherent, if irrational, whole. If Russia's troubles seem in his writings to go back to the evil of the October Revolution, Solzhenitsyn makes it quite clear that the original sin must be sought further back in time and space, that one must go back to the French Revolution—which he equates with Naziism—and beyond. We are doomed because we are godless.

Solzhenitsyn's credo as summed up here is not the fruit of my imagination; it will be backed up with chapter and verse. Enough has been said, however, to suggest that both his critics and his admirers within the western Left have landed themselves with a dilemma of their own invention. It is patently absurd to endorse Solzhenitsyn's philosophy because his description of the horrors of the gulag is accurate. It is equally irrational to reject his testimony because of his outlook. Dostoyevsky in *Crime and Punishment* attacks the corrupting power of money in the budding capitalist economy from the point of view of a reactionary romantic. His indictment is none the less devastating. So is Solzhenitsyn's. He is at his best describing the scene, conveying through one day the full horror of life in the camp. In his novels, and not just in *The Gulag Archipelago,* he shows how the concentration cancer grew, how it spread, attacking the whole social fabric, and how the entire body politic is still infected, even if the camp population is now incomparably smaller than in the past. To ignore Solzhenitsyn's heart-breaking contribution because one disagrees with his diagnosis would be sheer folly. On the contrary, those who reject his vision must follow him to the bitter end, and only then move beyond to find out what went wrong and when and why. This is the price that must be paid by those who see in October 1917, whatever happened afterward, the birth of a new era and not a calamity. Communists, trying to conceal the whole matter under the threadbare cloak of the "personality cult," are merely helping our rulers who are only too glad to confuse Marxism with the barbed wire.

But Solzhenitsyn is significant for us in more ways than one. Alexander Isayevich, born in the second year of the Soviet regime, is almost literally a child of the revolution. His ideological journeys cannot be put down to the heritage of the past. True, this exceptional man had a rather exceptional life, and I shall try to retrace briefly his itinerary, if only to explain some of the apparent contradictions in his work and his outlook. Nevertheless, when a young man starts by criticizing Stalin in the name of Leninism and ends by seeking a solution in heaven, his journey

tells us a great deal about the "socialist" environment in the
Soviet Union. Solzhenitsyn, for all his peculiarities, is also a
symptom, the sign of decay of Russian society, of its inability to
move beyond a certain point in its abortive attempt to get rid of
the Stalinist pattern. And this, in turn, explains why the Soviet
rulers could answer Solzhenitsyn only through censorship and
banishment. The central thesis of this essay is that Solzhenitsyn,
physically and mentally a victim of Stalinism, does not point to
the future, that his voice—tragic and moving as it is—is a voice
of the past. Why then is it still relevant in Russia today? Why
does it frighten the rulers in the Kremlin and their henchmen at
all levels in the party hierarchy?

Finally, there remains the problem of treating Solzhenitsyn in
political terms. No attempt will be made here to assess whether
Solzhenitsyn is "worthy" of the Nobel prize (after all, many
writers of smaller stature obtained this award) or to argue whether
as a novelist he can be called the equal of Dostoyevsky (though
such a claim, in my opinion, can only be backed by political
passion). This is not my purpose. But to look at Solzhenitsyn and
his work as a political phenomenon seems perfectly natural. It is
by now a cliché to recall that in Russia, in the absence of a
political opposition, prominent writers have often taken it upon
themselves to act as national spokespeople. Today in the Soviet
Union no political opposition is tolerated and Solzhenitsyn
chose to challenge the authorities on his own. Though a master
craftsman of the Russian language, he is no innovator, no ex-
plorer of unchartered literary roads. He is neither Joyce nor
Kafka. His greatness lies in his concentration on major themes,
or rather on one of the great issues of our time. Solzhenitsyn is
essentially a moralist, and politics lies at the heart of most of his
writing. Critics who choose to treat him in purely literary terms—
and they alone—must justify their approach.

Let us start with the easiest, though not least indispensable,
aspect: Solzhenitsyn the prophet and his message for the western world. Easiest because some of Solzhenitsyn's statements
are so preposterous as to speak for themselves. Indispensable
because, if his message carried in millions of copies goes un-

challenged, our establishments will have achieved their purpose—
turning Solzhenitsyn into a public warning against any radical
action. Strange though it may seem, Solzhenitsyn is not particularly valid as a weapon of anti-Soviet propaganda. Few people in
the West, even among members of European communist parties,
still view the Soviet Union as a workers' paradise or even simply as
a model of socialism. Since the end of the old cold war the points
that can be scored against Soviet rulers are of lesser importance,
and it requires Solzhenitsyn's passion to still see Moscow as the
headquarters of world revolution. But greater changes loom
ahead for western capitalism. If the French rising of May 1968
and the "hot autumn" that year in Italy herald the revival of
revolutionary hopes in western Europe, if the economic crisis
marks the end of a quarter of a century of exceptional prosperity
and false euphoria, if a whole rising generation questions the
rules of the game, then it is indispensable for the establishment,
as part of a counteroffensive on the ideological front, to persuade
the new rebels that any attempt to change society radically is
doomed in advance. And who is better placed to proclaim that
you start with Marxism and inevitably end up with barbed wire
than the articulate and passionate survivor of the gulag?

Solzhenitsyn in his writings often addresses the West, sometimes directly, sometimes in polemical asides. The zek, faithful
to his past, has a contemptuous hatred for all those distinguished visitors, the notorious "friends of the Soviet Union"
who at the end of their superficial journey were only too eager to
praise Stalinist freedom and democracy.[3] That the western Left
must take the blame for its shameful silence—and more—at the
time of wholesale purges and mass deportations is undeniable.
But Solzhenitsyn tends more and more to reserve his bitterest
comments for those European leftists who dare to protest crimes
committed not just in the Soviet Union but also outside the
Soviet bloc, for "the zealous champions of Greek democracy and
North Vietnam," for the "anti-fascists and the existentialists, the
pacifists, the hearts that bleed for Africa."[4] His favorite targets
are Bertrand Russell and Jean-Paul Sartre (not the fellow traveler
of the postwar period but the Sartre who in the last twenty years
of his life could not be described as tender toward the Soviet

leaders). In rather irritating remarks, Solzhenitsyn accuses them and their like of hypocrisy, of perceiving imaginary crimes in the West and turning a blind eye on Soviet atrocities. In his passion—understandable considering his background—he does not seem to perceive to what extent he himself is guilty of such double standards.

Take, for instance, the forced feeding of prisoners. Solzhenitsyn treats this as a horrible crime and compares it in a vivid metaphor to rape. Yet when the same thing is perpetrated in Germany against members of the Baader-Meinhof group, Solzhenitsyn keeps silent. Indeed, he tacitly approves, choosing as the publisher for the journal with which he was connected Axel Springer, the most outspoken supporter of such a system of repression. Or take Indochina: human beings literally caged like animals in Poulo Condor, one would imagine to be something comparable to Kolyma, something to excite the sympathy, the fellow feeling, of a zek. Yet Solzhenitsyn ignores their very existence, preoccupied as he presumably is with Thieu's culture and civilization. Back in 1965, feeling down and disheartened, he was cheered by the news of the communist defeat in Indonesia. What was the human cost of that defeat? According to western estimates, about half a million people perished. Considering the population of the country and the speed of the massacre, the mincing machine must have been working as fast in Indonesia as in the Soviet Union at the height of Stalin's purges. Not all the victims being equal for the ex-zek Solzhenitsyn, this massacre is for him a source of rejoicing.[5]

This is still humanly understandable. Victim of "communism," Solzhenitsyn cannot extend his Christian charity to communist victims. Let us therefore pick a different case. The latest appeal of Solzhenitsyn to his fellow citizens is not a call for rebellion. Instead, he makes a case for passive resistance. He pleads with his brethren, whatever their position, to speak the truth and damn the consequences. Daniel Ellsberg, product and servant of the American establishment, reaching breaking point and then putting his love of truth above the interests of his masters, would seem just the man for Solzhenitsyn's heart. Quite the contrary, however. Far from feeling sympathy for this American "seeker after truth," he is angry with Ellsberg's judges because of their leniency. He blames America, "in which a judge, flouting his obligatory independence to pander to the passions of society, acquits a man who, during an exhaustive war, steals and publishes War Ministry documents."[6] Here the victim borrows not only the language but the mentality of his torturers.

His Christian charity may be selective but our crusader is at least consistent in one respect. Unlike most Soviet dissidents, he is no admirer of the West. He pleads with western rulers to break economic relations with the Soviet Union, to stand up to that country in order not to lose the "fourth world war." But he thinks Russia's salvation must come from its own moral regeneration. He is not envious of western riches, which he finds merely corrupting ("excessive ease and prosperity have weakened their will and their reason").[7] He has no special love for democracy, bourgeois or otherwise ("when unlimited freedom of discussion can wreck a country's resistance to some looming danger and lead to capitulation in wars not yet lost; when the historical democracies prove impotent, faced with a handful of sniveling terrorists").[8] He has no objection to authoritarian rule as such, as he repeats time and again: "The autocrats of earlier and religious ages, though their power was ostensibly unlimited, felt themselves responsible before God and their own conscience."[9] In any case, if the twentieth century has a lesson for humankind it will not come from the morally debased West, but from the East regenerated through suffering. If there is to be salvation, Russia will be the redeemer.

Alexander Solzhenitsyn, in rejecting western influences, explicitly links up with an old tradition, that of the Russian Slavophiles. This, on its own, does not make him a reactionary: in Russia's famous ideological struggle of the nineteenth century one cannot neatly divide the protagonists into Left and Right, into progressives and reactionaries. Among the westerners some were dreaming of a socialist world of "free and equal" people while others were simply striving for capitalist exploitation on the western model. Among the Slavophiles a good number were undoubtedly seeking an ideological cloak for the preservation of existing privileges. Yet others were genuinely hoping that Russia should be able to jump from the *mir*, the commune, into a socialist commonwealth, by-passing capitalism, "history, like a grandmother, showing a partiality for the youngest grandchildren."[10] Solzhenitsyn, however, opts proudly for the most backward wing of the movement. He glances nostalgically back beyond Peter the Great and Ivan the Terrible. He dreams of a pastoral past, of a peasant Russia with its happy serfs.[11] Solzhenitsyn is not just appalled by the barbarian means used to modernize Russia; he is opposed to modernization whatever the methods. He goes on fighting the old battle and produces a modern toy—ecology—to clinch the argument. Teilhard de Chardin, the Club of Rome report, zero growth—he chuckles slyly. Weren't we reactionaries wise before the event?[12]

The West can bring no salvation; it is the source of poisonous modern germs which infected and contaminated Russia's happy pastures. Russia's undoing began when "the intelligentsia repudiated religious morality and chose for itself an atheistic humanism."[13] Solzhenitsyn is ready to admit that through the October Revolution Russia brought "its share of evil." "But did the so-called Great French Revolution, did France, that is, bring less? Is there any way of calculating? What of the Third Reich? Of Marxism as such? Not to go any further."[14]

A strange equation. Nevertheless, among humankind's many sins Solzhenitsyn has, naturally enough, picked Marxism as his target. He preaches on the subject, if not with authority, at least with assurance. Thus he asserts categorically that "in contemporary economic works—Lubell and others—it is proved that since the end of the manufacturing period, capitalism—belying Marx—has ceased to exploit workers. . . ."[15] In any case, Marxism is anachronistic, a vestige of the nineteenth century! Whereas the ideology of the Orthodox church is, by contrast, the latest product of the modern mind, even if according to Solzhenitsyn one should stick to the version preached in the fifteenth century, before the church got involved with modernizing tsars. It is unfair always to expect consistency and coherence from a reactionary romantic.

But from where does Solzhenitsyn draw his knowledge of Marxist theory? Certainly not from the principal work of the revolutionary thinker. Alexander Isayevich Solzhenitsyn, usually so contemptuous of people talking out of their hat, so full of scorn for instance for the editors of Novy Mir who dared to criticize an old emigré publication, The Landmarks, without having read it,[16] admits with full candor that he has never read Das Kapital. The passage in "An Incident at Krechetovka Station" is autobiographical. Like Vasya Zotov, Solzhenitsyn made many attempts to read the "book of wisdom" but found it too hard going. His knowledge of the "progressive doctrine," about which he lectures so often, is thus based on Soviet practice rather than on Marx's theory. In other words, to recognize his competence we must accept the one point on which Solzhenitsyn agrees, for once, both with the professionals of antisocialist propaganda and the masters of the Kremlin, namely that what is happening in the Soviet Union is socialism on earth and Marxism incarnate.

If Solzhenitsyn's value as prosecutor of socialism rested on his grasp of Marxism or on his increasingly unreal versions of world history, this whole section would have been superfluous. Our establishments have shrewder spokespeople. Faced with a rising generation questioning the established values of the ruling ideology, they have been forced to elaborate more sophisticated weapons of propaganda. They know that to appear plausible it is wiser to cover the anti-socialist message with a liberal coating, that it is cleverer to say a word against apartheid and not to show undue enthusiasm for the most notorious torturers of the western world. By comparison, Solzhenitsyn's message is crude, full of visible special pleading and obvious half truths. It is the sort of stuff that one only hears in the West on the lunatic fringe of the Right. But this is merely half the story. We should not confuse Solzhenitsyn with our home-bred reactionaries. Whereas they have class interests to defend, profits to collect, advancement to think of, Solzhenitsyn—victim and spokesperson for the victims—has nothing to gain. His courage cannot be compared with their hypocrisy. Solzhenitsyn's distorted world outlook is the product of his bitter experience. The universe of the Soviet concentration camp is not for him an abstract proposition.

> *"Don't break the mirror because the mug is ugly."*
> —Gogol, The Government Inspector

No literate and politically minded adult in the West had to wait for Solzhenitsyn to discover the Soviet concentration camps. A detailed bibliography of books published on the subject would fill more space than this essay: memoirs, eye-witness reports, analytical studies have been pouring out at least since the 1920s. Only for a short period, during the last war, were western publishers reluctant to print material "libeling" Uncle Joe, the indispensable ally. The refusal of a large part of the European Left to read or to believe that literature is another matter. It raises the whole question of the success of Stalinism outside Soviet frontiers, a problem much more complex than the now fashionable books by former practitioners suggest and one which can be explained only in the context of the social conflicts, the political struggles, and the ideological climate of the period. Here all that can be ventured is that the greater readiness of the European Left to listen today has probably less to do with Stalin's crimes than with the double failure of his successors: their inability to liberalize the Stalinist heritage beyond a certain point and their failure to preserve the illusion that what they are building is a different world, a socialist alternative.

All this in no way diminishes the importance of a great writer, his ability to render vivid what was abstract, significant what was vague; his capacity to force the reader to penetrate a strange world and there to look at its workings through the eyes of the victim. Solzhenitsyn is the first great novelist of the universe of the concentration camp and it is as such that he will go down to posterity. He had written constantly about the gulag and its shadow over the country at large, well before the *Archipelago*. (His only novel based not on his experience but on history, *August 14*, I personally found uninteresting, as I did *Lenin in Zurich*, but judgment must be suspended since the whole work is unfinished.)

In *Ivan Denisovich*, his early masterpiece, Solzhenitsyn gives us a glimpse of everyday life in hell, plain, ordinary, and horribly true. Though *The First Circle* is set in a relatively privileged detention center for scientists, a sharashka, drawing on a bigger and looser canvas the author can show us different kinds of inmates, trace their background, suggest their fears and hopes, the mainsprings of their struggle for survival. It is there, too, that we best perceive the thin frontier separating the outsider from the inmate in Stalin's time, the ease with which the mighty dignitary could be turned overnight into a helpless prisoner. In *Cancer Ward*, the gulag is apparently distant in the background. Only Oleg Kostoglotov, one of Solzhenitsyn's several semiautobiographical heroes, is a former political prisoner, a "fifty-eighter." Nevertheless, the gulag looms large over the whole story, particularly as it is set in 1954, when the entire system seemed for an instant threatened from within. Thus, Rusanov, the successful climber from working-class origin, suddenly remembers with fear how years earlier he had denounced a neighbor simply to get his apartment, while Shulubin, faced with death, accuses himself unjustly of cowardice because he merely had the courage to refuse a career, not the guts openly to defy the authorities. It is in this book, with its eloquent title, that we are best shown how the diseased cells invade the whole organism, and why Soviet history cannot be comprehended without the gulag.

Translating his own experience into a literary indictment was not in Solzhenitsyn's view enough to repay his debt to his fellow victims, especially when it became clear that the post-Stalinist process of change had come to a stop (the refusal to publish his own works was one of the signs of that reversal). He then decided to prepare for a more direct attack against Stalin's heirs. *The Gulag Archipelago* is, in once sense, a collective work of a unique kind: 220 testimonies were gathered secretly in a police state. But it is also very much a personal work, bearing the mark of its author, reflecting his outlook, his talent, his style. Solzhenitsyn is at his greatest telling a story, describing things seen, choosing the significant detail, investing a small fragment with significance for life at large. In *Gulag* he lends his pen to other sufferers and makes their experience come to life. Each reader will be haunted by a different scene: the young, blond girl standing in the night, swallowing her tears and waiting helplessly for her fate to be decided by a bully in uniform, whose

whim will mean life or death to her; or the agony of the train
journeys to the camp of the suckers, the *frayers*, in Russian camp
slang, robbed of all their possessions by the pitiless old-timers,
thieves and crooks, the subservient masters of this kingdom; or
kids turned into literally murderous little devils by their early
struggle for survival. Yet it is the cumulative effect of such
scenes which turns the reading of *The Gulag Archipelago* into
such a harrowing and indispensable experience, as if the description of hell lay in the accumulation of detail. No, nobody has
the right to write the history of the Soviet Union treating the
Archipelago as a side issue or even merely as a seamy side. It is
an integral part of the whole.

Although naturally more gifted in describing the concrete
than in conveying the abstract,[18] Solzhenitsyn is forced in *Gulag*
to venture into generalization. He is the historian of the gulag, its
geographer, its sociologist. He analyzes its legal providers, its
police supervisors ("the bluecaps understood the makings of the
meat-grinder and loved it"), its slavedrivers. He has a chapter on
the "magical work" of women and he does not forget the children.
At the end of the second volume he even turns anthropologist
to discover, bitter tongue in cheek, the strange habits of the
tribe of zeks.

To sum up the work of a brilliant writer is a waste of time; he
had better be read. Yet to recommend the reading of a best-seller
is even more ridiculous. The recommendation should be taken
metaphorically, as an appeal to the Left to take Solzhenitsyn
seriously—despite the hysterical absurdity of some of his latest
pronouncements on world affairs. The Right is a different matter.
Its passion for freedom is always curiously awakened when
bourgeois interests are threatened. It was greatly bothered by
democratic niceties in Portugal after the overthrow of Salazar's
dictatorship or in Chile during the presidency of Allende. But it
was blind to the performance of the Pide, Salazar's political
police, as it now prefers to hear as little as possible about the
atrocities perpetrated in Chile by the Pinochet regime. For the
Right such an attitude is normal, since it can only rule by fooling
the people. The Left can indulge in such hypocrisy only at its
own peril, however. Not that a revolution in any of the advanced

capitalist countries would face handicaps comparable to those experienced by the Soviet pioneers. But their precedent must stand as a permanent warning of what can happen when a movement departs—allegedly for a while, because of exceptional circumstances—from the principles of socialist democracy. And Solzhenitsyn's testimony, whatever his own views on the subject of revolution, is a reminder of the tragic catastrophe that may follow.

The mirror, therefore, should not be broken. Indeed, it should be kept as precious, showing that the mug was more terrible than even we imagined. But it still remains to be seen whether Solzhenitsyn's picture is complete and whether it does not contain its own distortions: Is the prophet guiding the pen of the witness? We must now look at the limitations of Solzhenitsyn the historian.

The Gulag Archipelago, in the words of its author, is a literary investigation and as such cannot be judged by normal historical standards. After all, a Soviet historian who asked the authorities for access to the secret archives would either have his head examined or, more likely, would be deported to a camp to study his subject from inside. Inaccuracies and approximations are thus inevitable. Solzhenitsyn's figure for the number of the victims of terror, for instance, seems very far-fetched. In *Gulag* he put it at between 40 and 60 million. Recently, in *From Under the Rubble*, he has raised the figure to over 70 million. To this one must add Soviet losses in the Second World War, usually estimated at about 20 million people. The total should be compared with the Soviet population which, during the period under consideration, averaged less than 200 million. Since the dead were predominantly male and essentially adult, we must conclude that within less than half a century Russia lost well over half its labor force. If this account were true, Stalin's economic achievement—very questionable by socialist standards—would be fantastic, extraordinary, unbelievable; indeed, as unbelievable as Solzhenitsyn's figure. But the doubtful nature of this figure does not invalidate the indictment: if the number of victims were a tenth of that figure, the tragedy would still be there. Its causes still would have to be searched and studied with passion by all those who, like myself, believe that what the Bolsheviks intended to carry out was a socialist revolution.

More worrying are Solzhenitsyn's biases, often setting at odds the analyst and the chronicler. Some of his prejudices are perfectly understandable. For example, the ex-zek has a contemptuous hatred for the orthodox, the *bien-pensants*, the Stalinists. He therefore tends to minimize their massive presence among the victims of their own system, playing down for instance the importance of the purges of the mid-1930s. He also tries to describe them all as time servers, bullying their subordinates and bootlicking their superiors, as privileged guests of the Archipelago. This just does not square with his own description. The deported Stalinists were fifty-eighters and as such shared the hardships with which "politicals" had to put up in the camps. Besides, if they were as "pampered" as he suggests, it is difficult to see why the waves of suicide he writes about should have been particularly frequent among them.

Whatever one thinks of Stalinism—and however passionately one was against it in its heyday—the phenomenon is not so simple, so unidimensional, as it is now being painted, often by its former admirers. If Stalin had relied only and exclusively on the fear of the masses and the avidity of the climbers, undoubtedly two important ingredients of his system, he would not have ruled for so long. The drama of the men who faced the Soviet execution squads with the name of their beloved tyrant on their lips, of thousands who perished in the name of the principle "right or wrong, my party," or of those who assumed that there was no way to fight the established system without endangering the revolution—this drama adds a vital dimension to the Russian tragedy, even if the illusions and scruples of the victims look strange in retrospect. It is a dimension missing from Solzhenitsyn's vision.

It is asking much even from a Christian preacher to feel sympathy for his persecutors the day when they in turn are swallowed by the meatgrinder. But strangely, or rather not so strangely, Solzhenitsyn hates with even greater passion all members of the Bolshevik opposition, of whatever faction. He goes out of his way to taunt them, to insult them, inventing imaginary charges to strengthen his argument.[19] His atttude is best summed up in his own words:

> If you study in detail the whole history of the arrests and trials of 1936 to 1938, the principal revulsion you feel is not against Stalin and his accomplices, but against the humiliatingly repulsive defendants—nausea at their spiritual baseness after their former pride and implacability.[20]

Is this not just the reaction of a man of courage disgusted by the apparently grotesque behavior of the defendants in these ghastly trials? It is nothing of the sort. Solzhenitsyn has no more love for oppositionists whose courage was, to put it mildly, no less than his own, for men who were not deported by accident but because they refused to abjure their principles and who in the camp did not just try to survive but went to their death sticking to their convictions. Whatever his prejudices, the author was bound to mention the resistance of the anti-Stalinist opposition, the strikes in Kolyma, the hunger strike which began in the autumn of 1936 in Vorkuta and lasted 132 days. The authorities gave the impression of merely yielding in order to gain time to prepare for savage reprisals. Solzhenitsyn describes this "final solution." Early in 1938 over a thousand remnants of the Trotskyist and "decemist" (i.e., democratic centralist), oppositions were gathered at the Old Brickyard in the Vorkuta. Gangsters were introduced into their tents with specific orders to humiliate and provoke the protesters; whenever they fought back they were shot by the guards. The survivors were marched off to a new destination: they were mowed down by machine guns in the tundra. Elsewhere opponents were literally buried alive. Solzhenitsyn the narrator tells their story briefly but movingly. The prophet cannot help interrupting with undisguised gloating: "At the old brickyard, in cold and tattered shelters, in the wretched unwarming stove, the revolutionary gusts of two decades of cruelty and change burned themselves out."[21]

Clearly, Solzhenitsyn's dislike for the opposition has nothing to do with their cowardice or courage. It has less to do with the past of the concentration camp than with the author's present convictions and with the political prospect for Russia. If all

Bolsheviks were not bloodthirsty thugs, if all revolutionaries are
not scoundrels, if all was not doomed from the start by definition, then the opposition to the present regime could be carried
in the name of a socialist alternative. This, as we shall see, is a
perspective Solzhenitsyn now refuses to envisage. The only
possible opposition must be moral and religious.

Once the spell is broken and Solzhenitsyn's political bias
perceived, everything falls neatly into a pattern. The priests, the
nuns, the believers in general, are upright, brave, and decent.
This can be taken for granted. Should a free thinker possess any
virtue the case must be stressed almost like a miracle. ("He had
never been a believer, but he had always been fundamentally
decent.")[22] Our populist also discovers the moral superiority of
the aristocracy: "And here is the kind of self-control this meant,
the sort of thing we have forgotten because of the anathema we
have heaped upon the aristocracy, we who wince at every petty
misfortune and every petty pain."[23] No wonder that for him the
White Guard officers who shoot workers and whip peasants are
"the exceptional few" as opposed to the "soldierly majority,"[24]
whereas for the Bolsheviks the opposite is true. This stands to
reason, since the Bolsheviks are the godless.

The contrasted description of Red and White guards gives the
game away. For ideological reasons Solzhenitsyn must prove
that Lenin equals Stalin, that the early 1920s were no different
from the late 1930s. If the White Guards were on the side of the
angels, if foreign intervention is not even mentioned in the
story, then the action of the Bolsheviks, the writings of Lenin,
the first detention camps, and so on, are taken completely out
of their context. If the Bolsheviks were not besieged, if they
were not struggling desperately for survival and then coping—
however inadequately—with major social upheavals, then their
actions can be portrayed as the ravings of madmen driven by
some metaphysical hatred of humanity, and hence Solzhenitsyn
can argue that everything was bleak, bloody, and hopelessly
cruel from the very start. Yet however hard the prophet tries to
prove his equation the task is beyond him. The witness con-
tradicts him time and again.[25]

The relationship between Leninism and Stalinism is a crucial element in any writing on the Soviet Union and I want to make my point perfectly clear. Only writers with an axe to grind—opponents of any radical, revolutionary change or Stalinists disguised—can blur the line between the two. Only they can confuse the political and moral climate of the early revolutionary period, when the pioneering Bolsheviks, besieged in their backward fortress, betrayed by the international labor movement, faced with a situation for which classical Marxism had no real counsel, had to improvise just to hold on, with the Stalinist period, when the allegedly necessary vices had been turned into virtue, into the model for the world at large, and a massive police state had been built to quash the faintest sign of dissent. No true historian of the Soviet Union will ignore this division. Yet just drawing the great divide will not do either. The seeds of the Stalinist nightmare must have been sown earlier. Where did things start going wrong? With the disbanding of the soviets? With undemocratic social relations in the factory? In the light of what was to happen, no concept, no instrument, no individual should be sacrosant. The party as a vanguard, the "dicatatorship of the proletariat," the action of Lenin, or even the teachings of Marx must be looked at again critically from our position of hindsight. Russia's backwardness alone cannot explain it all, though any judgment, however stern, will have to be set against the background of the country's primitive conditions. To pronounce a verdict in a social void is to condemn oneself to empty moralizing.

The fundamental weakness of Solzhenitsyn's approach is the divorce between the history of the gulag and the changing social and economic shape of the Soviet Union. Not that he does not bother about life outside the Archipelago. He mentions, for instance, the postwar famine, "to the point of cannibalism, to the point at which parents ate their own children—such a famine as Russia had never known, even in the Time of Troubles in the early 17th Century."[26] But the gulag remains a product of its own, or Bolshevik, wickedness somehow unrelated to the upheavals and calamities affecting the outside world.

What would we say of a historian of Naziism who would explain its rise without taking into account the galloping infla-

tion and the economic crises, driving the middle classes into
their hysterical frenzy? Yet the social conflicts tearing the Soviet
Union apart were even more tremendous: the bloody collectivization, equivalent to a second civil war, the breakneck industrialization, the turning of millions of *muzhiks*, accustomed to
the pace of rural life, into workers responding to the rhythm of
the industrial machine. This whole process of "primitive accumulation," as Marx called it, had taken cruel centuries in
England, the birthplace of the Industrial Revolution. In Russia it
was to be packed into barely a few decades. The misfortunes that
were to follow were summed up in advance by Preobrazhensky
in a formula that speaks for itself in its tragic contradiction:
"primitive socialist accumulation." Was the speed indispensable? Was post-revolutionary society bound to perform the
capitalist task and, in doing so, was it not condemned to pervert
the ends for which the revolution had been carried out? Today,
when the USSR generates over 1000 billion kwh. of electricity
and cannot show the shadow of a soviet, our answers to these
questions are more disillusioned and probably wiser than they
would have been in the past. But it is only in tackling such
questions in their proper context that one can hope to understand the gulag and not view it as a freak, as a cruel and
mysterious monstrosity.

A season in hell—the metaphor was used on purpose at the
beginning of this essay. Hell, too, needs no beginning, no end,
and is merely related to its imaginary counterparts: heaven and
purgatory. We emerge from Solzhenitsyn's *Gulag* volumes like
from a nightmare—shaken, guilty, terribly aware of what life in
this hell is and at the same time ignoring its origins, utterly
unarmed to fight against this phenomenon or its repetition.
Naturally, Solzhenitsyn tells us incomparably more about the
horrors of the concentration camp universe than Nikita Khrushchev did in his "secret" speech, but he adds little to our understanding of its causes. This is not surprising. God's wrath, the
original sin, or Bolshevik wickedness are no more explanations
than the euphemistic "cult of personality."

True, no history of Soviet Russia will be genuine unless it
includes the gulag at the heart of the narrative, not as an

epiphenomenon but as an instrinsic part of the system. The reverse is even more true. No history of the Archipelago will make sense unless it is conceived as part of a broader whole, as one of the elements in Russia's transformation, with its political conflicts, the social forces unleashed on a stupendous scale, its terror and its achievements, its broken hopes and twisted aspirations—in short, the more than half a century of Soviet history. This monumental modern tragedy is still to be written and, to avoid any fatalistic whitewashing, it should have as its motto: *tout comprendre n'est pas tout pardonner.* In any case, Alexander Solzhenitsyn, for all his experience, talent, and passion for his fellow victims was ill equipped to face this wider task. Indeed, by the time he was writing *The Gulag Archipelago*, his vision of the world meant that he did not even feel the need for such a rational explanation of the seemingly irrational.

> *"One and the same human being is, at various stages, under various circumstances, a totally different human being. At times he is close to being a devil, at times to sainthood. But his name does not change, and to that name we ascribe the whole lot, good and evil."*
> —The Gulag Archipelago *(vol. I, p. 168)*

A full-length portrait of Solzhenitsyn would present problems. He has violently dismissed his only biography published in the West,[27] and has often protested against the forgeries, half truths, and plain lies about his past spread by the Soviet police and its stooges. In fairness to a man for so long slandered by the professional machinery of a powerful state such materials must be dismissed. But for our purpose the obstacle is irrelevant. For a sketchy outline of his life, helping to understand his ideological journey, it is enough to draw on Solzhenitsyn's own writings, including some of his fiction, handled with due care.

Child of the new regime, Alexander Isayevich was born on December 11, 1918, in Kislovodsk, a Caucasian spa. He never saw his father, a former student of philology at Moscow University who had survived the First World War, during which he had served as an artillery officer, but died from the sequels of a hunting accident before the birth of his son. His widow took young Alexander to Rostov-on-the-Don when he was six years old. There, in the capital of the Cossack country, he was brought up in very modest surroundings, his mother eking out a meager wage doing all sorts of minor office work.

There must have been a religious background in the family, since years later, ashamed retrospectively of his own role as a bully, Solzhenitsyn exclaims: "And where have all the exhortations of grandmother, standing before an ikon, gone!" This, however, significantly is balanced at once: "And where the young pioneer's daydreams of future sacred equality."[28] Everything seems to indicate that his early days as a pioneer left an imprint on Solzhenitsyn who, apparently, was a very politically minded adolescent. Did he, like Zotov, consider that "his insignificant life only meant something if he could help the Revolution"? And did he, too, volunteer to fight in Spain?[29] This may be going too far. But it is very probable that, like his other alter ego, Gleb Nerzhin, "he did not run out to play after he had done his homework but sat down to read the newspapers. He knew the names and positions of all the Party leaders, all the commanders of the Red Army. . . ." The analogy with Nerzhin springs to mind because, like Solzhenitsyn, by the end of his secondary school "he could clearly detect the falsity in all the inordinate, gushing praise of one man, always that one man."[30] And it was this refusal to take part in the Byzantine cult which was to lead Solzhenitsyn to his destiny.

But let us not anticipate. It was not all politics for Solzhenitsyn. The youngster was so gifted that he faced an *embarras de choix*. By 1941 he had taken his degree in mathematics, a diploma he rightly claims really saved his life. He had also studied, by correspondence, at the Moscow Institute of History, Philosophy and Literature. He might even have become an actor were it not for some disease of the throat. War did not leave him much time for choosing. Freshly married, Solzhenitsyn spent the first winter of war as an ordinary soldier in charge of horse-driven vehicles, but shortly after he was sent to an officers' school. The days of an army without epaulets were gone and Solzhenitsyn emerged from the school proud of his rank and in no way perturbed by the hierarchical power it gave him over subordinates—a weakness he was later to describe in touching terms and to deplore. This is the sin admitted. The insinuations about Solzhenitsyn's "doubtful" war record are a pure fabrication of the official scoundrels ready to stoop to any level to discredit their accuser. In fact, Solzhenitsyn was in the front line as commander of a company searching for the artillery positions of the enemy. He fought the Germans almost to the end, until that fateful day in February 1945, the turning point in his life.

However learned and politically minded, young Solzhenitsyn must have been extraordinarily naive, a real innocent. Otherwise he would not have included in his letters to a friend thinly veiled criticisms of the Father of the People and Fountain of All Wisdom. Whatever his other qualities, Stalin remained the all-seeing, even in wartime, thanks to the secret police. The inevitable happened. The Smersh counterintelligence officers were waiting for him that February. Proud Captain Solzhenitsyn, cashiered on the spot, began at once the journey that was to take him to Moscow, the famous Lubyanka prison, and beyond.

The rest is public knowledge. Five months later, he was sentenced for anti-Soviet activity (under the notorious article 58) to eight years in corrective labor camps. He had just time to get acquainted with the gulag and its convoys when mathematics came miraculously to his rescue. To his great surprise, his background was taken into account and Solzhenitsyn was admitted to a special prison for scientists, the sharashka described in *The First Circle*. He was to stay there, near Moscow, between 1946 and 1950. We do not know whether he was to be sent away from these relatively privileged surroundings anyhow or whether, like Nerzhin, he really helped his fate in order to take his place among the "dead on probation." ("As the proverb says, 'You won't drown at sea, but you may drown in a puddle.' I want to try swimming in the sea for a bit," Nerzhin replies to a suggestion that he might stay in Mavrino.)[31] Be that as it may, Solzhenitsyn was to spend the next three years in the labor camp for political offenders at Ekibastus in Kazakhstan, working with trowel and mortar, a brother of Ivan Denisovich;

and he survived this ordeal. He was freed, the date is symbolical, in March 1953, just after Stalin's death, the beginning of the thaw. Freed, however, is too strong a word, since he was sent into exile to Kok Terek in South Kazakhstan.

What did this descent into the "sewers" of Soviet society do to Solzhenitsyn's outlook? He claims that in the first year he still assumed his opposition to Stalin was in the name of some form of "purified Leninism." He considered himself a Marxist. But his intellectual defenses were very weak indeed. More than a child of the October Revolution, Solzhenitsyn was a product of the Stalinist thirties, when the study of Marxism had been reduced to the veneration of the Holy Gospel and the learning by heart of its reduced authorized versions—The Short Course, The Problems of Leninism, and particularly the chapter on Diamat (dialectical materialism). Faced in prison with men talking a different language, Solzhenitsyn felt like a ventriloquist's dummy having to find his own voice. He was particularly shaken by his contact—in the Butyrki prison—with two men younger than himself, former Komsomols, or young communists, rebels, and believers in God:

> I don't recall that Ingal and Gammerov attacked Marx in my presence, but I do remember how they attacked Tolstoy and from what direction the attack was launched. Tolstoy rejected the Church? But he failed to take into account its mystical and its organizing role. He rejected the teachings of the Bible? But for the most part science was not in conflict with the Bible, not even with its opening words about the creation of the world. He rejected the State? But without the State there would be chaos. He preached the combining of mental and physical work in one's individual life? But that was a senseless leveling of capabilities and talents.[32]

The Marxism taught at Rostov University must indeed have been sterile if Solzhenitsyn was taken aback and unable to answer arguments so old and unoriginal. From one gospel and catechism to another the distance is surprisingly short. Solzhenitsyn was already ripe, but the actual conversion came much later, in the seventh year of confinement, during a scene worthy of Dostoyevsky.

Solzhenitsyn lies in the camp hospital after an operation.

Everybody is asleep. At the bedside of the feverish patient is a doctor, Boris Nikolayevich Kornfeld, a Jew converted to Christianity, who explains to Solzhenitsyn the reasons of his conversion and passes on to him his credo: "There is no punishment that comes to us in this life on earth that is undeserved. Superficially it can have nothing to do with what we are guilty of in actual fact, but if you go over your life with a fine-tooth comb and ponder it deeply, you will always be able to hunt down that transgression of yours for which you have now received this blow."

Dr. Kornfeld preached so passionately because he was frightened. That very night he was to be murdered, hammered to death by unknown prisoners. Does it mean that the saintly man was a stool pigeon? Solzhenitsyn leaves the question ambiguously unanswered, but he is struck by the last words of the dead man, especially that he himself was maturing toward a similar conclusion. In the very same hospital bed he writes a poem celebrating his religious resurrection and ending with the lines:

> "God of the Universe! I believe again!
> Though I renounced you, you were with me!"

There too, he discovers his new fundamental belief: Good and Evil are to be found in every person. Hence the "truth of all the religions" which fight the evil in individuals (every individual). Hence the "lie of all the revolutions," which merely suppress contemporary carriers of evil (and carriers of good, too, in their undiscerning hurry); but they inherit "the actual evil itself, magnified still more."[33]

God had given Solzhenitsyn his message; the sense of mission was to follow soon after. Life in camp had left its mark on Solzhenitsyn's body. In the autumn of 1953, plagued by a malignant tumor, he had to leave his distant place of exile to travel, like Kostoglotov, to Tashkent, expecting to die there in a cancer clinic.

In December the doctors—comrades in exile—confirmed that I had at most three weeks left. . . . I did not die, however (with a hopelessly neglected and acutely malignant tumor, this was a divine miracle; I could see no other explanation. Since then all the life that has been given back to me has not been mine in the full sense: it is built around a purpose).[34]

He has been fulfilling this mission ever since, with the pen as his weapon. We now know that Solzhenitsyn had actually started writing in the second year of his confinement in appalling conditions. For him the "pains of creation" had a more literal sense than for Flaubert. There was no question of rereading, pruning, polishing. One portion of the text memorized, the bit of paper on which it was written had to be destroyed; the penalty for absent-mindedness would have been death. Once out of camp Solzhenitsyn got down to writing with the passion of a man possessed and the caution of a crafty zek. "Rehabilitated" in 1957, he moved from Kazakhstan to Ryazan, south of Moscow. In both places he worked as a teacher during school hours and devoted the rest of his time to writing, or rather to writing and concealing his work. All drafts burned, the final version had to be microfilmed in primitive fashion in order to be hidden from the secret police. Solzhenitsyn seemed to write for eternity, or rather for the record.

Then, in the autumn of 1961, after the twenty-second congress of the Communist Party, he suddenly changed his mind and decided to stick his neck out. He sent the manuscript of *Ivan Denisovich* to the relatively liberal review, *Novy Mir*, edited by the poet Alexander Trifonovich Tvardovsky (or, to be more accurate, he had it submitted by Kopelev, the model for Rubin in *The First Circle*). It took a year between the first contact and the final publication. The complicated tug-of-war is vividly described in *The Oak and the Calf*. Here it is enough to recall that the timing was opportune, that *Ivan Denisovich*, as Solzhenitsyn put it, conquered the "superior *muzhik*" Tvardovsky, and appealed to the "supreme *muzhik*" Khrushchev. Indeed, in the hands of the latter the booklet became a weapon in the struggle against Stalinism.

Overnight the unknown Solzhenitsyn became a famous author (and, incidentally, the money advances enabled him to drop teaching in favor of full-time writing). But the honeymoon between Solzhenitsyn and the regime, or rather the period of diplomatic relations between the two, did not last long. By the end of 1964, and certainly in the following year, it became obvious that what Solzhenitsyn intended to publish—

particularly his two novels—would not get past official censorship. Indeed, the mid-sixties mark an ideological divide in his writing. Naturally, the break is not neat and the dividing line is blurred. Thus, *Cancer Ward*, begun three years earlier, was only completed in 1965, whereas in the previous winter Solzhenitsyn was already hard at work on the *Gulag*. Yet it can be argued that in his earlier works, including *The First Circle* and *Cancer Ward*, Solzhenitsyn still seems to be driven by his original beliefs, attacking Stalin in the name of Lenin, contrasting the reality of the Soviet Union with the promises and hopes of the revolution. Subsequently, and particularly today, he sends a plague on both their houses and curses all revolutions.

It may be objected that there is a difference between books written in the hope of official publication and those conceived when all such hopes are given up. Granted. But however much I may disagree with Solzhenitsyn's views, I would never accuse him of lack of courage. To have concealed his thoughts and withdrawn some passages from publication is one thing. It was not cowardice but wisdom. Once bitten, twice shy, Solzhenitsyn knew that for an unknown, a former zek, to reveal some of his views would have been useless suicide. Yet actually to write what he did not believe would have been quite a different matter and Solzhenitsyn would be the last person I would dare to suspect of performing such action just for profit or glory. To avoid any ambiguity, I will not quote from "For the Good of the Cause," the only short story Solzhenitsyn claims to have written to measure, for immediate tactical reasons. In fact, the two main novels provide more than enough material to prove my point.

Equality—to be more precise, its promise contained in the revolution and its absence in Soviet society—is an important theme running through both books. Thus, in *The First Circle*, Yakonov, the future MVD (Ministry of Internal Affairs) officer, explaining to Agniya why one should be on the side of the Bolsheviks: "But the main thing is they stand for equality! . . . Nobody will have any privileges based on income and position."[35] And much later, Ruska, the young rebellious zek, talking to Clara, the daughter of public prosecutor Makarygin: "Why did we have a Revolution? To do away with inequality! What were the Russian people sick and tired of? Privilege! Some were dressed in rags and others in sable coats; some went on foot and others rode in carriages; some slaved away in factories while others ate themselves sick in restaurants. . . .'' And he goes on to explain how privilege persists and "spreads like the plague."[36]

And here is the portrait of an old Bolshevik, hardly consistent with the views of the author of the *Gulag*: "Thus it seemed to Adamson that none of these people in the room was remotely comparable to those giants like himself who at the end of the twenties had chosen deportation to Siberia rather than to retract what they had said at party meetings. . . . They had all refused to accept anything that distorted or dishonored the Revolution and were ready to sacrifice their lives to make it pure again."[37] Or this comment about Makarygin's first wife, a Bolshevik revolutionary: "If she hadn't died when Clara was born it is difficult to imagine how she would have coped with today's world at all."[38] Or the comment of Radovic about a young officer who did not want to have special privileges: "This boy had been brought up a Leninist like us."[39]

The same theme runs through the passionate discussion in *Cancer Ward*:

"I haven't got a bean and I am proud of it—says Kostoglotov, I don't want a huge salary, I despise such things.

"Sh-sh,' hissed the philosopher, trying to stop him. 'Socialism provides for the differentiation in the wage structure.'

'To hell with your differentiation!' Kostoglotov raged as pig-headed as ever. 'You think that while we're working toward Communism the privileges some have over others ought to be increased, do you? You mean that to become equal we must first become unequal, is that right? You call that dialectics, do you?'"

Shulubin joins the discussion, quoting the April theses of the Bolsheviks: "'No official should receive a salary higher than the average pay of a good worker.' That's what they began the revolution with." And Kostoglotov brings the discussion back to his time: "It was called the Workers' and Peasants' Army then. The section commander got twenty roubles a month, but the platoon commander got six hundred."[40]

I could go on quoting, but I do not want to overstate my case.

An author is not responsible for the views of all his personages. In the same *Cancer Ward,* when Shulubin, after the moving confession of a man who just weathered the storm, preaches his wishy-washy version of "ethical socialism," it has more to do with the religious teachings of Soloviev than with the thinking of Marx. Throughout this novel and its predecessor one can already perceive the germs of Solzhenitsyn the Christian crusader. Nevertheless, the emphasis is entirely different. Then the author seemed to suggest that Russia could begin its resurrection by reverting to the early ideals of the revolution. Since then he has been preaching with increasing passion that all the misfortunes can be traced back to that revolution and to its ideas.

This is why Lukács, in an essay published in 1969, was entitled to maintain: "Nowhere [in the two novels] is there a figure whose thoughts and feelings are even remotely connected with a restoration, with the overthrow of the socialist regime, to say nothing of the reintroduction of capitalism."[41] He was wrong, and Solzhenitsyn told him so (to be more accurate, Solzhenitsyn was talking to himself while facing Tvardovsky): "If the novel [*The First Circle*] contained 'nothing against the communist idea' ... you've missed the point! It's much more dangerous than you think."[42] Still, Lukács' error was at least understandable. The critics who today try to paint the portrait of a "progressive" Solzhenitsyn have only their imagination and their own prejudices to build their case upon.

Why Solzhenitsyn changed so profoundly and roughly at that time can only be guessed, though the history of post-Stalinist Russia helps us to grasp his evolution. In the first ten years or so after Stalin's death hopes ran high and illusions prospered. It was then possible to imagine that the barbarian and anachronistic system built in primitive conditions had been artificially preserved by the aging tyrant and would somehow be dismantled after his departure. Various hypotheses were advanced in the West about the possible historical reversal toward democracy. The process of "substitution," analyzed by Trotsky and Deutscher—the proletariat standing for the nation, the party for the proletariat, the central committee for the party, and, finally, the general secretary for the society at large—was now expected to enfold in the opposite direction. As the frozen Stalinist society began to be affected by the Thaw; as Khrushchev to defeat his rivals in the politburo had to appeal to the central committee in 1955; as Stalin's statue was toppled from its pedestal; as hundreds of thousands of political prisoners emerged from the camps and timid moves were made to loosen the ideological straightjacket—it was not entirely absurd to assume that the road, however tortuous, full of zigzags and ambushes, might lead to a reforming of Soviet society. Then the advance got bogged down. Any further steps threatened not just the top leadership but all its accomplices and fellow profiteers, the whole mighty apparatus of the party. It became apparent, or at least it should have become obvious, that the system would not reform itself from within and from above, that Russia would have to go through a social upheaval from below.

That Alexander Solzhenitsyn, cautious, skeptical, mistrustful though he was, was himself influenced by this mood of hope is undeniable. About the year 1956 he wrote: "these were the freer months our country had known in half a century."[43] He hailed "the splendid promise" of the twentieth congress and the "sudden fury, the reckless eloquence of the attack" against Stalin launched by Khrushchev after the twenty-second congress.[44] Later, through *Ivan Denisovich*, his fate was in a way linked with that of Khrushchev, and after the latter's fall, Solzhenitsyn watched the tug-of-war attentively, fearing the victory of "Iron Shurik" otherwise known as Alexander Shelepin.[45] In fairness, it must be added that Solzhenitsyn was among the first—long before the Soviet intervention in Czechoslovakia—to perceive the intrinsic inability of the regime to move beyond certain boundaries. This awareness may partly explain the shift in his own position.

The shift itself is shown vividly in *The Oak and the Calf*. This is a strange book. It offers us a portrait of Solzhenitsyn himself, a complicated man, an *illuminé* mixed with a clever zek, a visionary with an eye on the main chance, an author claiming to have reached detachment, distance, charity, yet really feeling in his element with a club, a *dubinushka*, angrily raised above his head. The book also provides an insight into the Soviet literary establishment, its liberals and its diehards, its servitudes, its degrading subservience to the cultural section of the party. But above all *The Oak and the Calf,* half duel and half love story, is a record of Solzhenitsyn's relations with Tvardovsky and the latter's beloved journal, *Novy Mir.* Naturally, it is a one-sided record, since we hear only Solzhenitsyn's version. He is too clever a craftsman not to steal the limelight and too convinced of his mission not to see himself as the center of the world.[46] But any genuine stage manager would have had to put Solzhenitsyn in a favorable light. After all, while Tvardovsky and others more or less dirtied their hands during the Stalin era, the only mud Solzhenitsyn gathered was the mud of the camp. And even in the years described in the book, they are the *insiders* straining for compromise within the system, whereas Solzhenitsyn is the *outsider* seeking justice, and revenge, for the victims of oppression.

For all the author's efforts, the contrast to the reader is not so plain. This is probably due to the fact that Solzhenitsyn attacks his opponents not only for what they were and are, but also for what they pretend to be, for their aspirations. When Tvardovsky, during a discussion over *The First Circle* at the *Novy Mir* office, argues that the book raises the question, "What does socialism cost and is the price within our means?"[47] nobody objects that the Russian regime has little to do with socialism, least of all the author. When Tvardovsky claims, "But we are defending Leninism. In our situation it takes a lot of doing. Pure Marxism-Leninism is a very dangerous doctrine (?!) and is not tolerated,"[48] Solzhenitsyn does not question the value or coherence of their alleged Marxist critique, he merely sneers with the question and exclamation marks shown above. And when Tvardovsky and his team are finally kicked out of *Novy Mir* and some of them send a text to the *Samizdat* assessing the historical role of the review, Solzhenitsyn is a ruthless critic.[49] He rightly contrasts their boasts about the achievements of the review with concrete examples of its timidity (e.g., its silence over Czechoslovakia). Yet what drives him really mad is the epigraph taken from Marx and the suggestion that socialism alone can offer "the progressive historical alternative to the world of Capital," while the perversions of socialism may have something to do with the Russian heritage. "Are we, by chance, going to admit, comrades," he thunders, "that socialism *itself* is inherently flawed?"[50] The anger is not surprising, since by that time, Solzhenitsyn is searching his own "progressive alternative" and quoting as an example the Raskolniki, the Old Believers.[51]

This was the period of unrest among intellectuals, of the *samizdat*, of Solzhenitsyn's growing fame in the outside world, culminating in the Nobel prize for literature bestowed upon him in 1970. But these were also the years of Solzhenitsyn's exclusion from the Writers' Union, years of harassment and slander. Unable to answer argument with argument,[52] unwilling to embark on a debate bound to go beyond the meaningless condemnation of the "personality cult," the Soviet leaders resorted to the well-tried methods of the witchhunt. Solzhenitsyn's books remained unpublished in Russia, yet in public or confidential meetings they were being presented by the stooges of the regime as the work of an informer, a German agent, or even—who knows the prejudices of the public?—the Jew Solzhenitzer. Alexander Isayevich stood up magnificently to the mounting pressure. After a moment of panic in 1965, when part of his archives were seized by the police, he recovered with a renewed confidence in the power of the written word and a challenging contempt for the allegedly almighty rulers. From then onward he was ready to behave in keeping with the dictum of Innokenty that "for a country to have a great writer ... is like having another government." Here, for example is his reply to rumors about the Soviet leaders' readiness to allow him to emigrate: "I have the permission of my benefactors to abandon my home. And they have mine to go to China."[53] He did not yield to corrupting offers nor to bullying. He answered threat with threat, cooly calculating the weight of his response.

Unfortunately, while the stature of Solzhenitsyn as a resister was thus growing, his contact with Soviet reality was getting looser. He was no longer studying the present and the recent past in order to grapple with the future. He was looking further and further back into the past of Mother Russia for current solutions, dreaming nostalgically of a "future" in which the *muzhik* once again would be the backbone of society and not an "operatta *muzhik*."[54] While gaining respect as a resister, he was also losing touch with a good number of the small though brave band of Soviet dissidents. Bitterly conscious of this divorce, he pins his hopes on the future—as if unaware of the fact that his new posture really cuts him off from the incomparably stronger potential movement of Russian resistance:

> It is not from this letter, but earlier, from the appearance of *August 1914*, that we must date the schism among my readers, the steady loss of supporters, with more leaving me than remained behind. I was received with "hurrahs" as long as I appeared to be against Stalinist abuses only; thus far the entire Soviet public was with me. In my first works I was concealing my features from the police censorship—but, by the same token, from the public at large. With each subsequent step I inevitably revealed more and more of myself: the time had come to speak more precisely, to go even deeper. And in doing so I should inevitably lose the reading public, lose my contemporaries in the hope of winning posterity. It was painful, though, to lose support even among those closest to me.[55]

However strong or weak Solzhenitsyn's influence on the young generations is likely to be, his collision with the heirs of Stalin was inevitable. The question was only when and how. Stalin had carried Shaw's dictum that extermination is the extreme form of censorship to its practical conclusion. In his time there was no space for Solzhenitsyn, or for any form of open dissent. His successors, in spite of their camps and their psychiatric wards, did not quite know how to cope with an opponent too famous to be silenced without a major international outcry, a fuss particularly inconvenient for leaders whose whole policy rested on the premise of a detente with the United States. On the other hand, they could not leave Solzhenitsyn quiet either. When in August 1973 the secret police forced a poor old woman to reveal where one manuscript of *The Gulag Archipelago* was buried (and drove her for this reason to suicide), Solzhenitsyn replied by lighting the fuse of his time bomb: he asked his western publishers to release this very book. The conflict was reaching its climax (or anticlimax). On February 12, 1974, Solzhenitsyn was once again taken to a Moscow prison. Nineteen years earlier, for the young army officer coming from Germany, it was merely the beginning, the first of nearly three thousand nights behind bars. The celebrated writer was to spend only one night in jail and then, ironically, was to be sent back to Germany, as an exile. Deportation, it will be objected, is better than death. Undoubtedly. But for a man like Solzhenitsyn exile, a break with his native soil, was a particularly bitter and dangerous blow.

As a novelist Solzhenitsyn is, in a way, the social historian of the end of the Stalin era and of the beginning of its aftermath. He shows the stirrings below the surface, the contrast between the official image and the Russian reality, the hypocrisies which pretend to reconcile the two. But he is also the product of the period which he describes, of a Russia apparently unable to reform itself. When society is thus in stalemate, when its institutions no longer correspond to its stage of development but no social force is yet capable of breaking the deadlock, when the road forward looks as if it is blocked for ever, many people feeling trapped invent their own ways of escape. They seek God, find a nostalgic shelter in distant history, confuse past and future—just like Solzhenitsyn, though not, as a rule, with his talent and passion.

Some writers, even novelists, more intellectual, more abstract, can prosper in exile. Not so Solzhenitsyn. Naturally, with his sense of God-given mission and his prodigious gifts, he would have gone on writing even if exiled to the moon. But what hitherto kept this visionary from a total flight into fancy was the shrewd and brilliant observer within him, in permanent contact with his Russian environment. Cut off from his roots he is bound, if I may say so, to take off, to proceed inexorably on his already well-advanced journey into the past and the irrational.

> "The muzhik can only be resurrected in opera houses?"
>
> —*Solzhenitsyn*, From Under the Rubble

It remains to explain why a writer whose political message is so obviously anachronistic remains so subversive in the Soviet Union, so unbearable to the men in the Kremlin fifty-eight years after the revolution and already twenty-two years after the death of Stalin. The answer, we have seen, lies in the witness, the shrewd observer, hidden but hitherto not yet stifled, by the prophet. Even his maddest proclamations usually contain passages of plain, and for the Soviet leaders unpalatable, truth. *Letter to the Soviet Leaders*, to which we shall return, is a good example. The migration to Siberia, proposed by Solzhenitsyn, may be irrelevant, his appeal to the peasant soul and to the nationalism of the Russian leaders may be naive or unpleasant, according to taste. But in the same text Solzhenitsyn says that members of the Communist Party in the Soviet Union are not a heroic vanguard, merely a host of time servers, because the party card is a passport to promotion. He adds that in the Soviet Union the ruling ideology is "a sham, a cardboard theatrical prop," that "everything is steeped in lies and everybody knows it—and says so openly in private conversation and jokes and moans about it but in their official speeches they go on hypocritically parroting what they are supposed to say." Turning to the Soviet leaders, he asks: "Do you yourselves really believe for one instant that these speeches are sincere?"

What can they answer? In a country where for decades heretics were exterminated and dissent was a form of suicide, where even today an open debate with both sides stating their cases is unthinkable, and at the end of each conflict within the leadership we merely hear the version of the victors, in such a country Solzhenitsyn's plain speaking was dynamite. In a literary world in which for years, as a critic put it, it was enough to drive on a tractor into an editorial office to get published and in which the other function of the writer was to act as a social make-up specialist and remover of warts, the charge of realism—call it socialist or otherwise—contained in Solzhenitsyn's works was explosive. *Ivan Denisovich* got through. If other critical books were allowed into print, where would it all end? There can be no genuine freedom in literature alone.

Solzhenitsyn is particularly dangerous for the establishment in two respects. The first is his determination to explore the recent past. He has staked his claim to be the "historian of the revolution," i.e., to tell the true story of the last sixty years. The ambition is perfectly legitimate. A nation is politically paralyzed by collective amnesia just as an individual is and in the Soviet Union the basic facts about the development of the Soviet regime have been buried under layer after layer of successive distorted versions. The ordinary Russian does not really know what his revolution stood for, who made it, and how. Nobody has told him how the soviets were deprived of all meaning in the Soviet Union and how the workers were stripped of all power in the allegedly workers' state. He or she has only the faintest idea of how collectivization was precipitated and carried out, how the industrialization was conceived, how the party was purged and purged again, what the views of the "enemies of the people" were who stood in the dock. No wonder that one of the first temptations of many dissidents, such as Roy Medvedev or Solzhenitsyn himself, is to break through the wall of official lies in order to reconquer the collective memory. How badly this exercise was and is needed may be gathered from the gaps, loopholes, and errors in their works.[56] But here again the reconstruction of history is impossible without a free debate, while relevant questions about the recent past have a dangerous bearing on the present.

The scrutiny is the more subversive since Solzhenitsyn puts the emphasis on the bleakest and the bloodiest in the recent past. The ex-zek has heroically taken it upon himself to speak for those who have not lived to tell their woes, to seek redress for all the victims, and his accusing finger points in the direction of the guilty men in the Kremlin. So many years after Stalin's death are his accomplices still there? The revolution opened the gates to the young. The hierarchical system that evolved subsequently means that the prospective leader must climb all the rungs of the ladder to the top: the average age of the members of the politburo is 70. These men were in their prime in Stalin's day and were in some way cogs in the mincing machine. Nor were they just a handful. The Rusanovs, the Makarygins, the profiteers of the regime described by Solzhenitsyn are legion, and ready to defend their interests. The revelation of the whole truth about the camps, the terror, and their function in society threatens the entire edifice and is resisted accordingly, as the next chapter takes up in detail.

The second and even more dangerous weapon Solzhenitsyn wields is his egalitarianism.[57] We saw how, as a novelist, he contrasts the revolutionary promise of equality with the glaring inequalities of Soviet fulfillment and how he fully illustrates this contrast. Ruska, for instance, in the above-quoted conversation from *The First Circle*, goes on to tell Clara about the wives of bigwigs who never go to ordinary shops, about the full crate of macaroni he delivered to a party secretary in half-starved Kazakhstan, about special shops, special clinics, clubs for members only, and so on. A heresy for half a century, egalitarianism still haunts the Russian rulers who do not dare to throw the limelight on their privileged positions.

"He who drives in a car is incapable, absolutely incapable of understanding a pedestrian, even in a symposium," Solzhenitsyn comments wittily.[58] It is metaphorically from the point of view of a pedestrian that he attacks his fellow dissidents for their haughty contempt for the ordinary people. The intelligentsia, the "smatterers" as he calls them, pour scorn on the workers and peasants, guilty of political apathy, ready to sell their political birthright for a glass of vodka. This group forgets to look at itself in the mirror to see the one social group which does not bend its back to survive, but simply to preserve its privileges.

In the most penetrating parts of *From Under the Rubble*, Solzhenitsyn makes an important point, though he does not carry the argument to its logical conclusion. The professional intelligentsia, in the wide sense of the term, is now incomparably more numerous than in tsarist times. The democratic slogans of its dissident spokespeople are not at all irrelevant. The snag is that these slogans are devoid of social content, that they sound like the abstract preoccupations of an elite. In a profoundly divided, hierarchical country, in which the gap between the mighty and the mass of the people is still very deep, they look to the ordinary Russians as part of the struggle among the privileged. The intelligentsia will have a following if it dares to look beyond its own narrow interests and attack its own privileges in the process.

It is necessary to look at Solzhenitsyn's egalitarianism again to see whether it can provide such a lead. His feeling of equality

goes back to his childhood and youth, to the enthusiasms of the
young pioneer recalled by Solzhenitsyn (and Nerzhin). It grew,
deepened, and consolidated itself in the camp, where the zek
Solzhenitsyn shared the work, the dangers, the humiliations
and hopes of people thrown onto the very bottom of society. The
resulting profound sympathy for the poor and the downtrodden,
the genuine warmth toward the weak and the victims of injustice, are one of the most attractive features of Solzhenitsyn's
writing, and this Christian "populism" finds a response among
many young readers in the West. But this sentimental egalitarianism is not integrated into Solzhenitsyn's political outlook, nor
is it universal. Having blamed the present rulers for thus betray-
ing the ideals of the revolution, he now proceeds to attack the
Bolsheviks because they had tried to apply their principles. In
the first volume of *The Gulag Archipelago* he takes the defense
of the engineers downgraded by the new regime. He not only
approves their resentment as they, the possessors of knowledge
(science) were stripped of their hierarchical superiority ("How
could the engineers accept the dictatorship of the workers, the
dictatorship of their subordinates in industry, so little skilled or
trained and comprehending neither the physical nor the economic laws of production, but now occupying the top positions,
from which they supervised the engineers?"),[59] he is really in-
censed because "engineers were paid immeasurably low salaries
in proportion to their contribution to production" (presumably,
salaries not much higher than the wages of the workers). Privileges of the "upstarts" under the present regime apparently
disturb our author, while social differences under tsardom or in
the West leave him unperturbed. In any case, he has now come to
the conclusion that the "suppression of privileges is a moral not
a political problem"[60] and where this doctrine leads we may
gather from his fellow crusader Igor Shafarevich, who in the
same collection of essays sings the virtues of "spiritual equality"
preached by the church and points out the vices of "material
equality" sought by socialism. Justice in heaven is a message our
own priests find today too crude to serve unvarnished and we
shall not swallow it because it is served by eastern redeemers.

   The absence of a plan of action, of a plausible political solu-

tion, is also striking in Solzhenitsyn's *Letter to the Soviet Leaders.*
What does he tell them in substance? Remember that you are
Russians. Forget that silly Marxist nonsense. Leave it to the
Chinese, God help them. Stalin was almost fine when he was just
a patriot during the war. I, Solzhenitsyn, I am against revolutions, upheavals, and I have little faith in democracy for Russia. I
believe in social order and discipline. I don't want you to be
swept away by a movement from below. It could be dangerous.
Just stay Russian and drop your "progressive ideology." Solzhenitsyn gives here a good example of his split mind. Having
told us that the ruling ideology in Russia is a pretence, a sham,
he then picks one item of that ideology—internationalism—and
wants to convince us that this is the driving force of Soviet
policy, domestic as well as foreign. He must be one of the last
people genuinely to believe that Moscow is the headquarters of
world revolution and that Leonid Brezhnev spends sleepless
nights dreaming of true soviets from the Atlantic to the Pacific.
He is actually asking the leaders in the Kremlin to drop one of
the weapons in their arsenal of power politics and not any
"proletarian internationalism" to which, at best, they never did
more than pay lip service. While finding Solzhenitsyn's nationalist language quite congenial, they have no reason to yield to
his entreaties. Dangerous as a critic, he looks less threatening as
the inspirer of a political movement since historically, his political constituency—the peasantry—is dwindling.

For many years before and after the last war the Soviet leaders
saw the main threat to their regime in backward, rural Russia, in
the mass of forcibly collectivized peasants hankering after private property. No wonder. When Captain Solzhenitsyn was
thrown into jail, collective farmers and their families accounted
for roughly half the Soviet population. Now they account for less
than one-fifth. The vanishing of the peasant, the lengthening
shadow of the towns, and the likely political consequences of
this reshaping of the Soviet landscape will be examined in the
next chapter. Yet already here we may warn against expectations of instant results. The political future is not a crude and
immediate reflection of statistical change. Indeed, judging by
the performance of an admittedly young, small, and slowly

growing dissident movement, the trend is in the opposite direction. Amid Russian dissidents, both within Soviet frontiers and in exile, the westerners associated with the academician Sakharov have gained less ground than the Slavophiles following in the footsteps of Solzhenitsyn. In his footsteps and, unfortunately, beyond. Some of the apostles of Orthodox Russia as the only Messiah capable of bringing redemption to this rotten world have carried Solzhenitsyn's premises to their logical conclusions. They are admirers of an authoritarian state, contemptuous of the rights of non-Russian minorities, and openly anti-Semitic. Together with its voice, the old Russian Right has recovered the language of the tsarist pogrom-mongers, the Black Hundred.[61]

Less surprisingly, it is this jingoist opposition which managed to gain a sympathetic echo in sections of the ruling establishment. The Medvedev twins once assumed that "party democrats," as they called themselves, might be able to rely on the support of liberal and modernizing elements within the party hierarchy.[62] The hope for alliance between a democratic opposition and a technocratic wing in the leadership never really materialized. On the other hand, the reactionary opposition dreaming aloud of rural Russia, of the ikon and of traditions going back to tsarist times, obtained space for its views in *Molodaya Gvardya* (Young Guard) and *Krasnaya Zvezda* (Red Star). Thus, the journal of the Communist Youth Movement and the newspaper of the armed forces offered their columns to the preachers of Great Russian nationalism and when, the propaganda having gone too far, this whole campaign came under official attack, there were still men in the top leadership to protect the culprits.[63]

Solzhenitsyn, therefore, is not preaching entirely in the wilderness. The religious revival in Russia is a yardstick, the measure of the ideological desert created by the regime. The nationalism has stronger Soviet roots. Stalin resurrected Great Russian chauvinism and the cult of national heroes—Ivan and Peter, Kutuzov and Suvorov—as part of preparations for the last war. The conflict over, he discarded the crude nationalism and replaced it, once again, with "Marxism-Leninism" taught as a gospel. Stalin's successors are in a worse predicament. They have to serve the same primitive creed to a more sophisticated audience. Khrushchev's indictment of Stalin shook the believers, who were then not allowed to examine critically the new system and their own position. Threatened by the alternative of cynicism or religion, the authorities hoped to fill the ideological void by their own version of the doctrine of growth and prosperity. Hence, they are particularly alarmed by the slowdown of the economy. The combination of ideological emptiness with economic stagnation leads inexorably to a deadlock, and one can no longer exclude the emergence of a Bonaparte, not as a peasant emperor, but as a marshal produced by the social stalemate and designed to solve the deadlock. Adding the ideology of the Dark Ages to modern means of repression, his regime could inherit the worst features of both its predecessors.

The worst is never sure, and in this case the napoleonic solution is actually rather unlikely. The Communist Party has every reason to fight against a regime which would deprive it of its absolute power. The military dictatorship, with no obvious answers to major questions facing Soviet society, would at most be a stopgap. In the pages that follow I shall try to present more hopeful possibilities, arguing that the growing economic and social contradictions are offering scope for a different dissidence, for an opposition carrying its struggle in search of a socialist democracy. It is not illogical to expect that far from the spotlight turned on the star dissidents, far from the centers attracting foreign correspondents, in factories, laboratories, offices, and colleges as well as in the camps, a new generation is rising which may cast aside the bastards of October in the name of some new councils of urban and rural, manual and intellectual workers—a modern version of the soviets which back in 1917 not only shook the world but seemed to offer it new hope.

In order to move forward, this new generation will have to reassume its past, if only to grasp how the dream was twisted into nightmare, and in doing so it will pay tribute to the countless victims of this tragic period. Alexander Isayevich Solzhenitsyn will figure prominently in this metaphorical monument. He will figure there as an ex-zek who has somehow survived the horrors, as the heroic writer fighting passionately so that these crimes should be neither forgotten nor forgiven. But he will be there, too, as the mental victim of both Stalin and his successors, who, unable to reform Soviet society, have driven this man, for all his courage and talents, into an irrational deadend. In other words, they will show gratitude to the unflinching witness and compassion for the twisted prophet. Only when such reinvented soviets take over will the voice of Solzhenitsyn become what it should have been for a very long time—a tragic voice from the past. Until then, for all his aberrations, it will unfortunately remain relevant.

Two

The Soviet Union:
The Seeds of Change

On March 4, 1953, the world was stunned by the announcement that Stalin was not immortal. The "Father of the People" was dying. Five days later was the funeral and, in keeping with some strange Russian tradition, people were trampled to death.[1] The pictures of that funeral look like faded relics from a distant past. The speakers—Malenkov, Molotov, Beria—or the men bearing the coffin—Kaganovich, Voroshilov, Mikoyan, Bulganin, and Khrushchev—have all now left the political stage. This distance is a useful reminder of passing time. The Soviet Union has now existed longer (well over a quarter of a century) without Stalin than under his absolute rule.

The dramatic forecasts uttered on the morrow of the despot's departure also sound strangely dated. Reality proved more complex than the contrasting predictions. The pessimists then argued that the Stalinist regime, with its concentration camp universe, its byzantine cult of the leader, its bloody purges and ruthless repression, was eternal and immutable. They had to eat their words almost at once, as thousands and thousands of inmates were being released from the camps, as the frontiers of freedom began to be extended, as the "cult" was denounced and all sorts of reforms, admittedly haphazard and half-hearted, shook the foundations of the Stalinist empire.

Then came the turn of the optimists to be proved wrong. They had argued, accurately, that a system so obviously anachronistic, designed for a nation of illiterate *muzhiks*, would have to be modernized. Yet they also hoped that the ghastly offspring of the strange marriage between Marxism and primitive Mother Russia would, almost inevitably, be redeemed once the Soviet Union

61

emerged from its economic backwardness. Hence, they expected post-Stalinist Russia to move, inexorably if not smoothly, in the direction of socialist democracy.[2]

During the early years, known from Ilya Ehrenburg's title as the years of the *Thaw*, their optimistic assumptions seemed justified. Indeed, for over a decade, roughly till the fall of Nikita Khrushchev in October 1964, it was arguable that Soviet society was in a state of flux, that the reforms, however contradictory and inconclusive, were pointing in a progressive direction. Then came the long reign of Leonid Brezhnev, much longer than one would have assumed at its inception, and the argument ceased to be tenable. Something had gone wrong. The process of change was halted. Indeed, after the melting of the metaphorical ice, the political surface was refrozen in a new monolithic structure.

Changing yet immutable? It requires the blind passion of disillusion or the naivety (?) of latter-day Christopher Columbuses "discovering" the gulag in the 1970s to equate the empire of the epigones with its Stalinist original, nay, to paint it in blacker colors. Political prisoners had to be counted in millions; they are now numbered in thousands. The expression of dissent was unthinkable, now it is spreading throughout Russia and its bloc. Every communist party used to speak with the voice of a ventriloquist's dummy and follow at once the latest twist in the Moscow line; now, some are recovering their own voices and seeking their own roads. Many a Stalinist diehard in the Kremlin must sigh that "fings ain't what they used to be."

And yet in its essence the political system is also unchanged. Power still flows entirely from above. The hierarchical structure is unaltered and protesters still find out that the camp, the psychiatric ward, or exile are the penalties for dissent. Arbitrary rule, if one may say so, has merely been codified, while the supremacy of the party was confirmed in a new constitution. True, within Soviet frontiers, the regime has lost a great deal of its drive and its capacity to deceive, while outside these frontiers it is no longer viewed as a "socialist paradise" or even a purgatory on the way to a different world. Nevertheless, from its very survival the conclusion could be drawn that the post-Stalinist regime has weathered its transition, and that with more modest means as well as less grandiose ambitions it has found a new balance and a new permanence.

In the pages that follow I shall argue the very opposite, claiming that having solved nothing, Brezhnevism too "contains the seeds of its own destruction." But to suggest what is likely to happen, let alone what ought to be done, one must first grasp what has become of the Stalinist heritage. For this it is necessary to review the Khrushchevian decade of abortive reform, to seek the mainsprings and the limits of the Brezhnevian restoration. Then one must glance below the political surface at the profound changes in Soviet society, because today's predominantly urban Russia is quite different not only from the land which gave birth to Stalinism but also from the country that Stalin bequeathed to his heirs. Only then will it be possible to perceive that Brezhnev, shelving all problems or sweeping them under the carpet, far from providing solutions, has accumulated contradictions. This is the price the old men in the Kremlin had to pay for their long reign. It is also the reason why the protest movement, still so weak numerically, is for them so frightening. Behind a handful of divided dissidents they see the outline of real opposition; behind a motley group of victimized workers, the shadow of a genuine labor movement. Rightly, they are scared not of the dissidence as it is but of its historical potential.

The Soviet Union Without Stalin

Historical periods do not have a geometrical precision. As a rule, they do not end abruptly, and even when they apparently do, the old phase contains in embryo most elements of its successor. Thus in the last years of his reign Stalin's regime was obviously obsolete. Its methods of management were too centralized and bureaucratic to preserve efficiency in an increasingly complex economy. Its instruments of repression were also getting counter-productive. Designed to discipline illiterate *muzhiks* come to town, they were too hefty and clumsy for a more educated society. Since the conditioned reflexes of an omnipotent ruler were keeping the whole structure together, reforms were inevitable after his departure.

Similarly, Khrushchev's fall foreshadowed the main features of the rule of his successors. Though unable to carry any of them to their logical conclusion, Khrushchev stood symbolically for reforms. As such he threatened the privileged and, primarily, the apparatchiks, yearning for stability at last. By contrast, his successor stood for the consolidation of the vast hierarchical machinery of political and economic management.

Thus the two phases can be distinguished fairly clearly. The first, dominated by the exuberant personality of Nikita Khrushchev, was a period of turmoil and change, of reforms which could not be completed because they threatened the established structure of power, but also of a general awareness that the institutions must somehow be adapted to fit the transformation of civil society. The second, illustrated by the gray, pedestrian figure of Leonid Brezhnev, marks the more or less successful effort of the party leadership and of its bureaucracy to reassert their domination over society at large. If "change is inevitable" is the leitmotiv, the recurring refrain of the first period, the slogans best suited to express the mood of the second are "steady does it" and "don't rock the boat."

Khrushchevism or the Impossible Reforms

Half-peasant, half-townsman, half-statesman, half-clown, Stalin's henchman and then his iconoclast, the scourge of the bureaucrats and their prisoner, Nikita Khrushchev sums up in his own person the complexities and conflicting aspirations of Soviet Russia in transition. The former shepherd from Kalinovka in the Ukraine, cracking jokes, inventing Russian proverbs, preaching with earthly common sense, represented, in a way, the peasant burden of the Soviet Union, the diminishing yet still real weight of Russia's rural past. But, a fitter in a mine, a graduate from the party academy, he was also the mirror of the Soviet transformation. His self-assurance was that of the officials risen from the ranks, whose careers were linked with the reshaping of Soviet society; climbing in Stalin's shadow, they had avoided his unpredictable wrath.

Once at the very top Khrushchev himself looked unpredictable. The "liberal" who in the course of 1962 had by a personal decision rendered possible the publication of Solzhenitsyn's *One Day in the Life of Ivan Denisovich*, a few months later, at the Moscow Manezh exhibition, vituperated against modern art with the philistine venom of a narrow-minded conservative. The man who, in good Stalinist fashion, packed all the leading party organs with his nominees and surrounded himself with cronies (like his son-in-law Adjubey) was also feared by the party functionaries as the champion of a new deal, the reformer threatening the foundations on which their privileges rested. There was, however, some order in this apparent chaos and it sprang from Khrushchev's inability to carry out his threats. His famous "hare-brained schemes"—the craze for maize, the conquest of virgin lands in Kazakhstan, the chopping and merging of organs of economic management—had a logic of their own. The impulsive Nikita was seeking shortcuts and changing course all the time because a steady, comprehensive, and radical reform inevitably involved an attack on the stranglehold the party hierarchy had over society, and Khrushchev was not capable of leading such an assault. When meeting resistance, it never crossed his mind to appeal to the people against the party. For that he himself was too much a product of the system.

The road from Kalinovka to the Kremlin had been long. Indeed, the early career of Khrushchev was rather unspectacular. Young Nikita did not stay a shepherd for long. At fifteen he moved to the Donetsk basin, where he worked first as a miner and then as a fitter. Khrushchev did not take part in the October Revolution, but he fought in the civil war, and when he went back to the factory it was as a party organizer studying in the evening in the *rabfak*, the workers' faculty. Still, he was thirty years old when he became a full-time party official.

He then rose faster under the auspices of Lazar Kaganovich. The turning point came in Moscow, where he was sent in 1929 to attend the Industrial Academy. At the time, many students still had doubts and qualms of conscience. Khrushchev was not troubled by such scruples. The faithful and determined party-liner was rewarded with regular advancements in the party apparatus of the capital. The thirties, years of heroic exertions, saw the beginning of planned industrialization. They were also the years of delation, trials, and deportation. Khrushchev was prominent among the doers and the purgers. When he went back to Kiev in 1938, it was as party boss of the Ukraine, and a year later he became a full member of Stalin's politburo. After the war, he returned to Moscow in 1949 as one of the key party secretaries. The future censor stood close to the throne till the very end of the reign.

By the time of Stalin's death Khrushchev was an important political figure, though not one of the obvious contenders for the succession. A Molotov or even a Kaganovich had a more impressive record behind him, while Georgi Malenkov, though younger, stood higher on the ladder and was officially the heir apparent. But a week later Khrushchev was already better placed than any of his rivals. On March 14 Malenkov was forced to relinquish his party job "to devote himself" to his duties as prime minister, leaving Khrushchev as the most influential politician in the party secretariat. In the system set up by Stalin the secretariat of the central committee was, and still is, a crucial mechanism. If the main decisions are taken in the politburo, appointments, promotions, and other movements of cadres are settled in the secretariat. Stalin had shown that control of that body is the stepping stone to supreme power. Thus almost from the start, the rise of Nikita Khrushchev to the top was if not irresistible, at least very probable.

Contrary to the legend, he did not embark on this climb as the progressive hero fighting Stalinist diehards. The early liberal measures, such as the massive release of political prisoners, were taken collectively by a leadership conscious of the fact that it had to make some popular moves to consolidate its position. Actually, in order to discredit his chief rival, Khrushchev leaned temporarily toward the conservatives. In times of stress, in the exceptional periods of a struggle for succession, the fighting marshals, heads of the big battalions, and their natural allies, the so-called iron-mongers, do matter in the Soviet Union. To win their backing Khrushchev accused Malenkov of a dreadful sin, namely of suggesting that nuclear weapons make no distinction between social orders and would destroy socialist and capitalist states alike. In retrospect, the accusation sounds strange in the mouth of the future advocate of detente and champion of the consumer. It simply shows that in the struggle for power Khrushchev, too, was not choosy about his means.

Nevertheless, the association of his name with the "liberal" or "reformist" wing in the fight for Stalin's succession is natural. It is justified, for instance, by his performance at the twentieth party congress, a truly historic occasion. Khrushchev, it seemed, did not take the initiative. In the open proceedings it was the Armenian wizard and veteran survivor, Anastas Mikoyan, who criticized Stalin most harshly. But then, behind closed doors, in a special session, Khrushchev surprised his select audience by delivering his "secret" indictment of Stalin's crimes. The performance contains in a nutshell the duality of Khrushchevism.

As an assessment of Stalinism it is worthless. The document does not include any important facts unknown to the outside world. Nowhere does it go to the roots of the repression or study the system which bred this terror. In a most un-Marxist way it puts the blame on the "personality cult," that is to say, on the nature of one man. And it also tries to minimize Stalin's crimes, praising him for the repression of all the oppositions and taking him to task only for the massacre, say, of Kosior or Rudzutak, good Stalinists like Khrushchev himself.

Yet this bowdlerized version, this rather superficial document, was also plain dynamite—a time bomb. After a quarter of a century in which Stalin had been literally deified,[3] the sudden wrecking of his statue was bound to have a traumatic impact on the Russian people. The Soviet leaders could hope to exercise a considerable control over its effects within Soviet frontiers. They did not have the same means to influence communists living outside the Soviet bloc. The "secret" speech can thus be taken as the beginning of a still unfinished process which through first an eastern and then a western schism led to the total disintegration of the once monolithic international communist movement. Finally, within the borders of the Soviet empire the consequences were more immediately dramatic.

Stalin's successors approached the problem of the inherited

conquests pragmatically. Their master, having carried some kind of revolution "from above" in eastern Europe, treated the area as satellite territory but did not exploit it in the classical imperialist way. All countries were reshaped on the Soviet model. These little Russias built their own basic industries and developed their economies as if self-sufficiency were their ultimate aim. They were run by party hierarchies modeled on the Soviet pattern and strictly subservient to Moscow. But they were not treated as colonies destined to absorb surplus capital, goods, or labor from the USSR. Nor, despite the founding of Comecon in 1949, were they integrated into an international system of rational division of labor. The exploitation took the form of biased prices and mixed companies dominated by the Russians. Stalin's heirs realized that, without disbanding the empire, they could reform their eastern European domain through a combination of political flexibility and closer economic coordination; indeed, that they would benefit greatly from such a change. What they did not reckon with, despite the early warning of the East Berlin rising of June 1953, was that ferment from the center would become explosive when it reached the periphery.

As Stalin's heritage was being slowly dismantled in the Soviet Union, the echo of these moves was amplified in various parts of eastern Europe. Malenkov's "new deal" for Russian consumers led to the formation of the first liberalizing government of Imre Nagy in Hungary; and the reassertion of priority for heavy industry in the Soviet Union led to Nagy's first fall. The reversal of the trial of a group of eminent Jewish doctors as traitors—the notorious "doctors' plot" of Stalin's last year—the successive "purges of the purgers" in the Soviet Union, Moscow's attempt to resume relations with Tito's Yugoslavia—all this led to reshuffles at the top in most capitals of eastern Europe and to a revision of the ghastly trials which from 1949 onward had dispelled all the illusions about "national roads" to communism within the Soviet bloc. Most of the victims, however, were dead, and their rehabilitation—posthumous. Poland provided the exception: in Wladyslaw Gomulka it had an alternative leader, not a dead martyr. But Gomulka's return to office was at first vetoed by Moscow.

The Polish heresy, described in the following essay, united the divided Soviet leaders, and in October 1956 they rushed to Warsaw to bully the dissidents into submission. The pugnacious Poles were not ready to surrender, however. Faced with the certainty of a direct confrontation and the hope that the experiment might be contained within tolerable channels, the Soviet visitors decided to put a good face on a bad job. Wladyslaw Gomulka was carried to power by a popular wave and the Polish "spring in October" was hailed by optimists all over as a proof that the search for "autonomous ways to socialism" was now possible in the Soviet bloc. Yet the limits of this autonomy were spelled out tragically at once in Budapest. In Hungary, too, the Russians wavered for a while, then as the movement grew into a popular rising and as such threatened their system of rule, they answered the challenge with tanks. Barely born, the hopes were dashed and drowned in blood.

Coming so soon after the "secret" speech, the blow was a terrible one for western communists. Khrushchev, however, had no time to bother about their conscience, as he was fighting for his political survival. This external disaster could have precipitated his fall; instead it led to a confrontation in Moscow and to his victory. Admittedly, he had consolidated his personal position in the meantime. Back in September 1953 he was officially appointed the party's first secretary and in February 1955 he managed to remove Malenkov from the premiership. His opponents however, though down, were not out and could have taken advantage of his setbacks. Indeed, Molotov did seize this opportunity to argue that the wooing of Tito and the monkeying with the empire in general were, as he had warned, a certain road to disaster.

Not all of Khrushchev's opponents were fighting a rearguard action and the battle was not waged entirely over the future of eastern Europe. The clever Nikita switched it rapidly to the more convenient domestic front. Early in 1957 he launched a major overhaul of the country's machinery of management, sweeping away ministries and setting up a number of regional economic councils or *sovnarkhozy*. The official purpose was to decentralize planning, to allow some decisions to be taken at the

regional level and involve local people in the process of management. But the reform had also a political twist. Khrushchev was
mobilizing the party apparatchiks against the party technocrats,
the planners and managers whom Malenkov had favored.

Whether this challenge prompted the reforming technocrats
to strike a temporary alliance with disgruntled conservatives
cannot be proved. What is certain, on the other hand, is that
in June 1957 Khrushchev was outvoted in the presidium by at
least seven to four.[4] Refusing to resign, Khrushchev carried
the matter to the central committee, where the decision was
reversed and where he ultimately obtained a unanimous approval. Was it not splendidly democratic to resolve a conflict
within a higher instance by appealing to a lower and therefore
more representative body?

The snag with this interpretation is that, whatever the theory,
the practical outcome had nothing to do with democracy. The
267 full members of the central committee are no more elected
from below than their superiors in the presidium. They are
selected from above and in the four years of his rule over the
party secretariat Khrushchev had ample opportunity to pack the
assembly with reliable supporters. Besides, he also won the day
because he was backed by the armed forces, which flew his
supporters to Moscow and threw their not inconsiderable weight
on his side. As a reward, their most famous spokesperson,
Marshal Zhukov, was promoted to the presidium, the first
fighting soldier, as opposed to political marshal, ever to become
a full member of the supreme organ of the party.

Democratically or not, Nikita Khrushchev emerged from this
conflict as the undoubted winner. He could now eliminate his
opponents from the presidium, some at once, others by stages.
He was in a position to pack this body gradually with people
who had served under him or who otherwise owed him their
careers. He also showed at once that he regarded gratitude toward
a potentially dangerous ally as political foolishness: four months
after their joint victory, Marshal Zhukov, traveling in Yugoslavia,
learned that he was stripped of all his key functions in government and party. Above all, Khrushchev was now able to change
his posture and, stealing Malenkov's clothes, to acquire new

stature. On his way up he had to maneuver in the name of certain orthodoxy. Once at the top, the way to consolidate his position and to gain popularity was to tell the Russian people that after years of blood and tears, the time had come to profit from life. Forgetting the sacrosanct priority for heavy industry and the nuclear bombs discriminating between social systems, he now talked of goulash rather than guns and promised Soviet citizens a better deal for tomorrow and cornucopia for the not-so-distant future. From then on he built his new image as the champion of the Soviet consumer and the indefatigable commercial traveler of detente. Peace was linked in his slogan with plenty.

Though this may sound at first surprising, it is in foreign policy that Stalin's heirs made the smallest departures from his basic strategy. The supremacy of "socialism in one country" (or one bloc), the subordination of the interests of the world revolutionary movement to those of the Soviet state, and the search in this context for an agreement with the western powers were already the main features of Soviet diplomacy. The change was in the manner. Where Stalin had played his cards with the canny caution of a conservative, Khrushchev was going to throw them with the recklessness of a gambler.

He began triumphantly enough with the launching of the first sputnik into space in October 1957. Two years later he embarked on his crucial American journey, having just foreshadowed at the twenty-first party congress how the USSR would soon catch up with the United States. He could thus tell the Americans in the same breath that "we shall bury you" and let us ensure together the peace of the world. What mattered to him most was this understanding over the rules of coexistence with the other nuclear giant. The memorable meeting with President Eisenhower at Camp David was seen by many as the opening of a new era of competitive coexistence supervised by the two superpowers.

Khrushchev had to pay a price for this "spirit of Camp David." The conflicting cooperation between the two superpowers implied that on each side there was only one finger on the nuclear trigger. Moscow, going back on its pledge, chose not to help China with its atomic program. This was additional provocation for Mao Zedong, already critical of the USSR's domestic reforms and of its diplomacy designed, in his view, to preserve the political and social status quo. Faced with a disgruntled partner, Khrushchev, in the best Stalinist tradition, tried to bully the Chinese into obedience by cutting off Soviet aid. He merely precipitated the break between the two communist capitals, bringing the schism progressively into the open.

Coexistence, as preached and practiced by Khrushchev, was not a consistent doctrine applied without opposition: the eastern setback did worry the leaders in the Kremlin. Then the western powers showed little enthusiasm for the Soviet interpretation of the rules. The proposed Paris summit in 1960 ended in fiasco after the U.S. pilot, Gary Powers, was shot down over Soviet territory in the U-2 incident. The tension over Berlin drove the Soviet leader to increase military expenditure once again, thus putting additional strain on scarce economic resources. But amid these zigzags of Soviet diplomacy, Khrushchev's determination to build a bipolar world and to come to terms with the American president—Ike first, Kennedy afterward— was obvious. Even the Caribbean crisis can be fitted into this pattern. The Soviet leader wanted to prove that coexistence did not rule out the development of revolutionary movements in the uncommitted parts of the world. Instead of claiming openly that the USSR had a right to have nuclear bases too, he tried to cheat his way to equality. When his gamble failed ignominiously— allowing the Chinese to accuse him in their own language of both "adventurism" and "capitulationism"—Khrushchev did not switch his line. In 1964, when the Americans started their bombing of North Vietnam, it was no longer possible to pretend that the nuclear stalemate was an umbrella protecting liberation movements. Nevertheless, the bombing did not lead to a break between Moscow and Washington. If rumors spread at the time are to be believed, Khrushchev was then using personal diplomacy (the services of Adjubey, his son-in-law) to prepare major concessions over Germany.

The frantic nature of Khrushchev's latter-day diplomacy had its roots at home. It was there that his whole construction was gradually falling to pieces. The disastrous harvest of 1963, the second bad crop in three years, was only a supplementary blow.

The whole economic machine, spurred initially by the removal of some Stalinist fetters, was creaking and slowing down. The superficial overhaul of the Stalinist system of management was not enough and Khrushchev, unable to go to the heart of the matter, was jumping from half measure to half measure; his latest gimmick, in 1963, was to divide the party apparatus into two, one half dealing with industry and the other with agriculture. As the following year unfolded, Khrushchev's position was really paradoxical. On the face of it, he was at the height of his career, having inherited from Stalin, if not his absolute power, at least its trappings. He was preaching on every subject and his pronouncements were being hailed by the Soviet press in a parody of the "personality cult." All the key jobs in party and state were held by people apparently devoted to him, since they were his political creatures. And yet he proved perfectly dispensable, as on October 14 the alleged stooges removed him from the stage without even a whimper.

Like so many splendid constructions of formal logic, Khrushchevism had a consistency and a coherence, which incidentally exercised an attraction for communists throughout the world, badly shaken by the fall of their former idol. As long as one accepted unquestioningly its fundamental assumption about the renewed dynamism of the Soviet economy, the whole edifice did stand together. Advancing at a much faster pace, Soviet Russia was going to "catch up and overtake" the West in absolute production and then in output per capita in the relatively near future. There was no need to conquer capitalist countries; they would fall one by one like ripe fruit. Meanwhile, detente, dictated by the risks of annihilation, would help the Soviet bloc both to reduce the arms burden and to import advanced technology. Coexistence, in this interpretation, while precluding the export of revolution, ruled out the export of counter-revolution as well. This optimistic international version of Khrushchevism rested on the premise of rapid expansion in the Soviet bloc, speeded up by the gradual dismantling of the Stalinist heritage, fueled by progressive reforms, by the scientific revolution, by the mass entry into the economy of a new, educated generation ensuring a permanent and spectacular growth of productivity.

The resulting rise in the standard of living was to allow the regime to remove one by one the Stalinist vestiges of primitive accumulation and enable it to travel the way from repression to socialist democracy.

Heralded by the sputnik, by Yuri Gagarin in space, by Khrushchev's own daring predictions, this optimistic vision of the future—subsequently known as "goulash socialism"—captured the imagination of progressive opinion in the West and enabled the communists in particular to recover hope after the terrible shocks of 1956. The hopes, however, proved an illusion. Stalinism was not a superficial superstructure which could be discarded by piecemeal reforms and sporadic blows. As disappointment spread, the blame was put on Nikita on the grounds that, himself an accomplice of Stalin's crimes, he was incapable of purging the country of its Stalinist heritage. There was an element of truth in this argument: the author of the "secret" speech was ill-suited to carry the indictment beyond its limited original version. He could threaten his rivals with further revelations, and keep the "Leningrad affair" hanging over the head of Malenkov.[5] But as a purger of the students, the Muscovites, and the Ukrainians, he reacted violently whenever an attempt was made to extend the investigation further and look thoroughly at the mechanism of repression.

But the explanation must go beyond the personal complicity. Khrushchev was doomed because he was at once a part and the product of a system in which the power flows from above, where leaders at all levels are coopted and nothing is decided by the rank and file. The roots of this regime are to be found in the division of labor in the factory and the hierarchical order in the office, which are merely variants of the capitalist structure. Yet during the quarter of a century of Stalin's rule the system had created a mass of vested interests. It produced a multitude linked by varying degrees of privilege, weary of the purges, dreaming of peace and quiet, not of any upheavals of the status quo. Khrushchev's fundamental mistake was to think that he could reshape Soviet society with its privileged as his constituency, or turn the party apparatchiks against its technocrats, or seek popularity as the champion of the consumer. It never crossed his mind that to carry out the necessary reforms he might have to wage the struggle to the point of splitting the party. Appealing to the workers against the unions or to the people against the party was something he could not even contemplate.

This is the reason why he had to skip from project to project, from one magic solution to another. And yet even this bungling half-reformer was too much for the privileged of Soviet society, so eager finally to enjoy their advantages in peace. Did he not throw Stalin's ghost out of the mausoleum? And once you start delving into the past who knows where the search will lead you? Did he not threaten the permanence of privilege by suggesting a regular and compulsory rotation of party and state officials?[6] True, there were to be exceptions and those who went were to be replaced by other time servers and not by genuinely elected representatives. Still, once you start playing the democratic game there is no saying when the people will take it in earnest.

Khrushchev's potential greatness lay in this fear he tended to inspire, in the impression he gave of an awareness that the inherited kingdom was thoroughly rotten and had to be cleansed from top to bottom. His weakness resided in his narrow horizon, preventing him from envisaging the radical measures that had to be taken. It lay in his chosen constituency which ruled out the carrying out of the limited reforms he actually proposed. He did enough to frighten though not enough to break the opposition. Because of these contradictions, when he finally fell in October 1964 one could hear a sigh of relief in many Soviet offices and no voice of protest in the country at large. Nevertheless, it may be argued that with the unobtrusive fall of this tragicomic figure vanished also the hope of a gradual transformation of society from within and from above.

Brezhnevism, or the Lasting Provisional

On Khrushchev's fall, by the traditional standards of Soviet succession, the choice of an immediate heir was obvious. Leonid Brezhnev, a rather handsome middle-aged man with bushy eyebrows, was—partly through luck—the key man in the party secretariat. True, he owed his career almost entirely to Khrushchev's patronage. But gratitude is not the typical feature of a political climber and the two men, contrasting in character, also belonged to different generations.

Leonid Ilyich Brezhnev was born on December 19, 1906, in Kamenskoye (since 1936 called Dneprodzerzhinsk), a Ukrainian metallurgical center, where his grandfather had moved from southern Russia to find a job in the rolling mills. Thus Leonid was barely eleven years old at the time of the revolution and an adolescent during the civil war. The great ideological battles of the 1920s probably moved above his youthful head. The collectivization, on the other hand, was his own vital experience, since having just graduated from an agricultural school, he worked in the countryside during the bloody upheaval. This testing time also coincides with his admission into the party. Afterward, he went back to his home town to an engineering college. During the mass purges of the 1930s he was not so much an important actor as a faithful and skillful beneficiary, climbing over the bodies of falling victims. By the time war broke out, the thirty-five-year-old Brezhnev was party propaganda secretary in Dnepropetrovsk, an important industrial area of the Ukraine.

Brezhnev's war record, while not as crucial as it is now being painted, was quite impressive for a *politruk*. He served as the head of the political services of the Eighteenth Army, first on the southern, then on the Ukrainian fronts. As Soviet troops moved forward he took part in the liberation of Czechoslovakia, Poland, and Hungary, ending the war with the rank of major-general. The end of the conflict meant for him a return to the Ukraine and the beginning of the Khrushchev connection. During the period of reconstruction he served successively as party secretary in two important industrial districts of the Ukraine. Then, as Khrushchev went back to Moscow, Brezhnev followed and was sent at once to be the first secretary of Moldavia and thus to preside over the integration of this new republic recently seized from Rumania. In 1952, at the time of the nineteenth congress of the party (Stalin's last), he was admitted into the highest ranks: he was one of the eleven candidates to the enlarged party presidium (the new name for the politburo) and also one of the ten secretaries of the central committee.

His fate, however, was still very closely linked with that of his protector. After Stalin's death, as Malenkov seemed to hold the upper hand, Brezhnev was stripped of his newly conquered party posts and reduced to the rank of political head of the navy. Then as Khrushchev gained ground, he worked his passage progressively back as second and then first party secretary in Kazakhstan. When the "anti-party group" was defeated in 1957, Brezhnev was back in Moscow recovering his seats in both presidium and secretariat. There followed a rather puzzling setback. In 1960, while Frol Kozlov looked increasingly like the new heir apparent, the elegant Leonid was kicked upstairs. He became chairman of the Supreme Soviet, but this nominal presidency of the republic did not carry the same political weight as a seat in the secretariat. In 1963, Kozlov suffered a stroke, however, and Brezhnev went back to that crucial body, where he was well poised for the succession. A year later, whatever his own part in the plot against his benefactor, he profited most from his fall.

Brezhnev, who graduated from both an agricultural school and an engineering college, had more formal education than Khrushchev. Nor can he be dismissed as a purely decorative figure. A man who presided over the reconstruction of steel mills and water-power stations in the war-ravaged Ukraine, who then supervised such an enormous venture as the conquest of virgin lands in Kazakhstan, must have had drive, organizing capacity, and the knack of getting orders carried out. Intellectually, on the other hand, he strikes one as particularly dull, not just by contrast with the early Bolsheviks but also with his predecessor. Brezhnev's oratory, admittedly not helped by a speech impediment, is soporific. His "works," mainly speeches, now published in volumes, do not contain even a half-original idea. And his reminiscences, which earned him the Lenin prize for literature, whether his own handiwork or that of secretaries, are such a splendid collection of platitudes and clichés as to put a Victorian hack to shame.

Who could have guessed that, sixteen years after his accession to power, this dull man would still parade at the top of the pyramid, his tenure threatened only by old age and disease? To answer this question—less concerned with Brezhnev than with Brezhnevism, less with the personality of the ruler, or the absence of it, and more with a system of rule—we must turn back to the mood and interests of the vast though heterogeneous army of the country's privileged, which sighed with such relief at the time of Khrushchev's departure.

Privileges, whatever the Chinese may have said, did not suddenly reappear in the Soviet Union as part of a "capitalist restoration" under Khrushchev. As Stalin launched the country's industrial revolution, the expedients introduced by the Bolsheviks to tackle the problems brought about by backwardness and isolation were erected into a system and a creed. The old socialist dream of egalitarianism was condemned as a leveling heresy, the *uraunilovka*. Piece rates, norms, and record-breaking output—Stakhanovism—were proclaimed as a holy version of "socialist emulation." Trade unions lost their remaining rights as an expression of workers' interests and a single command system was consolidated throughout the factories. In society at large a rigid hierarchical order was established on the foundation of a vertical division of labor. As the reshaping of the country proceeded at breakneck speed, the number of the relatively privileged grew. They ranged from a new labor aristocracy at the bottom to Stalin and his henchmen at the top. In between they included local and regional party bosses, captains of industry big and small, the faithful scribblers and academicians, the dreaded police, and the obedient ministers.

The material advantages of these privileged people were comparatively more striking than they are now because the country was poorer. A *dacha*, a cottage in the country, is particularly impressive for families packed five to a room, a shining limousine shocks more barefooted travelers overcrowded in a tram, an exclusive shop full of food looks especially luxurious in a half-starving country. The gap between "them" and "us," between the privileged and the masses has if anything narrowed since Stalin's time, because the Soviet Union is richer, because the absurd differentiation of norms had to be reduced to take into account technological progress and a more educated labor force, because Stalin's successors were driven to increase the lowest wages, particularly the incomes of the poorest, the collective farmworkers or *kolkhozniki*.

The difference between privilege today and during the Stalin era, however, does not lie in the accumulation of material goods, but in the political climate, the uncertainty which at the time prevented the favored from enjoying their advantages in relaxed fashion. Stalin was creating the privileged in large numbers, yet at the same time he was not allowing the various social groups to organize so as to fight coherently for their share of the economic surplus and of political power. One of the byproducts, and possibly functions, of the reign of terror was to prevent such a crystallization of interests. In one respect at least, the privileged were if anything "less equal" than others: the Stalinist machinery of terror had a predilection for devouring its favorite children. The higher the position, the greater probably the risk of being purged. The classic example is that of the seventeenth party congress, held in 1934 and known as the "congress of the victors." Of the 139 full and candidate members of the central committee then elected, representing the victorious Stalinist faction, only 41 had survived by 1939, the date of the following and last prewar assizes of the party. And as the "doctors' plot" with all its implications made plain, on the eve of his death Stalin was preparing another massive purge, on the scale of that of the 1930s.

On the morrow of the tyrant's death the bulk of the privileged had very mixed feelings. They were grateful to their benefactor for having rebuilt the country in a way which had thrust them into commanding and favored positions. They were also relieved, sensing and hoping that the reign of permanent fear was over. Their collective aspiration was not toward any form of socialist democracy, which inevitably would have undermined their power. They wanted Stalinism without terror—or rather with a rational degree of repression directed only against those who really opposed the existing system.

But was such a combination possible? Khrushchev had to be discarded because his uncoordinated action suggested a negative answer, the feeling that tinkering with the system would not be enough. Brezhnev's bond with his vast constituency of apparatchiks and managers is contained in the unwritten oath that the categorical imperative of his whole policy, domestic or foreign, will be to not endanger the prevailing social relations and hence the structure of power and patronage resting upon them. His political longevity is due to the fact that he has been able both to keep this pledge and to reconcile the conflicting interests in the name of party rule, with his politburo seen as the keeper of common privileges.

This limitation did not spell immediate or permanent paralysis. In many fields measures initiated by Khrushchev were continued and even expanded. Thus the shift of resources into farming was speeded up so that the once neglected agriculture now absorbs about a quarter of total investment.[7] Similarly, the debate over managerial reform—the reduction of centrally imposed obligations and a greater reliance on economic criteria— was started under Khrushchev but gathered momentum after his fall, when the first measures began to be implemented.[8] Only afterward, when it turned out that further steps in this direction clashed with existing institutions and when the Czech precedent showed where economic reform could lead, was the whole scheme watered down beyond recognition.

By contrast, in two obvious matters the change of line was fairly rapid. First, the search into the crimes of the Stalin era was prohibited almost at once, not only because of the natural resistance of men with blood on their hands. A thorough analysis of the phenomenon, going beyond the pathology of one individual, would have revealed the nature of the state and the mechanism of repression, both rooted in a social inequality the leadership had no intention of eliminating. To rehabilitate Stalin completely was neither easy nor desirable. The natural solution was to leave the skeleton in the cupboard, hitting hard at the insubordinates daring to venture into the forbidden area. The second move, therefore, was the silencing of the writers. In the Soviet Union, where political dissent is banned, writers, if given scope, are tempted to play the part of the opposition. Pragmatic Brezhnevism saw no reason to give writers such an opportunity. Let scientists enjoy more freedom, within limits, and even establish contacts with foreign colleagues; this may be profitable. But if the writers are not satisfied with their golden collar, they will rediscover the consequences of their master's wrath. The trial of Sinyavsky and Daniel in 1966 was simply the first warning for their colleagues.

By such methods Brezhnev preserved the backing of his constituency and the ability to carry on in the Kremlin with his team of old men. Everybody is struck by this aging of the Soviet leadership. By 1980 the age of the full members of the politburo reached the venerable average of seventy, the time of retirement in most countries and professions. Yet this emphasis on gerontocracy misses several points about Soviet conservative rule and, in the first place, it wrongly suggests that Brezhnev was forced to stick to the same partners. He was not. While not indulging in any wholesale purges, he eliminated his rivals cautiously, step by step. Thus, the ambitious and relatively young neo-Stalinist Shelepin was deprived successively of his several power bases before being kicked out of the politburo in 1975. Shelest, opposed to Brezhnev's wooing of Nixon, was eliminated in 1972–1973, charged with too tolerant a view of Ukrainian nationalism. The original rival, Podgorny, was dismissed like a lackey, but only in 1977. Indeed, of all the men who took part with Brezhnev in the coup against Khrushchev only three were still in office at the beginning of 1980: his old companion of the Ukrainian days, Kirilenko; the veteran ideological watchdog Mikhail Suslov; and another old-timer, voicing in the politburo the interests of the party technocrats, Premier Alexei Kosygin.

The Top of the Pyramid

The chart on the next page lists the top Soviet leadership today. The men are not the same, but they are old nevertheless and this reflects the pattern of recruitment and promotion. After all, the likely substitutes, the candidate members of the politburo had reached the respectable average age of sixty-four by 1980. The October Revolution had opened the way to a new generation; Lenin at forty-two was referred to as *starik*, the old man. Stalin's periodic purges were always creating

The Politburo (full members)

Since		Born	Position
1957	Brezhnev, Leonid	1906	General Secretary; chairperson, Supreme Soviet
1973	Andropov, Yuryi	1914	Chairperson, state security
1978	Chernenko, Konstantin	1911	Secretary, CC
1971	Grishin, Viktor	1914	First secretary, Moscow committee
1973	Gromyko, Andrei	1909	Minister foreign affairs
1962	Kirilenko, Andrei	1906	Secretary, CC
1960	Kosygin, Alexei*	1904	Premier
1971	Kunayev, Dinmukhamed	1912	First secretary, Kazakhstan
1966	Pelshe, Arvid	1899	Chairperson, party control commission
1976	Romanov, Grigorii	1923	First secretary, Leningrad committee
1955	Suslov, Mikhail	1902	Secretary, CC
1971	Shcherbitsky, Vladimir	1918	First secretary, Ukraine
1979	Tikhonov, Nikolai*	1905	First deputy premier
1976	Ustinov, Dimitri	1908	Minister of defense

Politburo Candidates

Since		Born	Position
1976	Aliyev, Geydar	1923	First secretary, Azerbaidjan
1964	Demichev, Pyotr	1918	Minister of culture
1979	Gorbachev, Mikhail*	1931	Secretary, CC
1977	Kuznetsov, Vassili	1901	Deputy chairperson, Supreme Soviet
1966	Masherov, Petr*	1918	First secretary, Bielorussia
1972	Ponomarev, Boris	1905	Secretary, CC
1961	Rashidov, Sharaf	1917	First secretary, Uzbek
1978	Shevarnadze, Eduard	1928	First secretary, Georgia
1971	Solomentsev, Mikhail	1913	Premier, Russia

Secretaries of the Central Committee (CC)

Since		Born
1963	Brezhnev, Leonid	
1976	Chernenko, Konstantin	
1976	Dolgikh, Vladimir	1924
1978	Gorbachev, Mikhail	
1977	Kapitonov, Ivan	1915
1966	Kirilenko, Andrei	
1961	Ponomarev, Boris	
1977	Rusakov, Konstantin	1909
1955	Suslov, Mikhail	
1976	Zimyanin, Mikhail	1914

*On October 21, 1980, Gorbachev was promoted full member, while Masherov, killed in a car crash, was replaced as a candidate by Tikhon Yakovlevich Kiselev (born 1917), his successor as first secretary of Bielorussia. Two days later, Kosygin was replaced as premier by Tikhonov; it can be assumed that at the same time he ceased to be a member of the politburo.

plenty of room for advancement. Since his death, in the conservative, established society the newcomers must climb slowly all the rungs on the party ladder. To advance they must show ability, drive, determination, but above all a devotion to the system and its rules of the game, because at all levels of the hierarchy they are coopted from above. In the Soviet Union, like elsewhere, politicians like being surrounded by people they know and trust. Khrushchev had his "Ukrainians"; Brezhnev promoted several officials who had served under him while he was on the way up.[9] And on a lower level the same method of promotion functions throughout the country. The choosers are shaping the mold for a career. The established have no reason to favor critics likely to question the establishment.

Great hopes pinned on the arrival of the younger generation have thus been thwarted by the system of selection. The younger are not necessarily the better. Shelepin was less old than his colleagues, though hardly more progressive. Or to take the example of one of the newcomers to the top leadership, the politburo candidate Eduard Shevarnadze. At fifty-two he looks odd in this family picture of old-age pensioners. Yet, until he became first secretary of Georgia in 1972 he had spent most of his career in increasingly important jobs in the local office of the Ministry for Internal Affairs, the MVD. Clearly the selectors make no mistake. The change of guard will have a real political significance only when pressure from below and from outside the party sweeps aside the weighty machine of self-perpetuation, that is to say the whole system of Soviet rule.

Meanwhile, Brezhnev has contributed to stability in another way. The generation gap was neither the only nor the most significant of conflicts within the heterogeneous ruling circles. Ever since Stalin's death a tug-of-war can be discerned (more open while Malenkov fought Khrushchev, more concealed as Kosygin tried to resist the trend) between those who want to strengthen the autonomy and widen the powers of the apparatus of state and government and those who insist on total subservience to party rule. Brezhnev could not eliminate such conflicts, because the interests involved are real, but he has managed to institutionalize them within a politburo treated as the place where the common interests of the varying factions are being worked out. In 1973 he brought into that body the leading soldier, Marshal Grechko,[10] the leading policeman, Yuri Andropov, and Andrei Gromyko, the man responsible for foreign affairs, to confirm that all of the interests of the establishment are represented.

A second glance at the top of the Soviet pyramid of power, diagrammed above, is revealing in this respect. The politburo has in its ranks five members of the crucial secretariat, including Brezhnev, the general secretary. The party barons of Leningrad, Moscow, and the Ukraine are in by right (Kunayev the Kazakh more accidentally as Brezhnev's companion). But the state is also represented by the same Brezhnev in his latest reincarnation as president, by the premier and his first deputy, and, as just mentioned, by ministers of defense, security, and foreign affairs. If we move below, to the level of candidates, we find two more secretaries, four regional bosses, but also the deputy president and the premier of the Russian republic. The party is clearly dominant and this supremacy is plainly inscribed in the new constitution—which in Article 6 proclaims: "The leading and guiding force of Soviet society and the nucleus of its political system, of all state and public organizations, is the Communist Party of the Soviet Union. . . ." Nevertheless, an effort is made to mediate, to provide a forum for compromises, and who knows whether Brezhnev's ability to preserve a precarious balance is not the main reason why the so obviously semi-valid leader has been kept stubbornly at the helm.

A similar mixture of flexibility and opportunism combined with ruthlessness when vital interests are at stake is to be found in the regime's handling of external affairs, beginning with those of the communist world. Khrushchev when he tumbled was set on a collision course with China. His successors at first tried to avoid this confrontation. They put off the international communist conference, which was supposed to excommunicate the Chinese. They cooled relations with Washington for a time and Kosygin, on his way back from Hanoi in 1964, tried to see whether a deal could be worked out with Peking. The Soviet

leaders rapidly discovered that Mao was in no mood for concessions and, as the Cultural Revolution stressed the yawning gap
between their respective conceptions of revolutionary development, they changed course altogether. It was during the reign
of Khrushchev's heirs that allegedly communist troops fought
against each other on the Ussuri river in 1969, that rumors were
purposely spread from Moscow about a possible "preventive"
strike against China, that some fifty Soviet divisions were shifted
to the eastern front. Then, as Chinese diplomacy performed a
spectacular about-face and Washington exploited it adroitly to
bring about the end of the postwar bipolar world, the "yellow
peril" became an obsession of Soviet diplomacy. If Khrushchev
can be described as the architect of the eastern schism, the break
was completed by his successors.

The distinction between what is tolerable for the Kremlin and
what is considered unbearable is best illustrated by develop-
ments in the Soviet bloc. Moscow has put up with Rumania's
real acts, not just empty gestures of independence in foreign
policy, because Rumania, domestically more rigid and conservative than its neighbors, is no center of attraction. Hungary has
been able to go quite far with economic reform and market
experiments, Kadar assuring the Russians that this controlled
movement will not be allowed to get out of hand politically. In
Czechoslovakia, by contrast, political relaxation had unleashed
genuine social forces. Spurred initially by the intelligentsia, the
movement then had to lean on the workers. There was no guarantee what kind of regime would ultimately emerge, but potentially
here was an alternative, another model, a serious risk of con-
tagion spreading through the bloc and invading the USSR itself.
The frightened men in the Kremlin responded ruthlessly with
their tanks, caring little about the risks, admittedly small, of
foreign reaction and not at all about the consequences for
world communism.

The western powers, as expected, swallowed quite easily the
not-so-novel Brezhnev doctrine, reasserting Moscow's right to
interfere throughout the bloc. On the other hand, the entry of
Soviet tanks into Prague precipitated the disintegration of the

international communist movement. The former monolith now lies in small pieces and all Brezhnev's old horses will never put it together again. The western schism is written on the historical cards even if the world economic crisis, rendering more difficult the integration of western communist parties into their national political systems, has somewhat slowed down this process.

It is Brezhnev's relationship with the western powers that is at present most difficult to define. Ever since the intervention in Afghanistan, the Soviet Union tends to be described as the new dominant power, with a grand design and the means to carry it out. This fashionable vision of a dynamic Soviet diplomacy sustained by a long-term strategy corresponds neither to the nature of the Brezhnev regime nor to its record. We saw that Khrushchev's successors first tried to preserve good relations with Peking as well as Washington and managed neither. Once a decent interval elapsed after the invasion of Czechoslovakia, they opted for a deal with Washington and showed they had no more scruples than their predecessors to sacrifice obligations of socialist solidarity to the country's national interest. In June 1972 Nixon was feted in Moscow, having just bombed North Vietnam and mined its harbors. The Russians thus gave the impression that they were putting the search for a modus vivendi with the United States in nuclear and other matters above everything else. In fairness, this impression must be qualified. The Russians were simultaneously building up their military potential, particularly in missiles, so as not to find themselves in Khrushchev's predicament at the time of the Cuban crisis. They were also shipping arms to North Vietnam.

The American defeat in Indochina followed by Watergate altered, if not the basic balance of world power, at least its temporary equilibrium. The United States was provisionally unable to exercise the role of international gendarme which it had tried to assume fully after the Caribbean crisis. The Russians took advantage of the resulting void to advance their positions, usually by Cuban proxy, in Angola, Ethiopia, or South Yemen. But the external balance sheet of the Brezhnev era is not as aggressively triumphant as it is now being painted. It includes on the debit side one huge item—the defection of China—and a series of smaller setbacks, such as the complete loss of influence in Egypt. It must also be kept in mind that all the Soviet points were scored on minor fronts, where vital American interests were not involved, while up to now the Russians have carefully avoided going to the brink in cases of direct confrontation. (Though, admittedly, the last example, in the Middle East, goes back to 1973.)

It may be too early to decide whether the intervention in Afghanistan was a miscalculated gamble or the sign of a serious shift in Soviet policy. Precedent, however, pleads against suggestions of a planned and determined Soviet drive toward the southern seas and beyond. The old men in the Kremlin are ready to fill a void, to grab a prize when the danger is not too great and to fight tooth and nail when their own political survival is at stake. Otherwise they never seemed keen on radical solutions. Faced with the alternative of full collaboration with the United States and systematic struggle against American imperialism, Brezhnev was unwilling to take the risks of either and opted for a bit of both. The mistake of the policymakers in Washington may well have been to assume that the old Soviet leaders could be bribed or bullied into a deal visibly affecting their interests and therefore threatening their rule. Taking his reign as a whole, Brezhnev's leadership, in foreign as well as domestic affairs, is one of conservative consensus rather than of broad vision and bold initiative.

Beyond Brezhnev

Well over a quarter of a century after Stalin's death the record, as summed up here, may not look too impressive. The last fifteen years make particularly gloomy reading. Not just in Moscow, but in the ranks of western communist parties there must be many recalling nostalgically the good old days of glory and certitude when the Soviet Union, though bled by the war, was an inspiration for millions, when discipline under its banner was easily consented, when Stalin was still perpetuating the illusion that the pioneers working on the Dnieperostroy dam on the Dnieper, or on the distant town of Komsomolsk were building an

alternative society and thus preparing the "end of prehistory."
Yet such a judgment is unfair as is my own assessment written
from the critical viewpoint of a socialist. Judged by the criteria
usually applied in our own societies the picture is not so bleak.

Gray as he may be, Brezhnev is no more mediocre than most of
our rulers and if he soldiers on despite ill health so did, for
example, Georges Pompidou. However perturbing for the future
is the slackening pace of economic growth in the Soviet Union,
the country still compares favorably when set against western
stagnation and rising unemployment. Unprincipled hypocrisy
in diplomacy is not a Soviet prerogative either, as U.S. presi-
dents preaching the Rights of Man except in Teheran, where
they stopped to visit the Shah, know only too well. Our nostalgic
Stalinist, too, can be reminded that in spite of everything written
here, ordinary Russians are better off and less terrorized than
they were in Stalin's time. It is only measured by the socialist
yardstick that the record is abysmal.[11]

Most countries live without a vision, a grand design, without
an optical illusion capturing the imagination of citizens and
foreigners alike. Conservative governments unable to tackle the
fundamental issues of our time are a penny a dozen. That such
conservative rule can last and last long, Brezhnevism itself perfectly illustrates. To explain why I have nevertheless called it
provisional, implying that it is no more than an interlude, we
must now look below the political surface at the contradictions
accumulated in fast-changing Soviet society.

Soviet Society in Flux

When Stalin died the Soviet Union was only emerging from
its period of primitive accumulation. Barely more than a third of
a century had then elapsed since the October Revolution. Allowing for the ravages of two world conflicts, a civil war, and the
years required each time for reconstruction, Soviet Russia had to
pack into a very short span of time the cruel task which western
countries had accomplished, without tenderness, over centuries.

Because they do not take this crucial factor into account, the currently conventional explanations of Stalinism in terms of totalitarianism and the gulag cannot do justice to the subject. But my purpose here is not to apportion blame between the fatalistic and totalitarian schools of history. It is to show that below the political veneer of stability social change has continued at a fast pace. The conservative image of Brezhnevism is partly deceptive.

Without quite the convulsions and upheavals of yesteryear, millions of peasants have been leaving the land. On reaching the town, they join the ranks of an industrial proletariat, a vast urban working class, too atomized and disorganized to be a "class for itself," but no longer an army of muzhiks camping in town. And in recent years white-collar workers have been mushrooming in the towns, faster even than the blue: clerks, shop assistants, teachers, technicians, and in their midst a massive, though ill-defined intelligentsia, heterogenous, uncertain of its functions—and of its side of the fence. At the end of the brief journey through the fast-changing structure of Soviet society we shall perceive that there, as elsewhere, though in a different framework, the institutions are bursting at their seams under inner pressure or, to put in Marxist terms, the productive forces are clashing with social relations.

No Longer the Land of the Muzhik

At the beginning of 1979 38 percent of the Soviet population lived in the countryside. A statistic changes meaning with the angle from which it is viewed. Seen in the abstract and from outside, this figure shows that the weight of rural Russia remains tremendous, with 98.8 million people living in the countryside. This impression is strengthened by adding another vital statistical piece: nearly one employed Soviet citizen out of four is working on the land; the comparable American ratio is one out of twenty. But the figure acquires quite another meaning seen in Russia's historical perspective, even without going back to tsarist times. On the eve of the last war Soviet towndwellers accounted for merely a third of the total population, and even in the year of

Stalin's death 57 percent of that population was still rural. The balance is clearly shifting fairly rapidly.[12]

Land-hungry peasants, who had made the revolution possible, turned out to be its main predicament. Stalin leaned at first toward Bukharin's solution of a gradual transition of the countryside— "at snail's pace." When his plans were threatened by the forces of the market, he changed his line altogether and without any preparation, equipment, or industrial incentives, he launched an almost military offensive designed to liquidate the kulak, *kak klass i kak chelovyek* (as class and as individuals). The upheaval was equivalent to a second civil war, and Soviet farming in a way has not yet recovered from its bloody collectivization. The recovery was the more difficult in the first phase of the industrial revolution, since the countryside was treated as a provider of laborpower and the main source of accumulation. Agriculture and light industry were the twin Cinderellas of the Stalinist planners.

For farming the break with the Stalin era is real. All his successors grasped that the distorted growth—industry forging ahead and agriculture lagging behind—was in the long run poor economics and bad politics. In the spring of 1954, Khrushchev, with his predilection for the spectacular, launched the huge campaign for the conquest of the virgin lands in Kazakhstan and western Siberia, which was to lead ultimately to the reclamation of over 40 million hectares. In retrospect, the whole operation may well be viewed as a paying proposition. Originally, with its claim on the limited resources, it clashed with Malenkov's new deal for the consumer and it ran into all sorts of predictable difficulties. Even today the crops in the area vary considerably from year to year. Nevertheless, the Soviet Union has gained in the process a badly needed second granary comparable with the Ukraine.[13]

Yet Khrushchev himself was aware that the basic ills could not be cured by vast schemes extending the land under cultivation. What Soviet farming needed was more intensive methods of production and measures to interest the farmers in higher productivity; hence his own major drive to expand the chemical industry, partly designed to supply fertilizers on a massive scale. Hence, too, the moves he initiated to improve the peasant's lot. His successors carried out these projects. In particular, they granted the collective farmer a basic fixed salary (instead of a trudodzyen, labor day, from very hypothetical profits) and the right to an old-age pension paid by the state. They increased the incentives by raising substantially procurement prices, though not the prices in the shops, which had involved a big jump in the already high food subsidies. More steadily than their predecessor they poured into the countryside tractors, harvesters, trucks, fertilizers. They built more houses and improved social amenities. In the 1970s the share of agriculture grew to a quarter of total Soviet investment, a very high proportion for a modern industrial state. The Cinderella may not be a princess, but she now gets a big slice of the family income.

The results of this new and costly policy are not negligible. Soviet farm output is still dangerously susceptible to the vagaries of nature, but poor harvests when they occur, as in 1975 or 1979, are no longer as disastrous as in the past, while the continuing big purchases of western grain are mainly for fodder, to give a chance to the development of meat and dairy farming. Altogether, grain crops are now averaging 209 million tons compared with less than 100 million tons at the time of Stalin's death. Yields per hectare have roughly doubled over the period and the increased productivity has rendered possible the continued migration to the towns.

This undeniable progress should not be confused with the idyllic picture presented by Soviet propaganda, in which the March 1965 plenary meeting of the central committee, where Brezhnev outlined his agricultural program, is described as an almost miraculous opening of a new era. In fact, the increment so far does not correspond to the heavy investment. The Soviet planners have not found any new solutions. The collective farms, run bureaucratically by their heads, are no more a cooperative version of "associated producers" than the factories run by their bosses are a new form of socialist property. The recent achievements are due to bourgeois methods and capitalist-type technology. Only the planners have not yet found the way to make the Soviet peasants work with the same intensity on state or collective farms as they do on their small plots of about half a hectare, the last vestiges of private property, which still provide roughly a quarter of Soviet farm production. Elsewhere, precious fertilizers are wasted, machinery is lying idle at harvest time in need of repair. The distance still to be traveled is best illustrated by an international comparison. With one-twentieth of its labor force employed in farming the United States has a problem of farm surpluses; with nearly one-fourth of its labor power in agriculture the Soviet Union still has too starchy a diet, not enough vegetables, sudden shortages of meat. The gist of the matter can be put crudely: according to official Soviet statistics, productivity per farmer is five times higher in the United States than it is in the USSR.

What interests us here for the moment, however, is not the impact of this handicap on the international economic race but the political consequences of social change in the countryside. The rural landscape alters slowly and the tourist can still come upon sleepy villages, cut off from the world, straight out of the pages of a nineteenth-century Russian novel. Nevertheless, the social make-up of rural Russia has changed greatly just in the last quarter of a century. First, state farms, or *sovkhozy*, have grown considerably in importance. Taking up most of the newly reclaimed land, where there were no peasants to expropriate, they also developed throughout the country. These huge farms, on which the state is the direct employer, now number about 21,000 and have over 11 million people on their payrolls. They account for over a third of the meat and milk and well over a half of the eggs produced in the country: they provide nearly half the cattle and more than half the grain purchased by the authorities. Thus the state sector, once marginal, is progressively becoming dominant.

Second, the collective farms have ceased to be very different. The merging of the *kolkhozy* into larger units began before Stalin's death and has continued ever since. Their number has dropped from 250,000 in 1952 to less than 26,000 in 1980. In size, in the availability of equipment, specialists, and so on they are no longer so far apart.[14] Since the introduction into collective farming of basic salaries, their fairly rapid growth and the resulting relative decline of revenue from the private plot as a source of the kolkhoznik's earnings, even the pattern of their income is now getting closer. True, the forms of property are not the same, but as differences in working and living conditions are diminishing the transition becomes easier. Collective farms can be and are being turned into state farms without much fuss.

By the same token the distance is lessened between the kolkhoznik, the downtrodden of the Stalin era, and the urban wage-earner. In the last twenty years, according to official statistics, the real incomes of collective farmers have grown about 50 percent faster than those of the workers and employees and are now only 15 percent lower. These figures, misleading as are all averages, nevertheless reflect a trend that is perceptible in other ways. The levels of education are still much lower in the country-side, the rural population has fewer social and cultural amenities and buys fewer consumer durables, but the once yawning gap between the two cultures and modes of life is visibly narrowing.

Let us not hail this achievement as the fulfillment of the old socialist dream of "bridging the gap between town and country." The elimination of this difference and of many others—between mental and manual labor, between labor and leisure—was conceived as part of a general project involving the abolition of the hierarchical division of labor, the elimination of social inequality, the resulting withering away of the state. The project was seen as both part of a general historical process and a crucial element in this radical transformation. What we are witnessing in the USSR, rather than the fulfillment of a dream, is the belated Soviet version of a trend affecting equally western capitalism—the industrialization of agriculture. In the age of the tractor and of television, of mechanized farming and modern means of communication, there is no room for the peasant from Marx's famous bag of potatoes. The Russian muzhik is historically on his way out in the same way as the peasant has been vanishing in the western world. Already today amid the 27 million or so employed in Soviet farming, there are 1.4 million educated specialists and nearly 4.5 million mechanics and drivers.

Last but not least there is the continued contraction of the rural population. Just between the January censuses of 1970 and

1979 urban population climbed by 27.6 million, while rural population declined by 6.9 million, despite the fact that the birth rate is much higher in the countryside. The explanation is simple. In the growth of the towns only 12 million is accounted for by natural increase, the rest is due to migration from the country or to the transformation of villages into small towns. At this rate, by the mid-eighties only one-third of the Soviet population should be rural, exactly the same proportion as in France in the mid-sixties.

The international comparison is instructive. Continental western Europe has undergone in the postwar years the second phase of its agricultural revolution, with massive shifts of population. The original British pattern has spread. Farming now represents a rather small proportion of total employment, less then 9 percent in France and 15 percent in Italy. Though farm lobbies still exercise a disproportionate influence over policy, the political weight of the countryside, of its interests and moods, is no longer crucial. Something similar can be said of the Soviet Union, which is still at an earlier stage of the same process. The massive employment in farming strains the economy. Relatively backward rural Russia, with its nearly 100 million inhabitants, undoubtedly has an impact on the political and moral climate of the country as a whole. But the shape of the future is no longer determined there. The balance has clearly switched to the towns.

The early Bolsheviks, brought up on revolutionary history, were capable of discussing at length their own present in terms of, say, the French Thermidor. This analysis by analogy was carried on by their epigones, who were haunted by the idea of a peasant emperor, a Soviet Bonaparte, a military commander able to seize power harnessing the aspirations of land-hungry peasants. Such fears persisted well after the last war. They are by now obsolete. The men in the Kremlin need no longer spend sleepless nights worrying about peasant Bonapartism. Which does not mean that they can now sleep soundly. What they gain on the swings, they may lose on the roundabouts, as the more educated and more sophisticated towndwellers present them with new nightmares.

Soviet citizens are now predominantly towndwellers. Indeed, they are big-towndwellers. At the close of the 1970s 100 million

Soviet people lived in fairly large towns of more than 100,000 inhabitants and 33 million actually in the 18 towns of more than 1 million inhabitants. This concentration has a cultural as well as a social significance. Even today, for instance, there are three times as many graduates in urban than in rural areas and, according to Soviet authors, the educational level rises with the size of the town.[15]

If it is more educated, the urban population shares another feature with its rural counterpart: both are now less frightened. The Stalinist nightmare is gradually receding with the passing of time. Men born before the October Revolution are fit for a pension—or the politburo. Those who started working before the last war have today retired and even those who entered active life before Stalin's death are now distinctly a minority in the still expanding labor force. Though memories are lingering on and conditioned reflexes die hard, Soviet society is slowly awakening. Nobody would dare to suggest that flowers are blooming in hundreds or that conflicting interests are plainly expressed in open debate. The *psykhushka*, the psychiatric ward, is still threatening the genuine dissenter, particularly if he or she is not famous and lives far from Moscow. Still, no longer paralyzed by terror and slowly emerging from the melting pot, in which they were changed beyond recognition, the various social groups are beginning to grope toward an understanding of their collective interests, if not yet toward their expression.

Who are the actors thus getting ready to play their part on the political stage? In the idyllic official version, at least since Khrushchev's days, the Soviet Union is a "state of the whole people." It is not really a "classless" society: the cooperative peasants cannot yet be equated with the workers. The weight of the former, we saw, is declining, while that of the latter is rising; by now they are dominant, at least numerically. The legend that the workers, though deprived of all means of collective expression, are also politically dominant—the myth on which the rule of the Communist Party officially rests—does not help to clarify matters. The concept of the working class at least is fairly clear, whereas the same cannot be said of the third component of the official social trinity, the "friendly stratum" which stands next to the two "nonantagonistic" classes, the intelligentsia.

The vague term "employees," roughly the white-collar workers, conceals in Soviet statistics a strange mixture stretching from poorly paid elementary schoolteachers or shop assistants to the grossly rewarded academicians or party dignitaries. The ambiguity is not accidental: the authorities and their censors have no desire to facilitate the study of the ruling group and of its ramifications, no wish to lift the veil surrounding its mode of life or to reveal its direct or indirect share in the nation's surplus. Despite the revival of Soviet sociology this aspect is still largely taboo and social differentiation among the loosely defined "employees" is presented mainly in terms of education. This is why, after a short examination of the new proletariat, I shall sum up the results of the USSR's educational revolution before looking more closely at the ambiguous intelligentsia and its many temptations.

The Would-Be Masters

In normal times the working class absorbs newcomers into its ranks fairly easily. When the inflow is important, like in the recent example of southern Italians migrating to the industrial north, the integration is more complex and affects the temper of the body as a whole. In general, however, the working class, with its numbers, its traditions, its organizations, somehow manages to impose its patterns of life and labor onto the new migrants. Naturally, the process was not the same originally, in the early stages of the Industrial Revolution. Nor was it the same during Russia's unprecedented upheaval.

On the morrow of October the tragedy of the isolated revolution sprang from the contrast between the small, and shrinking, working class and the great peasant mass by which it was surrounded. At the end of the Civil War, with many industrial workers dispersed in the countryside and many others absorbed by the machinery of the ruling state, the revolutionary class had almost vanished and in their bitter controversies the Bolsheviks themselves were talking about the proletarian revolution without the proletariat.[16] By 1928, after several years of the New

Economic Policy, the working class, about 8 million strong, had roughly recovered its prewar level. Then, as the old social order was being destroyed in the countryside while fantastic targets were being set for industrial production in the towns, it climbed out of all proportions: within a dozen years it nearly tripled, reaching 24 million on the eve of the Second World War.

By the sheer weight of numbers the uprooted peasants were imposing their bewildered and resentful mood on the towns. Unaccustomed to urban life and particularly to its work rhythm, they had to fit in somehow, since the concentration camp was the penalty for genuine or imaginary sabotage. As the countryside, ruined by collectivization, was in no position to pay for the huge accumulation required, the growing working class had to bear the bulk of the burden. The fast-increasing urban masses had to contend for an almost unchanged supply of food and other consumer goods. Living in overcrowded quarters, underfed, the transplanted peasants were condemned to a bitter struggle for survival, while the communist leadership, forgetting the party principles of egalitarianism, was reinforcing the absence of solidarity through wage differentiation and Stakhanovism.

Obviously this was not the whole picture. The October Revolution did open up new prospects and release great resources of enthusiasm and abnegation. Young workers by their thousands did volunteer for pioneer labor in distant, unhospitable lands. Even the antagonized elders were impressed by the dazzling possibilities of educational and social advance offered to their children. Soviet propaganda did not rest on nothing. But it concealed the havoc wrought by "primitive socialist accumulation," the political, moral, as well as economic price paid for its sake by the working class.

This heritage must be kept in mind because it still weighs heavily on the workers as a class, despite the fact that the sons are so different from the fathers. Though no longer advancing by leaps and bounds, the working class has continued to grow steadily, climbing from about 30 million before Stalin's death to over 78 million in 1980. According to surveys carried out in big industrial centers the majority of newcomers are now recruited from working-class families.[17] Besides, the annual increments

Table I. Urban Labor Force, 1977

	Workers		Employees		Total[a]	
	millions	%	millions	%	millions	%
Industry	29.5	45.9	5.9	19.3	35.4	37.3
Transport & communications	8.5	13.2	2.7	8.9	11.2	11.8
Construction	8.3	12.9	2.6	8.4	10.9	11.5
Trade & procurements	7.3	11.3	3.2	10.6	10.5	11.1
Housing, communal services	3.3	5.2	0.7	2.3	4.0	4.2
Other (health, education, insurance, administration)	7.4	11.5	15.5	50.5	22.9	24.1
Total	64.3	100.0	30.6	100.0	94.9	100.0

Source: Compiled from figures in Nar. Khoz., 1977, pp. 378–81.
[a]Total number of "workers and employees" in 1977 was 106,393,000, but 11,451,000 among them were employed in farming and forestry, leaving 94,942,000 in nonagricultural employment. The corresponding figure for 1978 was 96,900,000. I am using the data for 1977 in order to compare this category with the number of specialists in the same branches (see Table II).

are by now only a fraction of the total. They merge into a huge urban army of labor, nearly one-half of which is employed in industry (this figure approaches three-quarters if building and transport are included).

Much larger, the new working class is also incomparably better educated. The figures, however striking, do not quite convey the change. On the eve of the last war only 8 out of 100 workers had gone further than elementary school; by 1977 this had increased to 73 out of 100. It will be objected that among the allegedly educated many have merely an "unfinished secondary education," i.e., some seven years of schooling. The argument is true, but the statistical picture is still partly a reflection of the past. Now, each year over 5 million young people graduate from the ten-year school or its equivalent and only about half of them can find a place at university or in a technical college. Today, most of the young workers have a complete secondary education and quite often a technical qualification on top of it. They view society differently than did the semiliterate muzhiks.

In a more eloquent mood Soviet writers present these worker-intellectuals (rabochyie-inteligenty) as the portent of the near

Table II. Urban Specialists, 1977[a]

	University graduates		Technical college graduates		Total		Specialists as % of employment in branch
	thous.	%	thous.	%	thous.	%	
Industry	1,983	19.7	4,308	31.9	6,291	26.6	17.8
Transport & communications	303	3.0	939	6.9	1,242	5.2	11.1
Construction	976	9.7	1,299	9.6	2,275	9.7	20.9
Trade & procurements	282	2.8	1,183	8.7	1,465	6.2	13.9
Housing, communal services	247	2.5	444	3.3	691	2.9	17.0
Other, including:	6,257	62.3	5,349	39.6	11,606	49.2	50.7
health, etc.	829	8.3	2,224	16.4	4,052	17.2	68.0
education, science	4,573	45.5	2,308	17.1	6,881	29.2	49.0
banking, insurance	47	0.5	180	1.3	227	1.0	39.4
administration	808	8.0	637	4.7	1,445	6.1	63.1
Total	10,048	100	13,522	100	23,570	100	24.8

Source: Compiled from data in Nar. Khoz., 1977, p. 394 and 378–81.
[a]By adding 489,000 university graduates and 1,119,000 specialists with secondary education employed in farming one obtains the total of 25,178,000 specialists in the economy as a whole in 1977 (see Table I).

future, when the difference between manual and mental labor gradually will vanish. Such propaganda, however, has little connection with reality and little prospect for fulfillment. First, the proportion of physical, nonmechanized labor is particularly high in Soviet industry, much higher than in the West; this is, incidentally, one of the main reasons for lower productivity. Second, and this is crucial, the Soviet Union has not altered in any fundamental way the capitalist division of labor and has not invented any ways for investing the immediate producers with genuine mastery over their labor. Hence even if automation were to spread very rapidly, far from eliminating alienated labor, it would merely extend it beyond the factory gates, here too following the western pattern. In their more sober moments, Soviet sociologists already mention timidly the frustrations and discontent of the young Russian workers. In a stratified and more stable society, they have less hope for advancement. They resent the fact that they were deprived of the possibility of further study. They are dissatisfied with their jobs, which are below their actual or potential qualifications. These frustrated young workers may well bring about the political reawakening of the Soviet working class.

Whatever the differences in numerical strength and levels of culture, the sons have no more effective political power than had their fathers. They too have to content themselves with the double fiction that the party represents their interests and that the factories are their own. They have no right to strike, to bargain collectively, to express their autonomous class interests. The labor unions are at best like mutual friendly societies, dealing with holidays, housing, working conditions, and at worst they are mere tools of management. Very occasionally, the pent-up discontent leads to an explosion, a wildcat strike, like the one in Novotcherkask in 1962 which was drowned in blood. The workers, the alleged masters of the land have as yet no political channels at their disposal.

Nevertheless, they count for more than did their fathers. Unable to wield the stick in Stalin's fashion, his successors are forced to use the carrot more often—not out of any deference to Marxist principles, but because of a healthy awareness of the potential power of the working class. Whatever the reasons, the wages of the workers have gone up in recent years, steadily rather than spectacularly, and their working hours have been shortened. Since 1956, when wartime legislation was finally repealed, they are no longer tied to their place of work and, in principle, can move after two weeks' notice. On the other hand, they cannot be fired so easily. Indeed, one of the main complaints made by the managers about the Soviet economic system is that they cannot take advantage of higher productivity because they cannot hire and fire at will.

While not fundamentally different in organization from the

western capitalist enterprise, the Soviet firm is not an exact copy either. Western communists visiting Soviet factories are often struck by the relatively leisurely atmosphere prevailing there. The difference should not be idealized: the mad rush at the end of the month and even more at the end of the year to fulfill the planned working target (the so-called storming) puts a heavy, if irrational, strain on the resources of the working people. Yet the impression is not inaccurate. In Stalin's time the threat of the gulag was, among other things, a means of imposing the rhythm of industrial work on raw, transplanted peasants. His successors have not found a substitute to deal with the more sophisticated labor force. Without the fear of unemployment and without a coherent set of incentives, the workers are not driven to produce surplus value at quite the same pace as their western counterparts. Indeed, one may talk here of a compromise, of an unwritten truce between the true and the alleged masters of the country, between the leaders in the Kremlin and the Soviet working class, in which the former tell the latter: leave all the decisions to us, don't meddle in politics, and we will not push the rate of exploitation to the full, leaving you with enough energy for some at least to moonlight on the side, thus helping to make ends meet.

I shall argue in the last section of this essay that this tacit truce, highly unsatisfactory for the workers, is drawing to an end, that diminishing returns on investment, a declining supply of labor, and a slackening rate of growth will soon force the leadership to break it in search of higher productivity. Even if this argument were accepted, one question would still remain: What will drive the Russian workers to united action as a "class-for-itself," to use the language of the young Marx? They have no memory, no tradition of solidarity, no channels for organized action. Atomized during the Stalinist upheaval, they have been torn apart by wage differentiation. A labor aristocracy has been bribed to some extent by wages close to the salaries of graduate engineers in production (though not in managerial jobs). Even if somewhat narrowed in recent years, the gap is still serious between, say, the wages of the skilled male workers in engineering or construction and those of the predominantly female workers in the textile industry.

Looking at it from a historical perspective, only one program may be able to unify this divided working class: the revival of egalitarianism in the widest sense of that term, an egalitarianism going well beyond the leveling of incomes, tackling the roots of the hierarchical division of labor, the problems of power and of decision-making, all social inequalities, including those between the sexes. The working class is fundamentally interested not in the mythical "state of the whole people" or the fictional merging of "friendly classes" but in a genuine classless society, which alone can eliminate its persisting handicaps and alienation. This is why in the Soviet Union, too, the working class remains potentially the revolutionary class—in the sense the term is used in *The Communist Manifesto*.

The trouble with historical perspectives is that they often loom distant. For the moment, far from emerging as a class-for-itself, the Soviet workers must still take the first steps to defend their elementary interests and act as a class at all. Even if they were to be stirred into action by the frustrated newcomers, they would still have to find allies. To suggest who these can be we must first look at the educational revolution, which has not only changed beyond recognition the Soviet working class but which has also altered relations within society as a whole.

Surprises of the Educational Revolution

Griboyedov's *Woe from Wit* is a Russian classic. The Soviet leaders often must be reminded of its title as each year a bigger number of high school graduates knocks at the door of the university only to find that there is no room for them at the top. The impressive spread of mass education was once viewed by the rulers as part of a scientific revolution which was going to solve their economic difficulties; and we shall see later why the expected miracle did not come off. But already the clash between the aspirations of the young generation and the possibilities offered raises a serious problem, increases tensions, and reveals a great deal about the structure of Soviet society.

The educational achievement of the Soviet state is undeniable, even if the content of that education is by now very far from revolutionary. On the morrow of October, during the period of hopeful if disorderly experiments, the reformers wished not only to restore equality by granting priority to yesterday's down-trodden, the workers and the peasants. They wanted to change the very nature of education, so as to turn it into one of the crucial instruments for establishing a classless society of equals. In the 1930s all such ambitions were condemned as Utopian nonsense. As the officers recovered their epaulets, the schools got back their golden medals, their academic traditions, and their respect for hierarchy. The fact that political courses in so-called Marxism-Leninism were preserved only made matters worse. The once revolutionary doctrine and critical method were gradually identified in the eyes of the people with the hypocritically flexible gospel of the establishment.

Yet in its scope the educational reform was revolutionary. For the Bolsheviks, faced with an almost illiterate country, the task was tremendous. They had to start from scratch, to teach primary teachers, to run crash courses in so-called workers' faculties to prepare gifted workers for university. Despite its poverty, the country devoted a high proportion of its scarce resources to mass education. Stalin's successors are no innovators in this field: they have collected cumulative dividends on past investment. If anything, they rather slowed down the process of expansion. As the wave of the educated did work its way through from primary to secondary education, Khrushchev tried to divert it temporarily into production and Brezhnev did little to provide new outlets in universities. In fact, the regime found itself in a dilemma.

Young Russians start school at the age of seven and "complete secondary education" (i.e., a ten-year school) means that they graduate at about seventeen or eighteen. High school education for all was launched as a slogan in the fifties, precisely at the time when the high school graduate ceased to be certain of getting a place at university. Hence the delay in carrying the program into practice. The conflict of interests which was involved in this issue led to serious studies and gave rise to one of the rare real debates authorized in the Soviet Union. To understand what it was all about, it is worth looking at the figures in the latest year for which detailed statistics are available.[18]

In 1978 just over 4 million young Soviet citizens obtained their high school diplomas of ten-year education. Three million got it from day schools, while more than 1 million had studied in the evening. In that same year the universities accepted 624,000 full-time students and 402,000 in evening and correspondence courses. In other words, depending on the definition, the graduate had one chance in seven or one in four to get into an institution of higher education, where he or she would study for four to five years. Another 896,500 got the second best, i.e., a place in the so-called specialized secondary schools, the technical colleges producing technicians, primary schoolteachers, junior staff in planning or in the medical services. There studies range from two to four years, because these colleges also admit students with only eight years of school (they actually took 547,000 such students in that year).

The eighth year is crucial in Soviet schools. Until then all youngsters are supposed to get a similar education apart from the inevitable differences between schools, especially between urban and rural areas. In 1976—sticking to comparable figures—over 5 million young people finished the eighth grade and, if statistics are to be believed, 97 percent of them went on to complete their secondary education. This is the sense in which it is claimed that the reform is virtually carried out. Not all the young Soviet citizens, however, are getting the same treatment. Out of the 5 million, as we just saw, over 3 million continued full-time study at school and over .5 million moved to specialized secondary education. The rest had to combine work and study, many of them in vocational professional schools. These lower grade technical institutes look like the provisional solution for the government; by extending the courses to three years it allows young people to learn a trade and officially to complete their secondary education.

The snag is that the prospects of each kind of education differ, and they show clear social distinctions. The vocational schools, preparing more or less skilled workers, are filled by children of laborers and collective farmers. The technical colleges, providing the "middle specialists," or the noncommissioned officers of the Soviet army of labor, have a good proportion of children of skilled blue-collar workers and of the unskilled "employees": the share of more privileged children rises as entry to higher education becomes tighter. The universities, which supply the officers' corps, show a clear bias in favor of what the Russians call the intelligentsia, that is to say the children of graduates from both universities and technical colleges. This so-called intelligentsia accounts for less than one-fifth of the labor force, but its children fill about half the places in the universities. The social contrast would be even more striking if Soviet scholars were allowed to study seriously the real upper class—the senior officials of the party and the state, the higher managers, the top layers of the scientific establishment and of the propaganda machine—or if they could carry out their surveys in some of the privileged special colleges, such as the Moscow Institute of International Relations.

To suggestions of class bias, the orthodox spokespeople reply indignantly with figures, claiming that "over 80 percent of the first secretaries of the CP in the republics, the krays, and the oblasts, of heads of republican governments . . . and 70 percent of ministers . . . began their activity as workers or peasants" and that "more than half the directors of the bigger industrial firms are former workers."[19] They thus plead the past to justify the present and conceal the future. Everybody knows that the October Revolution opened the way for an unprecedented promotion of the exploited, that in the early years it did not hide its bias in favor of the children of workers and peasants in the admission to university, that in its hurry to fill many commanding positions it relied on the *praktiki*, on trusted people appointed to jobs for which they did not have the formal qualifications. Yet there is a radical difference between a post-revolutionary regime sweeping aside the old order and an established, hierarchical society, particularly when the latter is threatened with a slackening rate of growth. Politically, the conservative nature of the present Soviet regime, based on cooptation from above, is obvious. Socially, the self-perpetuation of the privileged may prove its logical companion.

Two points are particularly interesting in the Soviet sociological literature on education.[20] In the first place, most children of the "specialists" expect to get into a university, and they actually do, sometimes even if their marks are far from brilliant. The ambitions of the children of the workers are not quite so great, but they are much higher than justified by the actual results. This widening gap between the great expectations and the sobering reality is potentially explosive. Secondly, the arguments used to explain the relative success of the privileged children have a strangely familiar sound: better housing, a higher cultural level at home, private tuition, and—hinted rather than emphasized— the pull and connections of the parents. The question is not whether class advantages still play a bigger role in the West; after all, there are differences in discrimination between capitalist states as well. The relevant point is that the problem is similar. Indeed, one wonders whether the tension is not more acute in the Soviet Union. In our societies the wealthy can ensure the future of their children to some extent through inheritance, bequeathing them stocks and other assets. In the Soviet Union, where higher education and a party card now are considered the two main keys to a comfortable position, the parents must fight harder still for the perpetuation of privilege.

To be fair, it must be added that the authorities did hesitate over the best way to tackle this explosive issue. In December 1958 Khrushchev introduced a two-year pause between high school and university, during which the aspiring students had to prove their worth in production. The move was interpreted as an attack on the privileged and was resisted as such. Politics, however, are ambiguous and Khrushchev had another purpose as well. He hoped in this way to frighten the intelligentsia and silence the students at a time when his own indictment of Stalin had given food for dissident thought. After the passage through the factory only the faithful and the orthodox would get the blessing from the Young Communist League or the labor unions, necessary to reenter higher education.

In any case, the pressure to drop class criteria and admit to the universities those who are "academically best" was so strong that Khrushchev himself was going to yield, and his successors dropped the productive interlude almost at once. Yet they, too, kept a small lever, setting up preparatory courses for admission

Table III. Population with Some Secondary Education

	Years of study[a]	1959		1970		1977	
		millions	%[b]	millions	%[b]	millions	%[b]
Higher complete	15	3.8	1.8	8.3	3.4	12.5	4.5
Higher incomplete	13	1.7	0.8	2.6	1.1	2.8	1.1
Secondary specialized	12	7.9	3.8	13.4	5.5	17.8	7.6
Secondary general	10	9.9	4.7	23.4	9.7	37.2	14.4
Secondary incomplete	8	35.4	17.0	57.3	19.6	53.9	20.9
Total		58.7	28.1	95.0	39.3	126.1	48.9

[a]Estimated average; for elementary education this is put at five years.
[b]As percentage of total population.

to university reserved for sons of workers and peasants. They thus have a politically reliable contingent and a quota which marginally redresses the balance. The general trend, however, is unmistakable, and it could not be otherwise: the Russians have not discovered the miraculous way to establish an equal education while preserving an unequal society.

The educational conflict is not transitional. Tensions have been building up and are bound to increase still further. The summary of the results of all this schooling shown in Table III is static by its very nature. To convey the dynamics of change it is enough to recall that only 2.4 million specialists with higher or specialized secondary education were working in the Soviet

Table IV. Education of Employed Population
(per 1000 employed in the national economy)

	Secondary education[a]		Higher education		Total	
	Country	Town	Country	Town	Country	Town
1939	60	210	3	32	63	242
1959	305	505	11	59	316	564
1970	474	658	25	90	499	748
1977	634	719	39	116	673	835

[a]Including incomplete; i.e., all people having more than five years of schooling.

Union on the eve of the last war; they numbered 12 million in 1965 and 26.4 million thirteen years later. The so-called technical and professional intelligentsia has ceased to be a small elite. Admittedly, it is spread unequally between the countryside and the towns: in agriculture the specialists account for about 6 percent of the labor force, while outside of farming they account for close to 25 percent. Even outside agriculture the distribution varies, with about half the specialists (as could be expected) in culture and education, health services, and the administration. What is significant, however, is that in industry and building, too, about one out of five employed is now a specialist, and the proportion is rising.

This image of a scientific revolution in progress must be somewhat qualified. The intelligentsia is a vague term. In tsarist times it referred to the educated, who were a rare commodity, and it had a moral connotation. Its members were assumed to be socially committed, striving in some way to change the shape of things. The current Soviet definition applies simply to specialists with more than 12 years of education, often narrow specialists who would not normally qualify as intellectuals at all. Among the more than 15 million technical college graduates (referred to earlier as the NCOs) about 7 million are really highly skilled technicians, working mainly in industry. The second biggest category, those employed in the health services, is so large because in addition to medical assistants (*feldchers*) it also includes qualified nurses. Health professionals are followed by elementary schoolteachers and the fast-rising group of accountants, statisticians, and other junior planning staff.

The university graduates, the real officers—though, unfortunately, they are lumped together without a genuine distinction of rank—have now passed the 11 million mark. By far the two biggest divisions among them are the graduate engineers (working both in production and management) and all sorts of teaching staff, mainly in secondary schools (in 1978 there were some 1.8 million graduate teachers just in the general day schools). Following far behind, each nearing 1 million, are doctors and economists and, still further, agricultural specialists.

In order to prove the growing homogeneity of their society,

Soviet writers like to emphasize the relatively small discrepancy between the salaries of specialists and the wages of workers. In 1978, it is claimed, the graduate engineers and technicians in industry earned on an average 208.4 roubles per month, which was only 18.3 percent higher than the 176.1 roubles earned by the average worker (in 1965 the alleged difference was 46 percent). Statistical averages indicate important trends but quite often they also conceal significant differences. Hidden among the specialists is the real upper class, with which we shall deal in the next section. Here it is enough to say that there are engineers and engineers. The engineer in management gets a higher salary, a bigger bonus, not to mention all sorts of extras, than does the run-of-the-mill production engineer. The difference in reward between the latter and the technician and between the technician and the skilled worker is not very big. Keeping in mind the traditional large variations in wages between branches in Soviet industry—essentially between heavy and light industry—and the increasing discrepancies between regions, aimed at spurring migration to, say, Siberia and the Far East, the figures look plausible. The shrinking gap reflects the narrowing difference in qualifications in the middle ranks. As the really privileged are lost somewhere within deceptive averages, however, the figures do not tell the whole story.

There is yet another reason for the apparently small difference in income between the loosely defined intelligentsia and the working class. To explain it I must mention briefly a crucial question, to which I cannot do justice in such a short essay, namely the discrimination against women. Properly, one should talk about womanpower rather than manpower in the Soviet Union, since women represent 51 percent of the labor force. The opportunities offered to women to go to work in impressive numbers is one of the achievements of the regime and the occasional suggestions, prompted by the falling birth rate, to send them back to the kitchen and the nursery represent there as everywhere the voice of reaction. But, having thus given the women an opportunity, the regime did not provide sufficient amenities to reduce their burden. Above all, after the original experiments of the early period, it restored the bourgeois family in all its traditional splendor. Hence the Soviet woman, too, must play two roles at once. On top of her work, she has the care of the family, the food, the children. She works longer hours and is handicapped in her professional life.

The discrimination against women is most obvious in politics, where with the fleeting exception of Ekaterina Furtseva, no woman has sat in the politburo. The lower you go down the ladder of power and decision, the higher the proportion of women in political institutions. Something similar can be detected in employment. At first sight this appears paradoxical, since Soviet women are if anything more educated than men. They account, for example, for 59 percent of Soviet "specialists" (though only 52 percent of those with university education). Whenever you probe behind this flattering image, sex discrimination rears its ugly head. Thus, four out of ten Soviet scientific workers are women; among professors and academicians the proportion drops to one out of ten. Women represent 83 percent of all heads of elementary schools; among heads of secondary schools they are only 31 percent. Women are as numerous as men in the collective farms, but among the 26,461 heads of the *kolkhozy* in 1977 there were only 507 women, or 1.9 percent.

Women are to be found in professions where salaries are relatively modest, or to put it differently, wherever women predominate wages are low. The proportion of women is particularly high in education (74 percent), culture (72 percent), and health and social insurance (83 percent). These, as we saw, happen to be branches in which the share of specialists is also exceptionally high and therefore salaries should be above average. Actually, they are about one-third lower than the wages of workers in industry. The glorious, uncharted road toward the elimination of difference between mental and manual labor, beginning allegedly by the narrowing of financial differences between the two, turns out to be a dead end, resting on the very traditional exploitation of women. I cannot end this too-brief discussion without stating the obvious: in the USSR as in the West, no egalitarian program for the radical transformation of society will have any meaning unless it involves woman's liberation at the very heart of its project.

Meanwhile, the competition for places in institutions of higher education will become more acute each year and will spread inevitably to technical colleges. The already impressive ranks of the technical intelligentsia will continue to swell as generations in which the specialists were the exception are gradually replaced by new ones in which they are the rule. The methods of selection are not innocent and their social beneficiaries are politically significant. The struggle over the shape of the educational system has been and remains so fascinating because the hidden tensions and the latent class conflicts have been allowed for once to come to the surface. Sooner or later, the social forces will break the political straitjacket. Then, when the class struggle is no longer fought furtively by educational proxy but comes into the open and gathers momentum, the loose amalgamation of the educated, brought together artificially under the name of the intelligentsia, will not act as "a class for itself"; it will break up and choose sides, in keeping with its contrasting inner interests. Yet to venture this is to anticipate my argument.

The Hidden Rulers

Having surveyed briefly the tremendous expansion of Soviet education and the resulting rise of the technical intelligentsia we may look more closely at the odd member of the Soviet trinity, the strange tribe of the *sluzhashchyie,* the nearly 33 million or so "employees" who together with their families represented about 23 percent of the Soviet population in 1978 and nearly one-third of total labor power outside farming. It is also by far the fastest growing category in the Soviet Union where since the 1960s employees are expanding at a quicker rate than workers, reversing the previous trend. Unfortunately, like "tertiary employment," its western cousin, this is an ill-defined social category, lumping together the most privileged with some of the worst exploited. To make matters worse, its frontiers are loosely drawn.

The official statistics define as *sluzhashchyie* all those who are doing nonmanual work outside collective farming. Yet the same statistics claim that 37.5 million people were doing "predominantly mental work" in 1977, when there were only 31.9 million employees. Even making allowance for those doing nonmanual work in collective farms, one is left with more than 4 million people unaccounted for, presumably workers considered as performing predominantly mental tasks. This impression of an ill-defined frontier is confirmed by the fact that whenever the general figures are cross-checked, the number of people actually doing specialist jobs in a given branch is smaller than the number of specialists allegedly working in that branch.[21] This leads to the politically interesting conclusion that already several million graduates from specialized secondary schools are employed in the economy as workers.

The *sluzhashchyie* are so obviously a mixed lot that Soviet sociologists themselves were compelled to draw a distinction between the nonspecialists and the rest. But to calculate the number of unqualified employees it is not enough to subtract the 24 million or so specialists from the total of employees since many qualified as specialists do not exercise their profession. Very roughly, the number of unqualified employees can be estimated at around 10 million. Clerks, junior office staff, and shop assistants provide the bulk of the white-collar workers. Once again, women predominate in these poorly paid jobs. In the Soviet hierarchy of incomes, the nonspecialist employees are close to bottom, just above the collective farmers and roughly on a par with the unskilled workers. Indeed, some Soviet social scientists have argued that they should be included with the working class.

Since they have been allowed to probe the reality of their country, Soviet sociologists, while sticking to the formula of "two nonantagonistic classes plus a friendly stratum," have embarked on permutations within this framework and on arguments about its content. The unqualified employees are not the only object of this debate. Some researchers, starting from the premise that what matters is relationship to the means of production, have argued that technicians and engineers employed in production should be amalgamated with the urban workers, while specialists in collective farms should be included with the *kolkhozniki*, in both cases as a layer of the same class. Others, while maintaining specialists as a separate entity, began dividing them into component parts.

Back in the 1960s for example, V. S. Semenov took 1959 population census data and split the intelligentsia into three sections: *cultural-scientific*, including teachers, doctors, scientific workers, and so on, he numbered over 5 million; *technical-economic*, including engineers, agronomists, planners, he estimated at nearly 5 million; and last but not least, *managerial*, in which he included 2.4 million people by adding up leading personnel in state administration and public organizations, heads of firms and their subsidiaries, as well as senior accountants.[22]

The same issue of managers was approached more recently by M. Rutkevich, a staunch opponent of the amalgamation of specialists with workers or collective farmers. Instead, he proposed to subdivide the intelligentsia by educational level, separating technicians from specialized secondary school and university graduates. Among the latter he then selected two interesting strata: the creative intelligentsia, in which he included the most qualified specialists in science, technology, the arts, and administration, and a larger section carrying out "organizing functions"; the latter comprised "heads (*rukovoditieli*) of enterprises and their subsidiaries as well as their deputies, chiefs of their structural subdivisions, i.e., of shops, laboratories, departments, university chairs, etc.," and its membership was estimated at "about one-fifth of all specialists." Having thus whetted our appetite, the author added at once that organizing is not just the prerogative of these managers, that "in the framework of Soviet socialist democracy it is carried out by millions of Soviet citizens—workers, *kolkhozniks*, employees and specialists."[23]

Whether Mr. Rutkevich was writing in earnest or tongue-in-cheek is irrelevant. Not all Soviet scholars are bound to pay lip service to a fiction so ostentatiously, though none are allowed to look behind the white collars at their rulers and then describe their position, at least not in official publications. Hence, it is without their direct help that we have to tackle the crucial question of who rules the Soviet Union. The answer is as difficult as it is vital, since there is no obvious class of private property owners, the revolutionary regime having nationalized all the means of production. Yet, if capitalism as described by the Marxist classics has been partly abolished, the reign of capital has not.[24] The hierarchical division of labor is unchanged and exploitation persists as surplus value is extracted in an unequal society.

Indeed, the weight of the state is felt more heavily and more directly under the Soviet regime, which cannot rely for this extraction on the automatic mechanism of commodity production, as in normal times a capitalist state more or less can do, but which has made no progress either, despite its economic achievements, toward the socialist solution to this dilemma, namely, the conscious organization of production by freely associated individuals. Thus political decisions taken from above must determine not only the line in foreign policy or the burden of defense, but also the global distribution of resources between accumulation and consumption. Within the limits set by the passive resistance of civil society, the rulers must determine everything, including the level of wages and the rate of exploitation in individual factories.

But who takes the decisions? Apologists and critics alike give the same answer: the party. Unfortunately, the answer merely begs the question. Except for propagandists on duty, nobody would seriously suggest that key decisions are taken by the 17 million or so party members. Even if the Brezhnev regime has succeeded in convincing the rank and file that their small advantages, such as priority on the housing list, are intimately linked with the system and the incomparably greater privileges of its main beneficiaries, it has not given them the illusion of sharing power. The ordinary members have as much influence on party decisions as the workers have on the management of *their* factories. If decisions are taken not by the 17 million, then are they taken by the twenty-six people at the top of the party pyramid enumerated in the chart at the beginning of this essay? No doubt the key decisions are taken in their offices, that is to say in the politburo and the secretariat. But Nikita Khrushchev, who had filled these very offices with his nominees, was cast out by them when he seemed to threaten some wider interests. Who then? The central committee and its growing staff? The secretaries of regional, urban, and district committees? Or the 300,000 or so full-time party officials?

The party apparatus, though itself manipulated from above, is at this stage unquestionably the dominant element in the Soviet power structure. Yet what I described earlier as Brezhnev's constituency extends well beyond the narrowly defined apparatchiks. It certainly includes all those in important jobs, figuring in the *nomenklatura*, that is to say where appointment requires the blessing of the central committee at the national or regional level. It really stretches well beyond if it is meant to absorb all people in commanding positions, the "managers" of Mr. Semenov or the "organizers" of Mr. Rutkevich. One should still add to this group senior officers in the armed forces and the police as well as the ideological servants of the state: the censors, the writers to measure, the journalists prompt to fulfill any order, the social scientists ready with the appropriate quotation from Marx or Lenin to justify the latest twist in the party line. The frontiers for what I would call the aspiring or potential ruling class are still loose, and its size cannot be defined precisely with the statistical data available. But, at a conservative estimate, it numbers around 6 million people or 5 percent of the working population.

Logically, the next step should be to find out the social cost of this establishment, the part of the surplus its position enables it to absorb. The share must be high, since its membership almost coincides with the country's top income bracket; only actors and ballet dancers seem to be missing. On the other hand, it is claimed that the ratio between the highest and the lowest wages was reduced from 5 to 1 in 1968 to 4 to 1 in 1975.[25] The reference is presumably to the highest and lowest 10 percent, but even so the gap looks suspiciously low. The minimum wage in 1979 was 70 roubles per month. The earnings of an academician, a minister, a party dignitary, or the "personal salary" plus premium of a top manager were eight to ten times higher and they were boosted by other advantages. A spacious apartment in town, a *dacha* in the country, easy access to special shops where scarce goods are available, better medical facilities, a comfortable place in a Crimean holiday resort, a chauffeur-driven car, and that supreme Soviet reward, the opportunity to travel abroad—these are only some of the privileges which make the life of the Soviet elite totally different from that of the ordinary citizens.

But the country's privileged are not, or not yet, behaving like a rising class. They do not parade proudly their conspicuous consumption, but as if haunted by the egalitarian ghost, they prefer to conceal it, and have given orders that it should not appear either in literature or in statistics. Dissident writers occasionally reveal some aspects of inequality—thus the Medvedevs briefly mention in *Khrushchev: The Years in Power* that the Soviet leader had four lodgings: a house in Moscow and a villa in the country due to his rank and another two due to his function—but they have not made a thorough study of the phenomenon. From the existing evidence one can draw two contrasting conclusions: the discrepancies in earnings are quite high by any, and shameful by socialist, standards: and the differences in incomes, earned and unearned, are incomparably greater in the capitalist West. Just as I was working on the Soviet data, the French satirical weekly, *Le Canard Enchainé*, published the income tax returns of the aircraft tycoon Marcel Dassault. In 1978, a rather poor year for this rich man, he declared income of 24 million francs (about $5.7 million), which was equivalent to the annual earnings of 1090 French workers on the minimum wage. The Russians are not in the same class. If I may paraphrase Marx, they are still at the stage of the "accumulation of joys" (and, admittedly, of power), not at the stage of the "joy of accumulation."

The social cost, alas, is not measured only in this direct share of the national surplus. In an unequal society of scarcity, the state is the product and keeper of that social inequality. Its cost must include the soldiers, police, prosecutors, and propagandists who defend this order within society at large, but also the managers, supervisors, and foremen who preserve the hierarchical division of labor at the workplace. In theory, there was to be one partial exception to this rule. The post-revolutionary state, while still an organ of repression (the proletarian dictatorship), was also supposed to be an instrument of self-destruction. Acting consciously against social inequality and the hierarchical division of labor, it was meant to prepare the ground for a classless society; the state, gradually rendered superfluous, was thus to "wither away." The Soviet Leviathan crushing with its overwhelming weight Russia's civil society more than sixty years after the revolution does not necessarily destroy the validity of the theory. It does prove, at the very least, that such an advance toward a classless society after the revolution is neither automatic nor inevitable. As to the social cost of the ruling establishment, this must be measured together with the interests it defends and the function it performs.

In *The Revolution Betrayed*, his major work on Soviet society, Trotsky attributed a dual role to the Stalinist bureaucracy: a positive one in defending state property and planning; a negative one in encouraging the bourgeois norms of distribution well beyond the requirements of development in a society in transition. The contradiction could not last. It had to be resolved either by the restoration of capitalism or by the overthrow of the bureaucracy. This most original book is still in many respects relevant and stimulating. But forty-four years have elapsed since its publication and the reality has proved more complex than the forecasts of a bold thinker. Private ownership of the means of production has not been restored, nor has the bureaucracy been swept away by the workers. The party hierarchy, clinging not just to state property but to all the means of control over the population, has presided over a tremendous transformation of Soviet society, its structure changing almost beyond recognition. True, Stalinist mass terror prevented these changes from crystallizing politically and the more selective repression introduced by his successors still does not allow the open expression of class interests. But below the surface this new social make-up is beginning to exercise pressure on the power structure, especially at the top. A conflict is opening up within the party hierarchy between its bureaucratic and its technocratic wings; still hidden and partly controlled, it may soon alter the nature of the ruling establishment.

Too narrow an interpretation of state property and planning as virture per se could lead to strange alignments in this conflict.[26] Logically, in certain circumstances, it should drive a socialist to back the conservative apparatchiks against the timid reformers, whose preference in management for economic indicators, profits, and the market might (although not necessarily) lead in the long run to the undermining of state property. Yet these diehard apparatchiks, symbolically represented in the leadership by Mikhail Suslov, the keeper of orthodoxy, are not only nostalgic for the Stalinist gulag and champions of censorship. Whatever they may proclaim about the marvels of the future fully communist society, their main purpose is to prevent any initiative from below. If their power were perpetuated and the police were strong enough to keep the lid on, workers would never take the very elementary steps needed to prepare them for the part of freely associated producers.

The fundamentally reactionary nature of the apparatchiks does not turn the would-be reformers into seekers of socialist democracy. They come from the same stable. The administration of the party, the state, and the economy have become so intermingled under Soviet rule that the career of a Kosygin, known as the patron of the economic reformers, differs little from that of a Brezhnev or a Suslov. Managerial reformers are as frightened of power from below as their colleagues. Political choice, freedom of expression, or the right to strike are not even hinted at in their projects. Actually, the first result of their policy would be to widen the differentials and strengthen the privileges. For a socialist the temptation is great simply to wish a plague on both their houses.

Of the two evils, the rise of the technocrats is preferable on purely pragmatic grounds. First, the distorting veil surrounding the workings of the Soviet economy hinders not only production, but also the awareness of social groups as to their position in the process of production and exchange. More transparent, more naked relations could speed up the development of class consciousness. Second, decentralizing decisions and granting more powers to the managers, the reformers might be forced to instill some life into the moribund trade unions and, if they did not, to precipitate unwittingly the spontaneous revival of a labor movement. Last but not least, as the Czech spring showed so strikingly, the reform spreads from economics into politics. Even if the Czech experiment was cut short, it did suggest that such prospects as the resurrection of workers' councils or the search for new forms of democracy are not too distant on the horizon. To put it in a nutshell, the rule of the apparatchiks at best might lead to a spontaneous explosion, without, for the time being, any political perspective. The rule of the technocrats could heighten class consciousness, thus opening up vistas when the conflict occurs.

Reform involves political risks for the rulers and this is why it has not been and will not be allowed to move beyond a certain point, according to some observers, though in the case of Czechoslovakia the process was stopped from outside by Soviet tanks. As to the Soviet Union itself, it may be argued that the Brezhnev regime represents the highest stage of rule by the party apparatus. In Stalin's time the party machine, used but also abused, was for long intervals eclipsed by that other instrument of the dictatorship, the mighty secret police. Brezhnev, as we saw, brought into the organs of central power the policeman and the marshal, the administrator and the manager. The politburo, assisted by the secretariat, can be described by analogy as the "executive committee" of the budding ruling class, provided one keeps in mind that it always gives priority to its still dominant faction, the party apparatus. The managers, the administrators, the specialists are now assured that their positions will not be suddenly threatened by the machinery of terror run amok and that their privileges will be protected. They also know that at least for the time being, however, whenever their interests clash with those of the apparatchiks, the latter prevail. The general secretary stands above the premier, and this supremacy, which is effective at all levels of the hierarchy, is enshrined in the Soviet constitution.

This supremacy is at one and the same time absolute and precarious. There are at least two reasons to believe that this highest stage of rule by the party may also be the last. The principal motive, which I shall try to develop in the last part of this essay, is economic. Brezhnevism, designed to perpetuate the structure of power and the political status quo, is progressively becoming unworkable as a system; the cumulative effect of various trends may soon force the leadership to embark on an economic reform despite its undoubted political risks. The second reason is connected with the changes in the nature and the social composition of the Soviet Communist Party itself.

At no stage did the "proletarian dictatorship" in the Soviet Union mean the direct rule of a class; at best it could be interpreted for a period as the party dictatorship in the name of the working class. In the early years, however, the party was bound to promote leaders who came from the working class. After a crash course, trusted workers were given commanding positions in management; they provided the bulk of the already mentioned *praktiki*, holding jobs above their formal qualifications. Other trusted workers acted as supervisors over the specialists of bourgeois origin, the *spets* whose devotion to the new regime was suspect. The situation was totally altered by the spread of education mentioned earlier and the consequent emergence of a professional intelligentsia which came from the working class. The number of *praktiki* has now dwindled and the party supervisors are themselves specialists. Brezhnev boasted at the last party congress that 99 percent of the party secretaries down to the level of the town and distict committees are now graduates, mainly in engineering. The social aspects of party recruitment are reminiscent of the biases we perceived examining admission to higher education: farmworkers and urban laborers are under-represented, the skilled and white-collar workers less so, while the professional intelligentsia has a bigger share in the party membership than in the total population.

The comparison with access to university should not be overdrawn. The party must have a fair number of workers within its ranks if only to preserve its image as the "vanguard of the working class." To run the country it also needs a good number of members in all social groups so as to be able to gauge the moods of these groups. Thus it is claimed that between the last two congresses (1971 and 1976) the number of workers and peasants recruited into the party corresponded roughly to their share in the labor force. This drive did not substantially alter the balance and the bias in favor of the intelligentsia, however, particularly in all executive positions above the mass of the rank and file. In its issue of August 1979 the theoretical organ of the party boasted proudly that workers and farmers "accounted for 30.2 percent of the members and candidates of regional, *kray*, and republican committees and their control commissions."[27]

The author forgot to add that they represented three-quarters of the labor force and that the remaining white-collar workers, or more precisely the "specialists" among them, held the bulk of essential jobs.

Occasional sociological surveys reinforce this impression of poor working-class participation in party organizations. Thus in a sample of collective farms the proportion of party members varied from 5 percent among the farm laborers to 86 percent among heads of *kolkhozy*. In a series of engineering plants investigated in Leningrad, working-class party members ranged from 13 percent among unskilled workers to over 60 percent among the managerial staff. Actually, the proportion is much higher than that among top managers, senior officials, heads of laboratories, or university departments. The "party of the working class" is dominated at most higher levels by the so-called professional intelligentsia.

This shift is not yet fully reflected at the very top. The cooptation, the *nomenklatura* are some of the means in the attempt to preserve the absolute supremacy of the party apparatus, whereas the gerontocracy is just a by-product. With the police, the judiciary, the vast machinery of ideological control at their disposal, the apparatchiks have plenty of weapons in their arsenal. Against this must be set the sheer weight of the main beneficiaries of the educational revolution. The managers, the administrators, the senior "specialists," though pleased with their privileges and the post-Stalinist security, cannot be satisfied with this state of things. To ensure and consolidate their position, they must stake their claim for a growing share of power. The conflict is thus inevitable, and it is important to know what it is really about. This is not a battle against the party dictatorship for the sake of some form of workers' democracy. It is a struggle within the party, within the establishment, and as such it will involve concessions, compromises, and shifting alliances. Yet though it is an inner conflict, it is nonetheless a crucial one and most likely to be bitter.

The struggle is crucial, because while the formal ownership of property will not be involved, at least not in the foreseeable future, the control over the means of production will be at stake and with it the manner in which privileges are perpetuated, power is exercised, and society is dominated. It is bound to be bitter because the apparatchiks, unlike the Rockefellers, Krupps, and other masters of the western world, cannot relinquish office and retain their hegemony. They have unprecedented, totalitarian power and no second line of defense (the two phenomena are to some extent connected), which is why they will fight tooth and nail. Finally, it may be ventured that the very nature of this conflict means that the so-called cultural and professional intelligentsia will play a vital part in it and in the heat of battle it will lose its superficial statistical unity.

The Three Temptations of the Intelligentsia

Few subjects have provoked so many contrasting assessments as the role and fate of the intelligentsia in eastern Europe. The contradictions are due not only to the difficulty of definition and the resulting variations, moreover. For some, bullied, gagged, underpaid by western standards, the intelligentsia is the main victim of the new regime. For others, on the contrary, it is the rising, conquering class. For Alexander Zinoviev, the professor of logic turned satirical analyst of the Soviet academic establishment, the intelligentsia is vile, subservient; it is thinking of advancement, rank, and career, dreaming of foreign travel not as a breath of fresh air but as the snob source of blue jeans or silk panties. Even the occasional exceptions, the few dissidents, do not change this picture; inspired by personal moral motives, their rebellion is a gratuitous act with no political consequences. The intelligentsia as such is for Zinoviev a pillar of the regime. For East German Rudolf Bahro, author of *The Alternative in Eastern Europe,* however, it is the probable agent of radical change.[28]

Bahro's is the most important Marxist text to have come from eastern Europe since the war, earning its author eight years in confinement.[29] Bahro had dared to restore Marxism, reduced to a clumsy instrument of apologetics, to its original function as a weapon of social criticism. Where with the exception of reactionary romantics hankering after an idealized past, most dissident writers are understandably impressed by the relative prosperity and freedoms in the West, Bahro is not. He sees at the root of evils in eastern Europe the survival of the "old division of labor," namely that inherited from capitalism. He is neither dazzled by the so-called consumer society nor paralyzed by a narrow productivist approach. In our common quest for goods he sees the search for compensation for our alienated labor and leisure. Not only the advanced capitalist West, but eastern Europe, is to Bahro sufficiently developed to embark on the urgent task of human emancipation. But if no conscious effort is made to tackle the traditional division of labor, to attack the relations of domination, to shift from the political economy to Marx's "economy of time," putting the all-round development of individuals at the heart of planning, the productive forces "will never be ripe for communism."

This struggle of the "forces of emancipation" against the "forces of compensation" is to be carried out through what Bahro calls symbolically a "cultural revolution." His program, conceived in eastern Europe, is strangely reminiscent of the French movement of May 1968, of the ideas and debates associated in the West with the New Left. Analyzing growth, he does not talk of conquering the environment but of people's insertion into and harmony with nature. Since domination, or as he puts it, "subalternity," lies at the heart of his argument, so does education. He advocates among other things higher education for all, though in very different universities, destined to produce citizens capable of mastering their society rather than narrow specialists geared to the reproduction of the system. The emancipation, obviously, cannot be limited to men, but Bahro tries to link women's liberation with such issues as the shape of the family, communal living, and raising children. Finally, he is concerned with the size of the unit that the immediate producers can control jointly and sees in the commune both the basis of self-management and the primary territorial unit for a federation allowing the free association of producers.

But let us not get carried away. A sober critic will object— rightly—that in the allegedly Marxist manifesto the working class vanishes as a historical subject. Preoccupied chiefly with the unjust distribution of labor and knowledge rather than income, protesting against the artificially narrowed horizon of the downtrodden, Bahro sees the inspirers and pioneers of his cultural revolution among those whose position in the process of production allows them to have the greatest "surplus of consciousness," in other words among the intellectuals. In this sense his views have a certain similarity with the ideas (doctrines would be too flattering a term), fashionable in the West in the sixties, proclaiming the advent of a new revolutionary class of scientists, researchers, technicians, and other professionals and reducing the proletariat, like the peasantry of yesteryear, to the role of a manipulated mass.

It would be unfair, however, to identify Bahro with our own prophets of the technostructure, of a postindustrial society, let alone of a new "meritocracy." Whereas they, whatever their disguise, expressed the dream of the intellectuals to climb to power on the backs of the workers, Bahro attributes a revolutionary role to the intelligentsia on condition that it must attack all privileges from the very beginning, starting with its own advantages of superior knowledge and education. In his loose program for action, a drive toward the equalization of incomes figures high on the agenda, and in the inevitable transitional period, higher wages as an exception are to be paid not for intellectual work, a reward in itself, but for hard, dirty, or monotonous labor. Indeed, his whole project aims at the elimination of subordinate functions. And since these will not disappear overnight, he proposes as a start that all managers, specialists, and so on should spend part of their working time in routine, if not necessarily manual, occupations.

What seems to me wrong with Bahro's vision is not his program but his proposed agents of change. The reasons for his illusion are probably subjective: born in 1935 Bahro is an intellectual product of the new regime. A former deputy editor of a youth magazine and an industrial organizer, the clash between his socialist convictions and the true image of "really existing socialism" drove him to express publicly his ideas, fully aware of the risks. He therefore assumes that other "party ideologues" think and are ready to act alike. Raising his own act of courage to the status of a categorical imperative, he forgets in the process that in the East as in the West the working class—however changed, heterogeneous, and atomized—remains the only class fundamentally interested in the elimination of all forms of social inequality and the only one having the potential power to do it. By contrast, any advance along the way of his "cultural revolution" is bound to split the educated strata. To recall the contrasting definitions mentioned above, the intelligentsia is neither the main victim nor a new ruling class, neither a pillar of the regime nor an agent of revolutionary change. In different and shifting proportions, it is a mixture of all these ingredients. To see how it can split into champions of the status quo, advocates of managerial reform, and proponents of socialist change, we shall go back to the Soviet Union and to the nascent struggle over the balance of power within the party.

A minority, but a substantial minority, of the Soviet intelligentsia has a stake in the perpetuation of the rule by the party apparatus. Incidentally, the apparatchiks themselves are no longer mostly workers raised to positions of trust; we saw that the party secretaries are graduates,[30] essentially engineers. This hard core of party secretaries, apparatchiks in executive or supervising jobs, is surrounded by a vast machinery of ideological control, a host of propagandists trained in the party's own schools.[31] The hacks who control the Writers' Union thanks to their obedience, the journalists whose pen is at the disposal of the party, the social scientists eager to change their findings to fit the twists in the party line are not the only ones interested in the preservation of the present system of power and patronage. So are the headmasters, the professors, the chiefs of institutes or laboratories, the many functionaries who owe their prominent positions less to their talents or to the appreciation of their colleagues and more to their known pliability to party orders. And one should put in the same category some of the managers who, while not *praktiki* in the old sense of the term, got their jobs through party blessing and are quite happy with a command economy in which the opportunity for bullying subordinates makes up for strict obedience to orders from above.

In this conservative coalition must equally be included the many graduates employed in the vast organism of repression, not just the officers or interrogators of the security police (the notorious KGB), but also their numerous accomplices, ranging from prosecutors to doctors in special psychiatric wards. The position of the armed forces is more complex and more ambiguous. Almost all officers are now graduates and almost all senior commanders are party members. The military hierarchy is represented in the higher party organs (it has 30 of its own representatives among the 426 members and candidates of the central committee elected by the last party congress) and is on good terms with the apparatus. The top brass get among the highest salaries in the Soviet Union and have an influential voice in determining military and foreign policy. And yet they are uncertain allies. The prospect of economic deadlock affecting the military potential might lead them to switch sides. (But on them are also pinned the hopes of the Great Russian nationalists.)

If the conservative coalition, tied by joint interests and enjoying common benefits, is numerous, the reforming alliance can rely on an even wider support from the intelligentsia. The natural leaders of that alliance, though not necessarily its principal spokespeople, are to be found among the modern managers, the chief engineers, senior economists, and accountants, all those who in recent years had taken such a keen interest in American methods of management and of human relations. In their subtle struggle against the party tutelage, these shackled captains of Soviet industry can woo the bulk of the Soviet intelligentsia, appealing to it not in the name of its own hegemony but with a Soviet version of the thesis on meritocracy, because whatever its social origins, the Soviet intelligentsia has by now acquired its own interests.

The managerial reformers cannot yet articulate a clear platform, but the broad outlines of their program may be gathered from hints and suggestions ventured in tolerated debates. A good example was provided by the proposal—put forward during the discussion over education—to divide students at the end of the eighth form into two distinct channels: 30 percent to prepare for academic studies and the rest for a technical education. The proposal was justified on seemingly rational grounds: the Soviet Union is now "a state of the whole people" in which no discrimination is required; the places in the universities are limited and they should go to the most gifted. The authors simply forgot to add that the proposed segregation would merely strengthen the already existing class bias.

A similar outlook could be detected behind the oft-voiced complaint that in the Soviet wage jungle graduate engineers frequently receive lower pay than skilled workers and supervisors. The critics, while duly paying lip service to the "leading role" of the working class, deplore that at this stage in Soviet economic development such trends, acting as a disincentive, lead to inefficiency. And they have logic on their side in a highly hierarchical society in which "to each according to his labor" is the official rule, while the promise of distribution "to each according to his needs" is a shibboleth, a pledge put off till doomsday. There is a great deal of hypocrisy on either side in this veiled controversy and a lot of uncertainty, too, about the immediate outcome. But seen in perspective, the ruling apparatchiks seem to be on the losing side in their confrontation with the managerial reformers.

The technocratic argument can be countered only by a bold egalitarian program of social transformation, and this, for obvious reasons, is beyond the reach of the authorities. To start with it could be the work of the radical intellectuals on whom Bahro pinned his hopes, for the time being a minute section of the intelligentsia, though one with tremendous scope for growth. Its first spokespeople may actually be recruited amid Bahro's party "ideologues," those with an unhappy conscience, compelled to preach the opposite of their beliefs, who hold in Marxism a mighty instrument for the indictment of their societies and have to use it as insipid whitewash. Double standards breed cynicism. They may also give birth to rebels. After all, the very word "intelligentsia" was once in Russia almost synonymous with anti-establishment. True, this was in the old tsarist days, when the educated were few and far between; less than 200,000 graduates from university or technical college employed in the national economy before the revolution compared with some 28 million in 1980. To spread today the radical intelligentsia must move beyond the purely intellectual circles and find new members among the graduates resenting their narrow specialization. It must appeal to the army of women and men filling the expanding jobs in education and the social services, whose absence of freedom and initiative is not even compensated by decent salaries; to the mass of technicians and engineers making the painful discovery that with their splendid diploma in the pocket, they are mere cogs in the machine.

The intelligentsia will split into its component groups through this process of increasing awareness. The process is particularly painful and the whole experience exceptionally difficult in a country where the possibilities of social promotion were once exhilarating and where the illusion that alienation may be uprooted in this way had and still has a powerful hold on the imagination. The mounting mass of the educated must thus gradually discover first that their jobs are not fulfilling, second that in the existing organization creative or commanding posts are few, then that both the system of rule and the existing division of labor have to be overthrown; ultimately they must realize, in the famous words of *The Communist Manifesto*, that "the free development of each is the condition for the free development of all." Not all will go as far or react in the same way. Some will resign themselves to the patronage of the apparatus. Others will search for more money and better status through the managerial reform. But a growing number will travel the whole way and will thus be driven to seek the alliance of the workers.

Confusion is inevitable for quite a time in a conflict where no side is able clearly to articulate its stand and where positions are shifting. In the first phase, that of struggle against the stifling tutelage of the party apparatus, managerial reformers and the radical intelligentsia may well look like they are fighting for the same goal. The apparatchiks will exploit this ambiguity, as indeed they already do. Concealing the advantages of the really privileged, they can parade in relatively egalitarian disguise as the defenders of the workers' interests against the appetites of a greedy intelligentsia. In a country in which the social division is profound and the gap between "them" and "us" is as deeply resented as in the capitalist world (if not more so), this is quite a weapon in the hands of official propagandists. The confusion will be lifted only as positions crystallize in the heat of battle, as the young dynamic sections of the working class join hands with the revolutionary intelligentsia forging a joint project and a common strategy.

At this stage, even my indulgent reader will understandably lose patience. Against the real background of the Soviet Union, still totally paralyzed politically by a huge web of repression, censorship, and thought control, this vision of workers as a class-for-itself uniting forces with the revolutionary fraction of the intelligentsia must seem, if not entirely Utopian, at least fantastically far-fetched. A word of explanation is therefore required. To discern a trend or perceive a historical perspective it is necessary to climb temporarily to a certain level of abstraction. The operative word is "temporarily." To prove that I am aware of the distance between the promise and its practical fulfillment, let me again sum up the tremendous obstacles lying on the historical road.

The working class is atomized. It is split apart by a complicated mechanism of wage differentiation aggravated by sex discrimination. It has no memory, its link with the revolutionary past of the Russian proletariat having been totally broken during the upheaval following the collectivization, and it is not allowed to develop new forms of political consciousness. Any move beyond passive resistance is punishable by law, any attempt to organize independently is considered a mental aberration and "treated" as such. Far from being a class-for-itself, seeking to accomplish a historical mission, the Soviet workers are not yet allowed to be a class-in-itself capable of defending its immediate interests.

The picture is not much brighter on the other side of the hoped-for alliance. Out of our three temptations for the intelligentsia the radical one, for the moment, is the least attractive. One Bahro, or even several, do not make a spring. This balance of power is confirmed by the course of political events. The hesitant, abortive way in which the dismantlement of the Stalinist heritage has been carried, or rather not carried, through from above may be explained only by the absence not of social pressure but of an effective movement *from below*. There is still one major point, to which I will return, namely, the discredit of the socialist idea among the people of eastern Europe. Within the Soviet bloc Marxism is symbolized by the Soviet tank. Within the Soviet Union it is identified with the primitive, flexible, and hypocritical gospel designed to justify the privileges of the establishment. To resurrect the idea as the promise and instrument of human liberation is no mean task in itself.

When all this has been said and admitted, there are also factors pointing in the opposite direction, mainly those connected with deep changes within both the working class and the so-called intelligentsia. To say that the young workers of today are less frightened and in many ways different from their fathers, the sullen, uprooted *muzhiks,* is not enough. What matters most is that each year now young people are entering the labor force having at least the equivalent of high school education and are offered broken-up tasks below both their qualifications and their ambitions. As the balance within the working class tilts in favor of these newcomers, the difference also narrows between them and the mass-produced technicians and engineers, sharing the feeling that they have no control over their performance and no understanding of its purpose. The aim of the establishment— apparatchiks and technocrats alike—is to set these two groups apart, competing for rank and reward in the hierarchical structure. The duty of a socialist opposition will be to unite them in the anti-hierarchical struggle over the control of the means of production and the shape of society at large. My last argument purporting that such an alliance is not just a flight of fancy is pragmatic: the prospect of such an alliance frightens the rulers and partly determines their policy. This ghost haunts not just Warsaw or Prague, but also the Kremlin.

Should skeptical readers give the benefit of the doubt to the author's perspective, they will still have another valid objection. A prospect should not be confused with its realization and, even should events move toward an alliance of this kind, the time factor may greatly alter the outcome. The Brezhnev era is a good illustration of the lasting provisional. It shows how a leadership with an apparently absolute control over the economic and political life of a country, over the contents not just of education, but of the books, films, plays, or television programs that will be tolerated, can for quite a long time resist seemingly inevitable trends. It therefore remains to show that this mastery is not total, that the economic difficulties accumulated in this period of postponement have reached an irresistible weight. In other words, it remains to show that the bell now tolls not only for the ailing Leonid Brezhnev, but also for Brezhnevism, the highest and last stage of the rule by the apparatus.

The Price of Stability

No modern state can stand for long propped up by bayonets alone. Stalin's regime combined terror with a ruthless upheaval of the social structure, opening up vistas of promotion for millions. It was also sustained by the hopes and illusions born of the October Revolution. His successors substituted for the apparently blind terror a more rational form of repression. But simultaneously the illusions gradually vanished. The Soviet Union ceased to be a model for leftwingers throughout the world. The Russians themselves, weary of waiting for the "bright communist future" always equally distant on the horizon, wanted some tangible, immediate reward after years of terrible exertions. The hopes of the new regime were therefore based on fairly rapid and regular economic progress, allowing a steady improvement in the living standards of the population. The slackening rate of growth thus threatens the basic premise of post-Stalinist policy.

The Soviet predicament should not be confused with the western crisis. Russia is not the victim of a trade cycle; it has no excess capacity and no unemployment. It is troubled by a diminishing return on investment and by a declining rate of growth, nothing immediately dramatic except for this prospect of an inexorable slowdown. The western crisis both hinders Soviet planners and provides some relief. It affects the Soviet economy to the extent that the Comecon is now part of the world market and East European countries find it increasingly hard to export goods. On the other hand, it cheers the planners, since the Soviet Union's rival in the economic race is virtually standing still. Back in the thirties, Stalin's industrialization drive looked even more impressive than it was against the background of a capitalist economy torn apart by the slump. In the sixties, on the contrary, while the Soviet economy was beginning to feel the effects of its sleeping sickness, the West was enjoying a boom unprecedented by capitalist standards. The underlying Soviet assumption—that a faster running late starter must overtake a slower rival—was thus being undermined, and this was one of the reasons why the Kremlin did allow a more serious discussion about economic reform. Now the leaders in the Kremlin can take some comfort from the western disease.

Yet no major country runs its economy exclusively in response to external stimuli. True, the western challenge is extremely important for Russia. Matching the American defense spending with a substantially lower national product means an incomparably heavier burden. Besides, since the Soviet Union has failed to change the division of labor or to invent a different pattern of production and consumption, another way of life, the comparison between the two blocs must still be made in traditional measures of labor productivity; the Soviet lag in this respect explains the inevitability of some kind of iron curtain. The outside challenge is thus undeniably vital, but the Soviet Union, even more than the western powers, needs growth for domestic reasons, to release social tensions. The declining increment in production threatens the unwritten truce with the workers and renders increasingly difficult the social integration of the mounting educated generation. The imperative need to reverse this trend will drive the Soviet leaders into uncharted and unwanted territory. If the first quarter of a century after Stalin was marked by desperate efforts to preserve a fundamentally unchanged structure of power, thus preventing any serious economic reform, the second quarter is likely to be dominated by the inevitability of economic change, leading to uncalculable political consequences.

The Slackening Pace of Growth

The declining rate of growth is illustrated in Tables V and VI. Table V compares the targets for 1980 set by Nikita Khrushchev in his "communist program" presented to the twenty-second party congress in 1961, with the plan for the same year established under Brezhnev's auspices. The shortfall is staggering, and it does not affect basic production alone. If Khrushchev's pledges had been kept, the Russians would be eating today twice as much meat and eliminating overcrowding, the worst plight of the Soviet citizen, since four times as many houses could be constructed than are at present. Table VI answers

Table V. Soviet Output in 1980

	Khrushchev's promise[a]	Brezhnev's fulfillment
Electric power (bil. kwh)	2850	1295[b]
Natural gas (bil. cubic meters)	700	435[b]
Crude steel (mil. tons)	250	157[b]
Grain (mil. tons)	300	209[c]
Meat (mil. tons)	31	15.5[d]
Milk (mil. tons)	175	93.3[d]
Housing construction (mil. sq. meters)	400	109.4[d]

[a]Speech to twenty-second party congress, October 18, 1961.
[b]1980 plan
[c]Average 1976–79.
[d]1979

Table VI. Gross Industrial Production Growth (in percent)[b]

	1951–55	1956–60	1961–65	1966–70	1971–75	1976–80[a]
Period growth	85	64	51	50	43	26
Annual avg.	13.1	10.4	8.6	8.5	7.4	4.7

[a]This assumes that 1980 figures correspond to planned targets announced by N. Baibakov on November 28, 1979. See *Ekonomicheskaya Gazeta* 50 (December 1979). The figure in the original plan was 36 percent or 6.32 percent per annum. The corresponding figures for 1981–85 are 26 percent and 4.7 percent. See Draft Plan in *Pravda*, December 2, 1980.
[b]Official figures.

the likely objection that in his propagandist zeal to prove how Russia would overtake the United States, Khrushchev was ready to invent utterly fanciful objectives. What was wrong was not his imagination but the very assumption that the Soviet economy would keep on growing at an unchanged rate. The huge difference between Khrushchev's promise and Brezhnev's fulfillment measures exactly the slackening pace of growth. According to the official Soviet figures, the annual rate of increase of the national income dropped from about 10 percent in the 1950s to a planned rate of 4.7 percent in 1976–1980 and an actual 2 percent in 1979. The corresponding figures for gross industrial production are 13 percent, 6.5 percent, and 3.4 percent.

A certain slackening of the growth pace was actually expected. Stalin's breakneck industrialization had been linked with a heavy rate of accumulation, an absolute priority for heavy industry, the emphasis on basic production, fuels, and raw materials. Investment in agriculture was reduced to a minimum and the social infrastructure was badly neglected. Millions of newcomers flocking into towns had to put up with appalling overcrowding, sharing rooms, kitchens, toilets, because little money was earmarked for housing. Light industry was the planners' last worry, its meager resources always at the mercy of a crisis in a sector considered more important. This mortgaging of the present for the sake of the future could not go on forever. But the post-Stalinist planners had taken the necessary shift of resources into account when drawing up their blueprints for the future. They assumed that the resulting drawbacks would be made up easily, partly through opportunities for rapid growth in hitherto neglected sectors and largely thanks to a "scientific revolution." The Soviet Union was going to switch from extensive to intensive methods of production. The new highly skilled and educated labor force rendered this transition possible. Indeed, it was to be the backbone of the "Soviet miracle."

Khrushchev, with his knack for coining a crude definition, provided a nickname for this optimistic vision: "gulash socialism" involved no change in social relations but predicted a rapid journey to the land of plenty—this cornucopia being somewhat confused with the standard of living prevailing in the most advanced capitalist countries. Externally, the project postulated that with its much bigger strides the Soviet economy would overtake the American in a short historical period. It went without saying that once this had been achieved, any form of iron curtain would become superfluous, at least on the Russian side. The Soviet system would spread by example until, as somebody quipped, an American Stalin would proclaim the funeral doctrine of "capitalism in one country."

At home, the greater the satisfaction of the Soviet consumer the lesser would be the need for the knout. Reforms would thus spring from a relaxation of tensions and would in turn feed the momentum of economic expansion. Soviet propagandists could not stress too much this aspect of freedom to come, since it would have underlined its present absence. But western communists and sympathizers saw in this prospect a new reason to believe (or to be less kind, they clutched to this straw with passion). If Stalin's Soviet Union had turned out very different from the image of their dreams, soon a democratic superstructure would crown the socialist foundations of the Soviet edifice. It would take them much longer (since some have not grasped it yet) to learn the second bitter lesson, namely that simply the nationalization of the means of production and crude planning from above cannot be identified with a "socialist base" on which to build.

Doubts about the optimistic vision developed inevitably because the miracle just did not come off. The global indices revealing a slowdown were confirmed by more specific signs. The productivity of investment, in which planners were now particularly interested, was declining (the increment in production resulting from an increase in fixed assets on the whole was diminishing). Efforts to reduce the time lag between the start of an investment and its completion—a lag roughly twice as long as in the United States—proved of no avail. The central element of the new policy, the rise in labor productivity, failed to reach its planned targets; it actually dropped from an annual average of 8.4 percent in the early 1950s to 3.4 percent in the late 1970s. This failure in productivity was no novelty, but in the past such shortcomings were made up by allowing industry to absorb more labor than was originally planned. Now the untapped resources of manpower have dwindled. They are in fact expected to drop dramatically in the mid-eighties, one of the pressures which is likely to force the leadership to initiate genuine change. But before we suggest what the rulers may be driven to do, we have to see what they have not done, why, in other words, we have to review the post-Stalinist tale of abortive reforms.

Stalin's successors were conscious from the start of the need to alter the country's economic policy. While they differed on timing and priorities, they all saw the necessity to put an end to the harmfully distorting lag of agriculture and to inaugurate a new deal for the Soviet consumer. It rapidly became obvious that such a shift of policy implied a wider reorganization of the prevailing methods of management and planning. Stalin's machinery had fulfilled its function and achieved striking results. Protected by the monopoly of foreign trade, the Soviet economy had been able to develop free from foreign domination. The planning mechanism, however crude, rendered possible the extraction of a big surplus and its channeling into basic production. Within ten years the USSR caught up with Germany in global output, though obviously not in per capita production. Then, having recovered from the terrible ravages of the Second World War, it emerged as the second industrial power in the world. This example naturally fascinates the countries of the Third World, unable to extricate themselves from their underdevelopment.

Whether it was possible to accomplish this and more without criminal improvisation, without such a human cost, and with the active participation of the masses is a much broader debate, one that will keep historians busy for a long time to come. Here it is enough to say that Stalinist planning produced apparently spectacular results so long as the main task was to maintain a high rate of accumulation, develop the raw materials base, and boost heavy industry. Then it became the victim of its own success. As the economy grew more sophisticated, requiring complex horizontal as well as vertical links, as the Soviet citizen ceased to be the utterly helpless consumer ready to purchase the shoddiest of goods, as the new stage of develop-

ment demanded invention, innovation, and initiative from below, the old system of almost military command from above
proved obviously counter-productive.

In keeping with his habit, Khrushchev tried to cure the disease
by a sweeping administrative reshuffle. In 1957 he abolished
most economic ministries (except those connected with defense)
and transferred their attributions to ninety regional economic
councils or *sovnarkhozy*. Setting a pattern that can be taken as a
rule of thumb, the reform brought some initial dividends by
eliminating a few sources of waste, then got bogged down because it had not tackled anything fundamental. In 1962 Khrushchev had to merge some of the *sovnarkhozy* and invent something new. This time he decided to split the party organs and the
soviets at district and regional level into two branches, one
dealing with industry the other with agriculture. The move was
clearly a gimmick which, though resented by local secretaries,
had little economic impact. In any case, by then the authorities
had to admit that to improve things it unfortunately was necessary to deal with the substance and not only with the forms of
planning. In September of that very year, foreign correspondents were struck by an article in *Pravda* which pled for the
reduction of planned constraints imposed on the Soviet firm and
advocated the use of profitability as a synthetic indicator. Profit
and the market conjure up the idea of a Soviet conversion and
the whole movement of economic reform thus became associated
in the western mind with the name of the author of the article,
the Kharkov professor Yevsiey Liberman. Actually, his was only
one of the very many contributions to a vast and lengthy discussion, the first relatively genuine economic debate in the Soviet
Union since the twenties.

It would be idle to try to sum up here this complicated controversy between all sorts of centralizers and all kinds of reformers,
which incidentally confirmed that the monolithic surface conceals all shades of opinion.[32] It is more interesting to notice that
whatever their inner differences the reformers all painted a very
gloomy picture of Soviet planning. They argued that because of
their vague conception of value and their inaccurate calculation
of prices central planners were operating with uncertain aggre-

gates. Instead of improving their tools and sticking to their own field of general planning, long-term prospects, and structural change, they were trying to determine the smallest detail in the remotest firm—with disastrous consequences. The various un-coordinated indicators drove factories to increase gross output, regardless of quality, assortment, or the possible saving on raw materials. With prices, the size of the labor force, and wages fixed from above, the manager of the Soviet factory had little incentive to cut cost to increase productivity. The so-called taut planning, a rigid system not allowing for any reserves, drove managers to conceal unused capacity so as to fulfill the next planned target and, more generally, to maneuver amid loopholes always on the borderline of the criminal code. If some critics loosely mentioned "producers," their main plea was for the liberation of the Soviet manager from the straitjacket imposed by the central planner.

Kept under constant check, the debate was nevertheless tolerated by the authorities both under Khrushchev and under his successors, determined at that stage to bring about some improvements. In 1965 Alexei Kosygin did finally introduce a reform, reducing the number of compulsory indicators and widening the prerogatives of the managers. But the reform had no precise timetable and looked like the prelude to a bolder overhaul. If such was really the intention of the Soviet rulers, their zeal was tempered by the Czech experience. Once again, the change led to a provisional recovery of the production curve which after a few years resumed its downward course. In 1973 a new decree provided for the merger of Soviet firms into associa-tions, a move which on its own favored neither the "marketeers" nor the centralizers. One had to wait till the autumn of 1979 for an almost open admission that superficial remedies had not cured the fundamental ills. To justify some additional changes in the management of the economy,[33] Soviet commentators had to restate all the old symptoms of the disease. Only this time the indictment was milder in tone because at this point nobody any longer expected radical departures.

Why have all the successive reforms and experiments failed to change the nature of Soviet planning? Why have they so far not been allowed to move beyond a certain point? The answer that first comes to mind is inspired by the contest within the ruling establishment analyzed earlier: pushed beyond that point the reform would have hurt the interests of the apparatchiks. True, most of the reformers denied questioning the principle of central planning. Some actually claimed that by restoring planning to its proper function, one would also revive its influence. But even if one were to take such claims at their face value—thus avoiding a lengthy debate on the logic of the market and that of socialist planning—the reform would still have had political consequences. The top party leaders might keep their control over key economic decisions; the apparatus as such would lose one of its levers of power. Acting as an economic watchdog is probably its main function. The party secretaries at all levels supervise the economic life of their appointed area, they sanction crucial decisions, interfere in the running of factories, act as match-makers with the higher bodies. A switch from "administrative methods" to "economic levers" would deprive them of this source of influence and speed up the shift in the balance of power in favor of the technocrats. The resistance of the apparatchiks thus makes sense, but it probably is not insurmountable, since it may soon be overcome under the growing pressure of economic events. The conservatism of the Soviet rulers has deeper reasons as well. They are reluctant to push the economic reform forward because they sense that it will unleash the social forces, break the tacit truce with the workers, and ultimately lead to the revival of a labor movement in the Soviet Union.

The scourge of unemployment is still one of the means to instill labor discipline under capitalism. Stalin's substitutes, we saw, were the labor passport and the threat of the camp. His successors weakened the repressive stick without furnishing an attractive carrot. In the economic debate we heard a chorus complaining about the wasteful utilization of labor power and it is worthwhile recording its main themes. Labor productivity in the USSR is lower than in the West and auxiliary workers are much too numerous, because Soviet management is put in a position where it pays to hoard labor. The director of a Soviet factory cannot easily recruit workers to expand profitable production or get rid of surplus labor to take advantage of increased productivity. When workers become redundant, they are usually shifted to another department. With the wage bill determined from above and only a small portion of retained profits available for bonuses, the manager has little opportunity to vary the set pattern of rewards in order to boost productivity.[34]

Behind this complaint of the Soviet managers one can detect envy for their western counterparts or for the textbook entrepreneurs of perfect competition. Soviet managers, too, would like to hire and fire, to manipulate differentials in order to increase surplus value. But if the authorities were to move appreciably in that direction, if they were to grant the managers real powers of decision, they would by the same token destroy the fiction of the workers as the co-owners of their factory. They could no longer argue that, as the Soviet sociologists put it, the factory director and his employees "stand in the same relation to the means of production." In more practical terms, the tacit truce between the leadership and the working class would be rapidly broken by this productivity drive. Faced directly with a boss who can decide on his own the level of employment and the size of wages, the workers would have to invent some forms of self-defense. Unless the labor unions suddenly ceased to perform their part as instruments of the state and auxiliaries of management, the workers would have to forge their own tools of autonomous action. Thus, on the horizon of economic reform the Soviet leaders can perceive a frightening prospect: the reentry of the workers into politics through economics.

Discussions on Soviet planning and its actual or projected reforms suffer from an almost unconscious handicap. Most participants, critics as well as apologists, tend to argue as if their value judgments implied praise or condemnation of socialist planning as such, when they do nothing of the kind. Socialism aims at a society consciously dominated by the associated producers. Within this context, decentralization, for example, would involve the transfer of power to the immediate producers and not the increase of managerial prerogatives. This revolutionary change at the level of the factory would have to be coupled with the difficult search for radically different institutions at all levels, capable of reconciling democracy at the place of production with central planning. The latter is necessary not only to coordinate the conscious control of the given society but also to eliminate as rapidly as possible all social inequalities. The state, whatever the fashionable anti-authoritarians may say, will not vanish by magic in an unequal society. I am not writing all this to suggest that the problems are simple or that I have a ready-made solution. I only want to show that changes in a socialist direction would require such upheavals, inevitably sweeping aside the existing structure of political power, that the Soviet leaders, no more guided by a wish of self-destruction than any other ruling class, cannot even contemplate similar steps. To view socialist planning through the prism of the Soviet establishment is about as fruitful as to invite Pope John Paul II to a constructive symposium on women's liberation. What is at stake here is something quite different.

Driven to Dangerous Remedies

The tragedy of the victorious Bolsheviks was to have found themselves at the head of a backward country destined to carry out the task of primitive accumulation in unexpected total isolation. The mistake not just of the Stalinist practitioners but of many of their socialist critics as well was to assume that, once this task was accomplished, things would sort themselves out, forgetting the link between means and ends, between itinerary and the destination. Now that Soviet output of electricity exceeds the limits of Lenin's imagination, while Soviet democracy is conspicuous by its absence, it is easy to see the connection. It would be wise to learn something from the tragic experience. The means are not innocent. The bourgeois norms of unequal distribution and the unchanged division of labor recreate in the changed framework a new social stratification, with its rulers (the self-perpetuating apparatus) and a wider caste of privileged.

Even more important for us is another post-revolutionary lesson. If the workers, the mass of the people, are deprived of the power to shape their own destiny—for whatever reason and however temporarily in principle—that power will never be handed back to them. They will have to conquer it all over again.

True, the social contradictions resulting from the Soviet economic crisis may soon give them an opportunity to become once again the actors of their own drama. But for the time being they are the relatively passive onlookers in a trial of strength between the technocrats seeking greater flexibility and the apparatchiks doing their best not to upset the political applecart. The immediate question is whether the Soviet leaders can find some by-pass to avoid the political pitfalls, whether they can give the Soviet economy the necessary new impetus without pushing the economic reform far enough to set social forces into political motion.

One panacea that was for a time fashionable can be dismissed at once: cybernetics will not save Russia's central planners. The computer may one day help a socialist economy in transition to reduce state interference to the strictest necessary minimum. On the other hand, the electronic machine which by definition can only reproduce what is fed into it, is in no position to solve the social contradictions blocking the development of Soviet planning, contradictions which are turning the problem of decentralization into such a politically sensitive issue. Incidentally, it is significant that at the height of the Soviet economic debate, the most prominent econometricians and cybernetics specialists did not side with the centralizers. On the contrary, they were among the chief advocates of economic reform.[35]

But could not Russia overcome its crisis by relying on borrowed technology and massive foreign investments? This second suggestion deserves a more serious treatment, raising as it does the whole issue of Russia's economic relations with the outside world. Before the last war, the Soviet Union had managed to survive the encirclement of a more productive capitalist world thanks to its own version of protectionism, based on the state monopoly of foreign trade. It succeeded in building within a short time a fairly powerful industry, which incidentally made it possible to repel the Nazi aggression. To achieve all this, the country was forced to forego the advantages of the international division of labor. In the thirties it lived in a state of almost splendid commercial isolation. Only after the war, when Soviet tanks had carried their version of "revolution from above" up to the Elbe, did Soviet trade expand, and even then not as fast as a proper division of labor within the Soviet bloc would have justified. One had to wait till after Stalin's death for this process to speed up, when the Soviet Union extended its ties with the Comecon and resumed trade with the capitalist world. The movement gathered further momentum in the Brezhnev era. From 1965 Soviet foreign trade has been rising about twice as fast as the country's national income.[36] And capitalist states have been getting an increasing slice in this fast-rising trade, their proportion in total turnover climbing from less than one-fifth in 1965 to nearly one-third in 1979.[37]

While the new attempt to integrate the countries of the Soviet bloc as well as the opening of Russia's frontiers to trade with the capitalist world are both important trends, one should not read too much into them. Thus, the claim occasionally made by the Soviets to have turned the Comecon into a separate independent market does not stand up to scrutiny. The oil crisis showed the very opposite. Until then, the members of the Comecon raised the wholesale prices at which they carried their exchanges every five years, on the basis of world prices for the preceding period. In 1975, so that the Russians could take some advantage of the boom in petroleum, it was decided to revise prices annually, each time averaging world prices for the previous five years.[38] Comecon prices may lag or differ, they may be affected by joint ventures and by political bargaining power, but ultimately they are dominated by conditions prevailing on the capitalist world market. But one should not jump to the opposite conclusion either: the Soviet Union has not been absorbed—some will say not yet—into the capitalist world economy.

Soviet trade with the West is that of a developing country. In 1979 fuel and raw materials accounted for over half of all Soviet exports and for the bulk of its exports to the western world, whereas industrial equipment and manufactured goods were the main imports. Only western shipments of grain disturb this rather classical pattern of trade and will do so until the Soviet Union completes its program in meat and dairy farming. Industrial imports from the West have undoubtedly helped Soviet progress, particularly in hitherto neglected branches such as chemicals, computers, or the motor industry (especially the two big projects, Togliatti for passenger cars and the Kama combine for trucks) and allowed planners to fill temporary gaps (e.g., wide-diameter pipes). Taken as a whole, however, the western contribution has remained marginal, resulting in no basic change in the nature and speed of Soviet development.

When Russia's frontiers were opened up, some enthusiastic western commentators talked of a new Eldorado and drew the picture of a Soviet Union flooded with capitalist goods. These sanguine forecasts proved untrue. The main reason is not, as often suggested, the absence of credits. Even if the Soviet Union has piled up a cumulative deficit estimated at around $30 billion at the beginning of the eighties, it remains a safe and attractive borrower by banking standards. Nor can the blame be put on protection, since sheltered walls elsewhere are an inducement for foreign investment. The chief obstacles remain the Soviet monopoly of foreign trade and the nationalization of the means of production, i.e., total command over the economy. It is possible to imagine further quantitative expansion on present lines, say, with European, American, or Japanese capital assisting in the development of Siberia and the Far East. A qualitative change, lifting the exchanges beyond the stage of credits paid back essentially through shipments of raw materials, would require an overhaul of the current framework of the Soviet economy.

Capital breaks frontiers in search of profit. If western capitalists were to invest heavily in Soviet industry, whether directly or through mixed companies, they would bring along their methods for extracting surplus value, and this differently managed sector of the economy could not long be isolated from the rest. Personally, I do not think this is a serious prospect for the near future, and not because I take Brezhnev and his colleagues for virtuous defenders of "socialist property": the Soviet leaders must simply be aware that to allow such an invasion at this stage of comparative productivity would be to invite political trouble. Right or wrong, my opinion is irrelevant to the argument. Foreign trade and investment kept within tolerable limits will help the planners without solving their predicament. A massive influx of foreign capital would not rescue the Soviet leadership from the need to revise its methods of management. On the contrary, it would precipitate the process of economic reform and its dreaded political consequences.

Thus, there remains only one final objection, the possibility the Soviet regime has of muddling through without any major changes in the economy, of soldiering on despite the steady decline. After all, the Brezhnev era has given an example of this capacity for survival. A slowdown, however, changes nature with time and the slackening of pace must be related to the original stride. When the Soviet economy was growing at a rate of 10 percent every year, the halving of that rate meant that without any reduction of accumulation or transfer from defense to civilian use, it was still possible to improve living standards and relieve social tensions in many ways. Now, unless something is done to redress the balance, the planners are heading toward zero growth and the societies of the Soviet type are probably less equipped for a period of stagnation than are the capitalist states with their tradition of cyclical boom and slump. This must be particularly true of the post-Stalinist regime in Russia, whose masters did not face the Soviet people promising them freedom and reforms in the hope that in the new relaxed atmosphere production, too, would pick up. Theirs, as we saw, was the reverse calculation. They banked on an improvement in living standards to consolidate their position and then, possibly, to contemplate relaxation and reforms. Naturally, one cannot rule out that a squeaky machine, patched up here, mended there, spurts for a moment or even keeps running at the old pace for a while. Here the snag for the Soviet leaders is that they must stage their uphill ride in exceptionally unfavorable circumstances. As the planners draw up their blueprint for the eighties and beyond, they are plagued by two handicaps: the steadily rising cost of the infrastructure and the steep decline in the supply of labor.

The big jump in oil prices gave the Soviet Union a temporary advantage, but at the same time it drew attention to the high cost of additional sources of supply. The suggestion that the Soviet ouput of petroleum will soon drop dramatically and that eastern Europe as a whole will have to become a heavy net importer of oil is a typical C.I.A. scare story. The reality, though different, is no less serious. The bulk of Soviet industry lies in the European part of the country, whereas the bulk of its raw materials lies in the Urals and beyond. Over 80 percent of the known sources of energy are to be found in Siberia and the Far East, in distant and inhospitable regions. Their development involves pioneering struggle against nature, requiring massive investment in housing, social amenities, and transport.

True, untroubled by any anti-nuclear movement, the Soviet planners chose to redress the balance partly by concentrating their program of nuclear power stations in Europe. But atomic stations are also expensive, and their output will be far from sufficient for the requirement of the European regions. To exploit the new oil and gas deposits in the permafrost areas of northwestern Siberia, to harness the power of the Ob, the Yenissey, the Lena, and the Amur, to lay the track of the second trans-Siberian railway (the BAM, or Baikal-Amur railway), and then to build pipes, tracks, and transmission grids to transport oil, gas, coal, iron ore, and electricity over thousands of miles—all this cannot be done without an enormous outlay. This eastward drive is not unexpected and should not be viewed through Malthusian spectacles, but its fulfillment is largely dependent on the more efficient running of the Soviet economy as a whole.

More dramatic, though equally predictable, is the drop in the supply of labor. The early years of Soviet and east European planning will probably go down as a period when everything could fail—capital investment, productivity, the crops—but massive doses of labor were always available to improve the general picture. This era is now drawing to an end. The young people entering the labor force in the eighties are, if one may say so, the grandchildren of the last war, and for that reason they are not too numerous. The other, less accidental, reason is the decline in the birth rate, following here the pattern of all industrialized countries toward smaller families. The rate of births dropped from over 25 per 1000 inhabitants in the fifties to around 17 per 1000 inhabitants in the sixties. As a result, the natural increase of the population dropped from over 17 per 1000 to less than 10 per 1000. With the inevitable time lag, this slump is now being gradually reflected in the population of working age.

In an economic sense, the trend is even more worrying if one looks beneath the global figures at regional development. Judging by the official census data, the annual rate of growth of the Soviet population was only 0.96 percent in the seventies (compared with 1.36 percent in the sixties), but this average conceals enormous discrepancies, ranging from 0.65 percent in Russia, Byelorussia, or the Ukraine to about 3 percent in Central Asia: Uzbeks or Tadjiks are expanding five times as fast as Russians.[39] Since the republics of the Caucasus and of Central Asia, where the baby boom still goes on, happen to be regions of Moslem concentration, there has been much talk of an Islamic threat to the Soviet regime. The danger should not be exaggerated. Lumping together all the republics where the Moslem population is important, one reaches 45 million people, or 17 percent of the Soviet population, still less than the present share of the Ukraine, and outsiders, particularly Russians, are quite numerous in all these republics.[40] The fact that the ethnic Russians are in the process of losing their numerical supremacy in the Soviet Union does not lie at the heart of the serious national problem facing the Kremlin. Its gravity springs from the absence of real democracy in the federal structure, from peripheral nationalisms responding to the Great Russian chauvinism at the center, from the ideological void, in short, from the political failure of the regime. The danger is serious, but it is not essentially numerical or Moslem.

Let Soviet marshals bother about the mounting share of Moslems amid future recruits (or even future officers). What interests us here is the economic impact, which is immediate. To put it crudely, Moslems breed but don't move. The parts of the country where the families are still large are those where they tend to stay put. In Transcaucasia, while not leaving their republic, they at least move to the towns. In Central Asia they are reluctant to move altogether. (Between 1970 and 1979 the proportion of towndwellers remained stationary in the Turkmen republic and actually went down in Tadjikistan.) The regions of potential labor surplus are not the main sources of migration, which will render the quest for laborpower in the developing regions of Siberia and the Far East still more difficult.

The natural increase does not directly determine the size of the working population, even less that of the urban labor force. The age at which young people leave school and old people retire, the proportion of women employed, and the scale of migration from the countryside are among the many factors to be taken into account. The trouble for the Soviet planners is that none of these factors can help them greatly. Schooling will not be shortened; women already represent more than half of total employment; the reserves of labor in the countryside are not as large as the bare figures would suggest, because the rural population is relatively old, many young people having already gone to town.[41]

To make matters worse, the age pyramid of the Soviet population is highly unfavorable, with the proportion of people of pensionable age rising steeply; their number is expected to climb from 30 million in 1975 to 50 million in 1990 and 80 million in the year 2000.[42] The Soviet authorities, which had granted the working people the right to relatively early retirement (age sixty for men and age fifty-five for women) were compelled in 1979 to pass legislation—authorizing some pensioners to get a second salary—designed to take them back to work. Rather than a solution, this is a sign of the gravity of the situation. The stark truth is spelled out in official Soviet forecasts. The annual increment in the urban labor force, in the number of "workers and employees," which averaged 3 million in the sixties and 2 million in the seventies, is expected to drop spectacularly in the early eighties and vanish altogether in the second half of the decade.

In itself this prospect is far from tragic. There is no magic in numbers and an economy can prosper with a rising or a declining population. But a rapid increase in productivity has become imperative if the Soviet Union is still banking on growth. The cumulative effect of the trends described here will force Brezhnev or rather his successors to begin in earnest the overhaul of the Soviet economic machinery, despite their justified political misgivings. Here 1984 will not look like a passage from Orwell's utopia in reverse, with Big Brother lording over a country where everything is rigidly fixed, controlled, dominated. The odds are that the 1980s will witness a society in turmoil. The economic reforms from above, imposed on a reluctant leadership, will unleash forces from below, crystallize interests, reveal and intensify class conflicts. It may even see the beginning of a revival of a labor movement in the alleged land of proletarian rule.

The Missing Subject?

Is this the proverbial *Hamlet* without the Prince of Denmark, a play on the impending upheaval in the Soviet Union leaving the heroic band of dissidents off the stage? It is true that I have dealt so far with the dilemmas facing the leadership, the conflicts among the privileged, the growing contradictions in a changing society, or the economic crisis likely to bring matters to a head, and have barely mentioned the new subjective phenomenon of the post-Stalin era, the emergence of men and women brave enough to challenge openly the almighty state. I have done it on purpose. For all the courage of its members, the dissident movement is still a political force of the future and its dual nature—its weakness and its potential power—cannot be understood without the social background. The Soviet leaders know they have little to fear from the dissident movement as it stands, without popular roots. If the leaders in the Kremlin, with their army of judges, stool pigeons, police thugs, and ultimately with the tanks at their disposal look both formidable and frightened, it is because they are dimly aware of the scope opening up for a genuine opposition.

At this stage, it must be admitted, Soviet dissidence is politically weak. Its famous pioneers, graduated through camps and psychiatric wards—Solzhenitsyn, Amalrik, Bukovsky, Sinyavsky, Plyushch, the ex-general Grigorenko, and a host of others—are now dispersed throughout the world from Vienna to Vermont. Their fellows who stayed behind are to be found in lunatic asylums, in the jails of Moscow, Kiev, and Vladimir, in distant camps, or if they are still free, are awaiting arrest. The omnipresent academician Andrei Sakharov, who had once ensured an air of continuity in Moscow, was deported to Gorky after the intervention in Afghanistan. True, the ruthless official drive to divide, deport, destroy the budding opposition should not be a surprise and the movement manages to survive despite the persecution. Somehow, the diary of the dissident movement, the *Chronicle of Daily Events* is being produced and there are still volunteers for martyrdom, men and women ready to replace the protesters grabbed by the secret police. What is disquieting is the apparent inability of the dissidence to spread beyond a limited circle; at least so far they have not found an echo in the country at large.

And yet the rulers in the Kremlin treat it with the violence and passion of frightened men. A regime sure of itself, its legitimacy, and its prospects could cope with dissidents in a different manner, seek other methods to isolate them and render them ineffective instead of using the sledgehammer to crack the smallest nut. This disproportion between the apparently minimal menace and the maximal response is best shown through the case of a newcomer to the community of protest, the Free Association of Soviet Workers.

In the first ten years of its existence—taking the protests against the trials of Sinyavsky and Daniel in 1966 as its organized beginning—the dissident movement seemed unable to expand beyond the ranks of the intelligentsia. Then in the autumn of 1977 victimized workers from all over the Soviet Union, who had met in Moscow where they had come to seek redress, gathered to sign a petition and then to hold a press conference, with the miner Khlebanov as their first spokesperson. They had no political program and no platform. They just wished to air individual grievances, claiming that officialdom, including the trade-union establishment, refused to listen to them. Only the following year, having come under heavy attack, did this group become more political, talking about the right to strike, asking the International Labor Organization to recognize it as an independent trade union and the western labor unions to back the whole venture.

The contrast is striking between this persecuted association of a few dozen workers—jobless would be more accurate, since those who still had jobs were thrown out of work, while Khlebanov was at once submitted to "psychiatric tests"—and the mighty official organization of Soviet trade unions, with over 100 million members, a huge staff, plenty of money, holiday resorts, clubs, and so on. Yet the authorities immediately smashed this timid challenge to their monopoly of labor control.[43] Behind the thin substance they saw the lengthy shadow, the vision of mass strikes as in Poland. . . .

If the apprehensions of the leadership are not irrational, why has dissidence failed so far to gain further ground? The reason cannot lie in what is considered to be the slogan uniting all oppositions throughout eastern Europe, namely, the defense of civil rights. The struggle for democracy is so obviously indispensable there and a socialist can endorse it echoing the well-known words of Rosa Luxemburg: "We have always revealed the hard kernel of social inequality and lack of freedom hidden under the sweet shell of formal equality and freedom—not in order to reject the latter but to spur the working class into not being satisfied with the sweet shell but rather, by conquering political power, to create a socialist democracy—not to eliminate democracy altogether."[44] That in the seventh decade after the revolution, instead of enjoying such a flowering of freedom, Soviet subjects should still be deprived of elementary rights, that the demand for freedom of expression should be considered in the Soviet Union as proof of mental aberration, is shameful; it is the worst indictment of the regime and reason enough in itself to use quotation marks whenever the word "socialist" is coupled with the name of Russia. Yet the battle for democratic freedoms there is crucial on practical as well as moral grounds. Without the right to strike, debate, and organize the political awakening and the development of class consciousness will be a most painful exercise, with a high risk that discontent will burst out in wild explosions without a future.

The trouble is not with the dissident program of civil rights but with its content, or rather with its lack of social content. Rights are conquests, not gifts from heaven, and eastern Europe will not be an exception to this rule. In the West feudal fetters were broken and freedom of movement and formal equality of status established by the rising bourgeoisie which required such a framework to impose its superior form of exploitation. Once in power, it would have gladly stopped the process there. Further

freedoms, such as free universal suffrage or the right of association, had to be conquered from below by popular movements, in
which the working class was to play an increasing part. In the
Soviet Union, where the state is not only the barely hindered
jailer but the sole employer as well, it takes courage, conviction,
and deeply felt motives to brave its wrath. In a country where
Orwellian double-talk has been raised to a fine art, where lofty
Marxist principles are used to conceal a system of injustice and
repression, the mass of the people will not be driven to action by
abstract slogans alone.

In order to rally a real opposition the movement will have to
produce a project, presenting a global alternative, and link it at
the same time with concrete, down-to-earth proposals affecting
the everyday life of the people. Freedom, for instance, is not just
the right to write or paint freely. What will it give the workers
beyond the right to strike? What control will the workers have
over their own work? Or how will it enable the *kolkhozniks* to
shape the policy of their so-called cooperative? Or take equality.
What, for instance, will it mean for women? Equality naturally
will have to be translated prosaically into wages and salaries.
Will it also be raised to tackle the problem of hierarchy and of
privileges, which are not all material? Free elections are an
obvious part of the program, but who is to be elected, where, and
for how long? Should genuine elections be limited to political
representatives or extended to posts at all levels in the factory, in
the office, on the farm? And how provisional should such delegation of power be? These are only some of the questions that
must be answered by the movement as it grows and if it wants to
gather momentum. Step by step, it should thus elaborate a vast
egalitarian program capable of winning workers, attracting
kolkhozniks, mobilizing women, and splitting the intelligentsia.
Only in this way can it build a homogenous social bloc ready for
sustained action in the conquest of power.

Up to now the dissident movement has made little advance in
that direction and this is hardly surprising. Though still small in
numbers, it is rich in political complexion, a motley crowd
stretching from "party democrats" (as the Medvedev twins called
themselves) through liberals like Sakharov, representatives of

persecuted religions and oppressed nationalities to Great Russian chauvinists. The common denominator used to describe them collectively as defenders of civil rights is rather metaphorical. The reactionary romantics standing behind Solzhenitsyn or even to his right may be using civil rights as a stick with which to beat the authorities; they are themselves dreaming of an ancient autocracy, with its own knout and its own intolerance.[45]

A clarification of the project will lead inevitably to further differentiation and splits. The Russian nationalists, whose ideological allies are to be found, not so paradoxically, in the most reactionary circles of the party, the army, and the police may be the first to go their own way. Even liberals like Sakharov will object when criticism of privileges connected with the party card turns into an attack on privileges as such, including those resting on educational status (and achievement). Dissidence can grow into opposition if it gradually develops its egalitarian project to its logical conclusions and it will do so only if socialist elements become the driving force within the movement.

The main purpose of this essay is to argue that conditions are now ripening in the Soviet Union for the emergence of such a socialist opposition. This bold statement must be qualified at once. I am well aware of the differences among possibility, probability, and certainty. Where there is a way there is not necessarily a will, political consciousness lagging traditionally behind apparently obvious class interests. History is not linear and inevitability is usually written into it after the event. Admittedly, a restoration in the USSR of capitalism in its classical form, with the break-up of collective farms and the handing over of factories to private owners, seems unthinkable. On the other hand, when the development of productive forces clashes with social relations and this stalemate is preserved by powerful conservative rule, all sorts of things can happen. In such a society with no tangible way out, cynicism or resignation are not the only possible moods. Nationalism rears its head, religion recovers its attraction, and reason everywhere gives the impression of bowing before the irrational.

In such circumstances, one can imagine a confrontation of conflicting nationalisms threatening the whole federal structure, a military commander emerging, not as the emperor of a dwindling peasantry, but as the champion of Russian nationalism trying to keep the empire together. Since such a military dictatorship would solve none of the social problems, it might be driven to foreign ventures, and these being blocked by the nuclear stalemate, a move in the opposite direction cannot be ruled out, that is, opening the country to the full blasts of capitalist competition. I am not trying to sketch here the full list of possible Soviet scenarios, especially since none have sufficiently solid foundations to last. I want simply to show that in describing the most likely course of events I am not blinded by the faith of a fatalist.

Even if my more probable and optimistic assumptions were to come true, the future would not read like a socialist fairy tale with a proletariat in full political armor, a class-in-itself, sweeping the Soviet Union and guiding it overnight to a classless and stateless Utopia. In the best of cases, the remaking of a working class, the revival of a labor movement, and the development on such foundations of a socialist opposition will be a long and painful process. In many ways, its new pioneers are facing harsher times than did their revolutionary ancestors from tsarist times. The state is stronger than it was, it has totalitarian weapons at its disposal, while the opposition has to bear the burden of broken promises and shattered ideals. They will have to invent a new language, and not only to prevent any confusion with the present masters disguised as Marxists. They will have to redefine the road leading to social equality, to the abolition of classes and the withering away of the state, taking into account both past errors and the unpredicted complexity of modern society. In one crucial respect, however, they are better placed than were the early Bolsheviks. Should they emerge victorious, they will not come up against the same gap between their project and the economic surroundings, between the dream and the rugged reality.

Pessimism or optimism are rather vague and relative concepts. After the long nightmare during which Stalin while carrying out the process of "primitive accumulation" also crushed all opposition, after a brief interval of illusion about possible "reforms from above," and the unmistakable disillusionment during the Brezhnev period of uninspired restoration, hope flickers again on the Soviet horizon. The deepening economic crisis will soon give the Soviet leadership no choice but to embark on a serious reform of their system of management, thus upsetting the artificially preserved political stability. Class conflicts should come to the open, giving rise to a movement from below for the first time since the 1920s. Here lies an unprecedented opportunity for a socialist opposition in the Soviet Union. Will it be seized? Our duty is to survey Soviet society, to look beyond the traditional limelight to perceive stirrings of this political opposition in the factories and on the farms, in the offices and on campuses. It is also to keep the interests of this rising revolutionary generation in mind in whatever we do or say about the Soviet Union and even when we draw our own plans for the future. Such at least is the natural obligation of all those for whom the Bolshevik revolution is not a curse, a calamity, or a historical aberration, but a grandiose (though unfulfilled) attempt to create conditions for the conscious control of society by the associate producers. Or to put it in even wider terms, such is the obligation for all those for whom 1917 is a crucial link, more complex and tragic than our elders imagined, in the chain along which humankind is struggling for mastery over its fate.

*   *   *

When so many pundits have dismissed the working class—changed or unchanged, old and new—as an agent of historical change in the western half of Europe, is it reasonable to pin hopes for radical transformation largely on its revival in the eastern half? Political arguments, unlike some controversies in physics or chemistry, cannot normally be clinched by an experimental test. An upheaval throws sudden light on the social scene and provides a retrospective answer. The French rising of May 1968 and the Italian hot autumn that followed were such reminders of the social weight the working class still carries in the advanced capitalist countries. Only that and nothing more, since this rediscovery has had few political consequences so far and has almost fallen back into oblivion.

In eastern Europe such sudden insight into the real balance of forces was offered by the Polish strikers in the winter of 1970–1971. There too the newly discovered social weight has not been fully translated into political terms. The Polish workers, though they had to pay for it with blood, merely conquered veto power, that is, the negative ability to prevent the government from doing certain things and not the positive power of shaping their country's destiny. In the pages that follow, therefore, Poland is not shown as a model. It is presented as an example, an illustration of how the workers can suddenly enter the political stage all over eastern Europe.

Three

Poland: The Workers
Enter the Stage

Opening their newspapers on Sunday, December 13, 1970, Poles could hardly believe their eyes. Though the radio had already announced a rise in consumer prices, the details in cold print must have taken their breath away: beef up by 19 percent, pork by 17 percent, lard by more than a third. Shock after shock awaited them as they went down the list. Flour and kasha were up and so were fish and dairy products. The price of jam was raised by 38 percent and that of ersatz coffee was nearly doubled. True, the prices of some manufactured goods were brought down at the same time, but many were to argue later that this had only made matters worse. In Poland, where food still accounted for over half a worker's budget, to raise food prices sharply and simultaneously cut the cost of television sets (still a relative luxury at the time), car radios, or tape recorders, was to make the distinction between the haves and the have-nots only too obvious. For the workers the blow against their living standards was also an open challenge.

To justify the move, the Polish leaders used the classic arguments about the need to mop up excess purchasing power so as to balance supply and demand. Capitalist economists and politicians were bound to approve the reasoning in its apparently classless neutrality. The reasoning, though not the performance. Even the most narrow-minded of western technocrats would not have proceeded in so clumsy a fashion. It was dangerous enough to concentrate the increases into such a big package, resulting in an immediately tangible reduction of real wages, but to time this sharp rise in food prices for mid-December, in a country where Christmas and New Year festivities are the eagerly awaited national bout of eating and drinking, was sheer folly.

Fools, then, or knaves? Did the Polish Communist Party (PCP), as the United Polish Workers' Party is generally called, misjudge the mood of the people or did it provoke their wrath on purpose? A balanced judgment points to miscalculation, or more accurately, to the blindness of a leadership too sure of its power and too ignorant of the social realities. But this merely raises another question: How did Gomulka, brought back to power fourteen years earlier on the crest of a popular wave, get so out of touch with the mood of the workers? Thus, before examining the historical consequences of this foolishness—the bloody conquest by the Polish workers of the right to say no—we must stop for a moment to ponder how the Gomulka regime, born amid hopes in particularly auspicious circumstances, gradually drifted into disaster.[1]

From Ambiguous Consensus to Conflict

Maybe the Polish "spring in October" was too good to be true from the very start. In 1956 the whole nation was apparently standing behind its communist leader, Wladyslaw Gomulka, a victim of Stalinism though an honest Stalinist himself, who was miraculously back in office. Gomulka could rally around him, at least provisionally, the socialist hoping for a new deal and the nationalist attracted by his defiance of the Russians. In the long run, Gomulka proved unable to satisfy either faction, and in any case, this consensus was too artificial to last.

The enthusiastic unanimity of that autumn of 1956 was itself the result of a movement which had gathered momentum over a couple of years. Changes after Stalin's death were not mechanically transmitted from the center to the periphery. Their scope depended on national circumstances and in Poland the movement went further and deeper than elsewhere. The release of innocent communists held in jail on trumped up charges raised the whole issue of the security police and its performance. Doubts were thus cast on the enthusiasm with which peasants had entered collective farms and the workers had welcomed the ruthless labor discipline. People imprisoned simply because during the war they had belonged to the London-directed underground were next to be freed. In a new mood of reconciliation many policies were being revised, including the attitude toward the Catholic church. (Cardinal Wyszynski, virtually a prisoner, was one of the first beneficiaries.) Most striking, however, was the change in the general climate. People began to speak up and even to write in an entirely different manner, though the censorship was never abolished.

How far would this undoubted shift in party policy be allowed to go? The question was put to a first dramatic test in June 1956. Witnessed by foreign visitors gathered for the annual Poznan fair, the workers from Zispo, the town's biggest engineering factory, had downed tools and marched into the center of the city. The original reaction of the authorities was grimly traditional. The workers were first shot at and then attacked as counter-revolutionaries, imperialist agents, and what not. If things had been left at that, the continuity would have been tragically perfect. But they were not. Journalists, writers, and party activists were this time allowed to probe and ask awkward questions. Zispo, standing for the Stalin engineering works of Poznan, was only a new name for the old Cegielski plant, a proletarian fortress. How was it possible that this stronghold of the working class should have turned against the regime? The message implicit in this query shook the whole party, including its leadership.

While the Poles were thus breaking with precedent, the Russians, who had set the whole movement in motion through their indictment of Stalin, were trying to stop the unrest or keep it within bounds. The divergence between the two capitals was not limited to the post mortem over the Poznan riots. It was everybody's secret that after the death of their party secretary, Boleslaw Bierut, the Poles had put a stop-gap in his place, determined to give the job back to Gomulka, whose return was to be the symbol of a break with the past. The Russians were categorically opposed both to the new man and to the new deal. Forgetting their own inner divisions, Khrushchev and Kaganovich, Mikoyan and Molotov landed in Warsaw on

October 19 to attend the plenary meeting of the Polish central committee and there to veto the proposed takeover. The bullying visitors were in for a series of surprises. Stooges ready to toe the Moscow line were on this occasion hard to find. The party was united behind Gomulka and for once it had the full backing of the country. Even the armed forces, ignoring the top commanders borrowed from the Red Army, were ready to fight. True, the Soviet forces were strong enough to crush the military opposition, but rather than pay the high political price, the Soviet rulers chose at the last minute to give in and see whether the new Polish leader would not preserve the Soviet model. Their reluctant gamble came off.

A man hailed by the Poles as a national hero because of his defiance of the Russians and then ensuring the preservation of their pattern of rule may be suspected of duplicity, yet the suspicion is unfounded. Gomulka's responsibility and his personal tragedy have more complex causes. The man is best described as a true believer, an honest though narrow-minded Stalinist who never concealed his convictions. The misunderstanding springs from the twists of Polish history and from Gomulka's own record. Born in 1905, he became a PCP member well before the war, when joining the party was a passport to prison rather than to honors and success. He owed his personal rise to Stalin indirectly: as a provincial labor leader he would never have emerged at the top of the communist resistance during the war if Stalin had not beheaded the PCP in a bloody purge just before the conflict. The debt was more direct as well, since his party would not have come to power in Poland at the end of the war without the aid of Soviet tanks. Grateful and faithful, Gomulka nevertheless took too seriously the postwar talk about a "Polish way to socialism," allowing for substantial variations in the prescribed journey or the pace of advance. When, with the coming of the cold war Moscow imposed an entirely new strategy, which the stubborn Gomulka was not flexible enough to survive, he was removed from his job, kicked out of the party, and thrown into jail. If he himself was not tortured, some of his close collaborators were. No wonder that to his compatriots he subsequently appeared as a patriotic leader, a Polish standard-bearer against the Russians.

Gomulka did not gain popularity under false pretences, concealing his brand of communism. If to begin with he granted important concessions to the church, he did not hide his atheism and his hostility toward the clergy. If he allowed peasants forcibly enrolled into collective farms to leave them at once, this was a concession to freedom and not to the doctrine of private property in the countryside, let alone in the towns. Those who welcomed the "spring in October" as the first step on the road back to capitalist normalcy knew that Gomulka was not their man, at least not in the long run. The real victims of illusion, or rather of self-delusion, were Gomulka's most fervent supporters, the students, writers, and intellectuals known at the time as the "revisionists."

A revisionist in this Polish context should not be seen in the strict Marxist tradition as a follower of Herr Bernstein, arguing that socialism can be built gradually by reforms within capitalist institutions. Though they wrote a great deal of lively stuff, Polish revisionists did not produce a coherent doctrine. Twelve years before the Czechs they tried to prove the realism and topicality of the tautology about socialism with a human face. While differing on many issues, the Polish revisionists held some common beliefs. Despite the crimes of the Stalin era, they still believed in socialism as a project, assumed it could be built in eastern Europe, and relied on the Communist Party as the main instrument for this construction. The youngest and most radical among them saw in the workers' councils, then being revived all over Poland, the embryonic tools of socialist democracy. As their hopes were disappointed one by one, the ex-revisionists moved in all political directions.[2]

The honeymoon between the reforming intellectuals and the new regime was short-lived. It was brought to a formal end in the autumn of 1957 with the closing down of the weekly *Po Prostu* (To Put It Plainly), which had played a very active part in awakening people and stimulating debate. Gradually, the censor's office recovered its power and the press, while not so subservient as it had been formerly, was no longer allowed to act as a political pioneer. The divorce became absolute in 1964 when two young radicals, Jacek Kuron and Karol Modzelewski, were actually arrested, tried, and jailed for writing *An Open*

The Road to Gdansk

Letter to the Party, in which they described the ruling bureaucracy as the exploiter of the working class.[3]

By this time Gomulka also had lost the support of the workers, who together with the peasants had been the main beneficiaries of the transition. They had got rid of a ruthless Stalinist labor code and through strikes or threats of stoppage achieved a substantial increase in their real wages. Pleased with this improvement in their living standards, according to all accounts, they did not fight in most places for the consolidation of their newly won rights in the factory. Even if these accounts are true, Gomulka and the party themselves could have encouraged the development of workers' councils as potential organs of political hegemony in otherwise hostile surroundings. Yet this very hypothesis is absurd, since it assumes Gomulka conceived the exercise of power in terms other than those of pure party rule. In fact, the new regime did exactly the opposite. In 1958 it diluted the elected workers' councils within the Conference of Labor Self-Government, including representatives of official trade unions, the party, and the communist youth, thus depriving the councils of any autonomous influence. The experiment in workers' democracy was rapidly over.[4]

Thus after a time, the only people with no reason to be displeased with Gomulka's rule were the very men in the apparatus who were so frightened at the time of his return. They need not have worried. Gomulka did eliminate some of the worst culprits and bring back his victimized colleagues, but otherwise he left the structure of the party unchanged; a radical break was probably beyond his imagination. Yet even the apparatchiks were not too happy, since they saw no scope for advancement. Gomulka, so cautious with the economy that he slowed down expansion in order to avoid inflationary pressures, also left the hierarchy undisturbed, once the initial reshuffle was over. In addition, after the intellectual excitement of the transitional period the party, like the country at large, must have experienced an awkward ideological void. To fill that void and simultaneously provide scope for promotion, the minister of the interior, General Moczar, and his followers, known as the "partisans," opted for the nationalist game.

Playing with nationalism is rather perilous in a country where its open expresson is bound to be directed against the eastern neighbor. On this score Moczar could only proceed through hints and allusions. His version of nationalism had to look backward, appealing to the anti-German feelings of wartime and to prewar anti-Semitism. Only a few thousand remnants were left out of a once lively Jewish community of more than 3.5 million but anti-Semitism apparently dies more slowly than do the Jews, and the "partisans" thus relied on the basest conditioned reflexes to gain popularity. Moczar hoped to achieve several results at once. Though few in number the remaining Jews had been politically active, so the fathers could now be attacked as Stalinists and the sons as radicals. Starting with the latter, one could then extend the offensive to the whole liberal opposition.

Making political capital out of an attack on the survivors of the holocaust was quite a thing even in a morally debased party, and a Moczar was in no position to develop this line without Gomulka's blessing. Since this is a terrible accusation it must be both circumscribed and made more specific. A communist of prewar vintage, Gomulka personally had no racial prejudices whatsoever. Moreover, hostility toward Zionism is an old and perfectly legitimate communist attitude. Gomulka's crime, after the Six Days' War, was to have allowed the line to be blurred in Poland between Zionist and Jew, thus bestowing an air of respectability on a campaign which until then could not come out into the open. Thus if various factions in the leadership played a more or less active part in this shameful performance none can disclaim responsibility.[5]

Against this background the actual preparation for the purge can be summed up briefly. The pretext was provided by a play, *Dziady*, written by Poland's most famous poet, Adam Mickiewicz. Staged in a Warsaw theater, it was rapidly closed, allegedly because its anti-Russian historical passages had given rise to topically demonstrative applause. Whether the whole affair was a provocation or not, by March 1968 the Warsaw students had been maneuvered into a position where they were forced to stage a protest, and when they did, the authorities were ready to pounce. "Angry workers" were brought to Warsaw university by the police to beat up the students. This was the signal for the mass arrest of protesting students throughout Poland, for the purge of people of Jewish origin from the party, the universities, and other responsible positions, and for the elimination of non-Jewish intellectuals who would not keep silent when the party stooped so low. General Moczar's calculations had worked. By analogy with Marshal Pilsudski's Poland of prewar days, I almost wrote that this was the successful purge of Jews and communists. . . .

Putting the blame on Jews or cyclists[6] may distract popular attention from economic difficulties but does not solve them. Facing a growing unbalance between supply and demand, Gomulka was told by his latest economic advisers that the time had come to take harsh measures, to revise production norms and cut down popular consumption. Hence the already mentioned plans combining doubtful technocratic wisdom with plain political blindness. Did Moczar and his "partisans" or Gierek and his followers push their leader intentionally so as to precipitate his fall? Allergic to conspiratorial explanations of history, I rather doubt it. A workers' rising was too dangerous for the party establishment as a whole to run such a risk. I am more inclined to think that they collectively underestimated the strength of hidden discontent. Having just humiliated the intellectuals, they felt ready to take on the workers and tame them in turn, but they were in for a surprise. And this is how the ground was prepared, fourteen years after Gomulka's triumphant return, for his shameful fall back into oblivion. The man's personal tragedy is certainly worth retelling. Censorship one day permitting, a Polish dramatist should revive these strange peregrinations of a sincere Stalinist. Given its scope for ruthless wit plus human compassion, it should make fascinating and revealing reading.

A Tale of Three Cities

After this long digression, we can get back to 1970 and the Polish winter of discontent.[7] For the moment we are interested not in Poland as a whole, but in its most northern part, the maritime provinces. Between the wars Poland had only a small outlet to the Baltic Sea, the famous "corridor" between German lands leading to Gdynia, an artificial harbor built out of nothing. The postwar change of frontiers turned Poland into a maritime country. The "free town" of Danzig became Gdansk, the biggest Polish harbor and a sort of twin to Gdynia; together with the smaller town of Sopot the three became one major agglomeration. Some 300 kilometers further west, Szczecin, on the estuary of the Oder, also became a Polish harbor.

With a wide coast and three major ports, Poland inherited a shipbuilding industry—or rather the ruins of one, which had to be rebuilt and then expanded. Progressively ships became one of Poland's staple exports. Indeed, it was a rather strange industry, exporting about 70 percent of its output and tied to one customer, as the Soviet Union took on an average three-quarters of the Polish exports. In 1970 the industry was still underequipped and overstaffed. The labor force in the Baltic shipyards, some 50,000 strong, was very mixed, combining highly skilled craftsworkers and laborers straight from the countryside. The population, particularly in the Szczecin region, was also of varying origins, many migrants having moved there after the war from eastern areas taken over by the Russians. But on top of this by now traditional working class, the shipyards recruited for unskilled jobs young peasants living in hostels and barracks. Wages in the yards were above the Polish average, though the relatively high level resulted from massive overtime. Many workers could not keep this rhythm for very long in difficult conditions, and the turnover rate was high.

In their drive to improve productivity the planners had put shipbuilding on top of their reforming agenda, possibly because the industry purchased some of its sophisticated equipment with dollars while it sold its products for roubles. Where the workers complained about overcrowding, unhealthy conditions of work, and too long hours, the planners talked of heavy costs and high wages. Indeed, they had prepared a wholesale revision of piece rates or premiums and the scheme was already being tried out. The workers, relying on overtime and bonuses for half of their income, felt threatened, fearing (not without reason) a cut in their wages. The yards were seething with rumors and tension was building up all over the place. The rise in food prices provided the fuse for an explosion which, within a week, was to reshape the political face of Poland.

It all started in Gdansk, an ancient Hanseatic city whose restored old quarter is a well-known tourist attraction. But the real heart of the town now beats in the Lenin Shipyards, the biggest in Poland, employing together with subsidiaries some 16,000 people.

On Monday, December 14, 1970, the huge yards were both idle and bustling with activity. The workers had laid down their tools and were busy discussing the best way to respond to the challenge. Then they walked out, department after department, and a big crowd gathered in front of the management building. But the bewildered managers were in no position to offer anything or even to embark on negotiations. So a column marched out through the gates headed for the symbolic center of decision, the local party headquarters, setting from the start the pattern of things to come. The helmeted workers singing revolutionary songs acted as a magnet, and by the time they reached the building of the regional party committee[8] the crowd was several thousand strong. Since the first secretary was in Warsaw, attending a session of the central committee, a lower official came out to speak. It was by then too late for a dialogue, since rumor spread that the delegates who had walked into the headquarters to present the demands of the workers had been arrested. Fights broke out between the militia, the Polish police, and younger demonstrators. A van with loudspeakers was seized by the crowd which paraded through the town chanting "We want bread," and "The press is lying." They proclaimed a general strike for the day after and called for a mass demonstration that very afternoon.

The response was uneven. At the Gdansk Polytechnic the students stayed put: the hour had not struck for the joint struggles of workers and intellectuals. At the radio station the marchers threatened to break up the place if their message was not read and then did not carry out the threat. The swelling crowd marched back to the center of town. The militia could not contain this human wave, which broke through and hurled itself several times against the party headquarters. Troops had to be sent to rescue the building. Skirmishes were to last throughout the area till well after dark. Meanwhile, the authorities appealed to the workers both on radio and television to respect law and order, thus isolating "hooligans and wreckers." The speakers could not have had very much confidence in their own appeals: Warsaw was already on the alert and that very night two of Gomulka's closest lieutenants flew to the coast to supervise operations. They sensed they had more than a riot on their hands and they were right. Tuesday was to be Gdansk's Bloody Tuesday.

That very morning it was obvious that the workers from the Lenin Shipyards did not stand alone. Their comrades from the Northern Shipyards and the Repairs Shipyards joined the strike at once. The harbor was paralyzed by the dockers and news of solidarity strikes poured in from factories stretching well beyond the town. At seven in the morning the crowd facing the management building was much larger than the day earlier, yet it did not get any more response. A quarter of an hour later, the head of the big procession reached the party headquarters. There, too, there was nobody to listen to their grievances, let alone to propose some remedies. And so the growing thousands marched on to the building of the militia and the adjoining prison demanding the liberation of demonstrators arrested the previous day. Greeted with tear gas and truncheons, they replied with anything they could lay their hands on. The battle hung in the balance for over an hour.

Finally the demonstrators were driven back to the party headquarters, from where most employees had been evacuated. The crowd, by then over 10,000 strong, was in a fearless mood. The troops had just been given permission to use their arms and when they shot in the air the warning was greeted with laughter. Young people set the building on fire and the smoke mingled with that from exploding grenades. A helicopter hovered over the roof in a vain attempt to rescue a couple of trapped officials. By the time the reinforcements, including tanks and armored cars, managed to clear the area, it was nearly three in the afternoon. Most workers had gone back to their factories and yards to elect delegates, elaborate platforms, and consolidate the sit-in strikes, but despite the curfew the skirmishes still went on. The official announcement deliberately underestimated the casualties for the day, listing 6 dead, 300 wounded, and 128 arrested. Orders were given to take the ships in sailing order to sea, while troops were rushed into the area. Gdansk, Gdynia, and the neighboring towns were virtually in a state of siege.

On Wednesday morning, while the strike was spreading, the limelight was still on the Lenin Shipyards, where some 5,000 workers stood in front of the management building asking for a reply to their democratically elaborated demands over wages, prices, reprisals, and so on. They got only a warning not to walk out as the shipyards were surrounded by troops. What happened next was summed up succinctly by the local paper: "A group of young people decided to run against the tanks and test in this way the reaction of the soldiers. It ended in tragedy . . . two dead and eleven wounded."

Everywhere strike committees were being set up and everywhere the authorities refused to deal with them seriously. At worst, they denied altogether their claim to represent the workers; at best, they asked them to go back to work, promising to consider their demands in due course. At the Gdynia shipyards, named after the Paris Commune, the strike committee issued a three-point ultimatum: its recognition as the only authority in the shipyards; the liberation of the arrested members of the all-Gdynia strike committee; the immediate acceptance of economic demands. The authorities replied by sending the troops to occupy the shipyards. Indeed, that evening Stanislaw Kociolek, vice-premier and politburo member, appeared on television to announce that the shipyards in both towns were to be provisionally closed. But at the end of the same speech he appealed to shipwrights to return to work. The resulting confusion may well have contributed to the bloodshed that followed.

Ancient Gdansk and modern Gdynia lie next to each other. If the harbors became twins after the war, the two towns have tended to become a single agglomeration. No wonder that an upheaval in the former had an immediate echo in the latter. Yet it was only on Bloody Thursday that the center of the conflict shifted to Gdynia. Gdynia Shipyards is the station facing the Paris Commune Shipyards. Opposite the station, at the intersection of three roads, tanks and armored cars were stationed from dawn, while at six in the morning, trains coming from both directions had unloaded their normal quota of workers. Between the mounting crowd and the troops blocking the way a collision was inevitable. The tanks shot first with blank cartridges and then in earnest, leaving four dead and many wounded. If the commanders hoped in this way to frighten and disperse the crowd, they were mistaken. This was not the end but the beginning of a six-hour battle. Some workers stayed on the spot, trying to reach the yards despite tear gas thrown from helicopters and bullets bouncing off cobblestones. Others marched in successive processions to the center of the town, carrying the corpses shoulder high on uprooted doors. Seven times they attempted to storm the town hall only to be thrown back. At noon it was over: the official body count listed fifteen dead and seventy-five wounded by firearms.

Gdynia was not the only place requiring reinforcements: Szczecin entered the fray that same Thursday. Like Gdansk an old Hanseatic city recovered from the Germans after the war, in 1970 Szczecin was Poland's seventh largest town, with 340,000 inhabitants.[9] Though Gdynia was next door, while Szczecin was quite distant, the scenario was almost the same. There too, it all started at the main shipyards (ironically bearing the name of Adolf Warski, a prominent Polish communist liquidated by Stalin), employing some 10,000 people. There too, the shipwrights vainly attempted to establish a dialogue with their own bosses and the local party leadership. When the party's first secretary virtually vanished in the hour of crisis, the workers decided to go to the party headquarters. Outside the gates of the shipyards they were met by the militia, first with truncheons, then with bullets. Mad with rage and using metal tubes and bolts as weapons, the shipwrights broke through the cordon and marched on the regional party committee, their ranks swelling on the way. They invaded the building, burned some smart furniture, and set the symbolic seat of party power on fire. Things might have ended there and then if the militia had not tried to disperse the huge and angry crowd, thus extending the battle before the armed forces managed to restore a precarious truce. Some looting and a great number of sadistic beatings by the militia occurred during the mopping-up operations, once the main confrontation was over, and here too a lot of blood was spilled. The official toll of seventeen dead was treated in town as a sinister joke.

If the events in Szczecin were similar to those in Gdynia and Gdansk and need not be retold here in detail, we have more documents about the democratic control of the workers over their movement in Szczecin. The Warski Shipyards were divided into thirty-six departments or sections. In the December strike each section elected three delegates, who could be recalled at any time and had to get their shop's approval for any major decisions. The delegates in turn elected a five-member strike committee which at first was significantly dominated by party members. To complete the description of this structure we should mention the presence of delegates from other factories, because by the third day the strike became almost general and the Warski Shipyards were turned into the headquarters of its general staff; striking bakers or printers went on working only with its specific permission. However dim their revolutionary recollections, the rulers of Warsaw began to perceive the nightmarish vision of Lenin's "dual power." Enough was enough.

By mid-week the party leadership in the capital still behaved as if it could keep the situation under control through repression. On Thursday, a state of siege was proclaimed through-out the country, allowing the militia, the security forces, and other organs to "use all legal methods of coercion, including the use of weapons" to restore order. That same evening Premier Cyrankiewicz addressed the nation in pathetic and rather vague tones. But the basic assumption was still the same: these local disturbances were the handiwork of vandals and counter-revolutionaries who had led misguided workers astray. By the end of the week the rulers had to recognize and admit the obvious: these were not riots, it was a workers' rising.

Even so, the leaders probably were able to cope with it in military terms. They had enough tanks and ammunition to face the disarmed workers. Politically, it was a different matter. Destroying the myth on which it rested, the alleged "workers' state" had to take on the working class, judging by the speed with which the ferment was spreading, not only along the Baltic coast but on a national scale. It was worthwhile sacrificing a few political heads to avoid such a risky confrontation. On Sunday, December 12, a week after the publication of the new prices, Wladyslaw Gomulka's reign came to an end when he and four of his closest supporters were removed from the politburo. His place as the party's first secretary was taken over by a tall and neatly dressed man, the fifty-seven-year-old Edward Gierek.

Gierek's parents had been driven out of capitalist Poland in search of work and he himself had worked several years in French and Belgian mines. A communist, he went back home after the war and rose rapidly in the hierarchy, reaching the rank of party boss in Poland's showpiece, the prosperous and disciplined mining region of Silesia. Known as a pragmatic, Gierek was asked to make peace with the pugnacious Polish workers. The very first evening he addressed the nation on television, and his tune was already different: "The recent events have reminded us painfully of the basic truth that the party must always preserve close links with the working class and the whole nation, that it has no right to lose a common language with the working people." While not saying that the strikers were right, he nevertheless granted their actions sprang from "honest" motives.

Within one week the political surface of Poland was undoubtedly altered, but at what a price? Taking Gierek's figures at their face value, there had been 45 dead and 1,165 wounded (153 by firearms). The unofficial estimates count the dead in hundreds and the wounded in thousands. Since most funerals took place at night and some corpses were buried furtively in nylon bags, the actual figures will not be known until the archives are opened and the existing secret report on the events is made public. In any case, the human cost was high. It was not very easy to determine, however, what the workers from the Baltic harbors had gained with their blood. After that memorable first week, the temptation was to answer both a great deal and very little.

In one sense their victory was unprecedented. Never before in the history of the Soviet bloc did workers, fighting on their own, topple the party leadership and bring down the government. (Three days after the party change, parliament duly endorsed a reshaped government with a new premier and new ministers of defense and internal affairs.) But they had not changed the structure of power, the way in which decisions were reached and carried out. The place of the fallen dignitaries had simply been taken over by their colleagues. Similarly, the concessions made by the new leadership were essentially verbal. There was no longer a question of dismissing workers as hooligans. Rather, the events were described as "a labor protest of a socio-economic nature." It was admitted that previous economic policy had not always been very wise and regretted that "sincere talks" had not been started with the workers from the very beginning. Behind the sweet words, however, the economic policy remained the same. Customers had to pay the new higher prices. Indeed, it was after some hesitation, sensing the need to consolidate his still shaky position, that Gierek granted a partial compensation, a special allowance for people with the lowest incomes.

All this was enough to relax tension temporarily, to secure peace for Christmas and the New Year. The troops returned to their barracks and the sit-in strikes were interrupted. In the maritime provinces, however, the shock had gone too deep for a rapid return to normal. The militia was still settling accounts on the quiet. The workers were licking their wounds and airing their grievances at all sorts of meetings improvised on every possible occasion. The focus was once again on Szczecin's Warski Shipyards. A new stoppage was just avoided there early in January and when the workers struck again on January 22, their action was precipitated by an outburst of moral indignation, by their refusal to be cheated in once-traditional ways.

While leaderships change, old habits remain. The local propagandists were convinced it was their duty to produce examples of the workers' enthusiastic support for the new regime and with the help of a few supervisors and party faithfuls, they staged a ceremony of pledges of plan overfulfillment in the tube section of the shipyards. The skill of the scribes and the art of the make-up specialists did the rest. On January 20 readers of the local paper learned about this splendid example of devotion and collective zeal, along with television viewers throughout the country. The 500 or so workers from the tube section, questioned by their puzzled comrades, were mad. Two days later, these "heroes of labor" were the first to put down their tools, bringing the whole shipyard to a stop.

This time the organization was somewhat different. Each section had five delegates but also elected directly one member of the strike committee. The latter was no longer dominated by party cardholders but led by the workers most radicalized during the previous weeks, such as the head of the strike committee, the ex-sailor Edmund Baluka. The commission on resolutions was busiest of all, having to deal with scores of proposals, ranging from details concerning one shop to proposed solutions for national problems. Surrounded by troops, threatened, the Warski Shipyards paralyzed by the strike was a school for democracy. Yet even in such hothouse conditions political consciousness can grow only at a certain pace. The requests of the workers were broadly the same as in December, except for one proposal invented by Baluka on the spur of the moment: the demand that Gierek and the new premier, Piotr Jaroszewicz, should come to the shipyards "so as to establish a direct and constant dialogue with workers' representatives, i.e., with the strike committees."[10]

The nine-hour confrontation between the party boss and the proletarians, between Gierek with a galaxy of dignitaries and the strikers of the Szczecin shipyards is now part of a legend and as such surrounded with inaccuracies. It is not true, for example, that the Polish leader responded at once to the call from Szczecin. The authorities first tried to break the strike, surrounding the shipyards with the militia. Supplies were cut off and leaflets dropped from helicopters warned workers against alleged "bandits" who had taken over. Only the fear that the strike might be the start of another upheaval drove the rulers to the shipyards. If you can't beat them, join them.

It is equally untrue that the encounter was entirely improvised, Gierek the bold just walking into the workers' den. He actually landed in Szczecin in the morning, together with the premier, the minister of defense, Wojciech Jaruzelski, and Franciszek Szlachcic, the new minister of the interior. The latter was sent to negotiate with the strikers, since Gierek did not wish to face a mass meeting with all the workers. As a compromise it was decided to stage a meeting in the recreation hall, holding about 300 people, and relay the proceedings outside by loudspeakers. On the other hand, it is true that Gierek and his colleagues arrived in the shipyards earlier than expected, hoping to surprise the strike committee and pack the hall with supporters. The move was only partly successful: if many reliable party and management members did get into the hall, the "fives," the elected delegates of the workers, were more numerous.

Even stripped of its legendary trappings, the meeting was an extraordinary occasion, providing insights into the strength and the weaknesses of the nascent labor movement, the strategy of the ruling class, and the ambiguous relationship between the two. It was also unique in the sense that the whole debate was secretly recorded and the tape then smuggled out. The precious document makes it possible to reconstruct and analyze this historical occasion.[11]

The general manager of the shipyards acted as chairperson and opened the meeting. Immediately after, Baluka read the eleven-point platform of the strikers, which can be summed up under three headings. First, economic demands: that prices be brought back at once to their former level. Second, guarantees for the strikers: no victimization or payment for the period of the strike. One might add here the demands for a correction over the alleged "pledges," the punishment of the culprits, and, more broadly, fair information both on a local and on the national scale. Third, political demands, or democracy: immediate new elections to trade unions, workers' councils, and "in keeping with the will of most members—democratic elections in party and youth organization at the level of each department and of the shipyards as a whole." The strike committee was to be turned into a Workers' Commission with all the powers and guarantees required to supervise this democratic overhaul.

Gierek, who got up next, knew that this was not the usual ceremonial occasion and he performed quite acutely. He started by describing the gravity of the situation and putting the blame on his predecessor. Quite cautiously, however. Gomulka had rendered great services in the past, but then he became authoritarian. The speaker hinted that he and his colleagues did their utmost to alter policies, but in vain. Gierek also went out of his way to exonerate the Russians, incidentally revealing that during the crisis they had intervened twice—Brezhnev on the phone and the politburo by letter—to recommend "political and economic solutions."

"I, like you, am a worker. For eighteen years I have worked down in a mine. . . ." In an effort to establish an identity between himself and his audience, Gierek played his main card, and the ambivalence of his position is well shown in the following passage: "I am not frightened of you, comrades. I'm not frightened in the sense that you know that I am a worker—don't you?—and if we can't come to terms, who can?" Gierek was laying it on a bit thick. "I'm fifty-eight years old, I can soon retire. I am entitled to a French and Belgian pension, too." He went on: "Each one of us [leaders] would prefer to stand next to his machine, like you, and not to have all these troubles on our mind. But in this hour of crisis one must make sacrifices." (More than 10 years later the sacrifice still lasting, one may draw conclusions about the permanence of Poland's crisis.)

All this and a very gloomy picture of the economic situation of the country was clearly designed to prepare a negative answer on prices. "You may disagree, but I am putting my heart on a plate and telling you there is no way back, no way back." Aware of the loudly expressed discontent of the audience, Gierek made his first concession, on new elections. But he at once emptied the proposal of all its explosive potential. The strikers were thinking of a really revolutionary change: all bodies, genuinely elected, should be the true expression of the will of the workers in the shipyards. Gierek talked in terms of cooptation: there are certainly valuable people in the strike committee; let them enter various bodies so as to facilitate the task of management. The strikers were dreaming of a new form of government from below; the party boss translated this aspiration in terms of more efficient rule from above.

He similarly downgraded the demand for "genuine information about the political and economic situation both in the yards
and in the country." The strikers used the example of the invented "pledges" as an illustration of a general system of ma-
nipulation and cheating, but Gierek took it as a specific demand
and granted a simple correction—only that and nothing more.
The very publication, he argued speciously, will be a sufficient
punishment for the culprits. What he really feared was made
plain when he later categorically rejected the suggestion that the
whole discussion and the platform of the workers should be
published. But we've explained here, he objected, that some of
your requests cannot be met. "And such requests which cannot
be met cannot be published either, because it is, it would be a
call—you understand—a call to all crews: do as we do—right?—
and so on and so on." At the very idea of a program uniting the
working class, the party secretary stammers from apprehension.

Altogether, however, Gierek emerged rather well from this
ordeal, cleverly mixing pleas of solidarity, professions of faith,
with an anguished "we'd love to but we really can't." His subordinates, though speaking at length, added little to his general
strategy, except perhaps an emphasis on the German danger, a
patriotic hint in Szczecin, Poland's western outpost. The shorter
speeches of the workers' delegates—the "fives" and the members of the strike committee—cannot be summed up so easily.
They are concrete, specific, and range over a score of subjects.
They describe how the parody of pledges was performed. They
tell in detail about varnishers and others working outdoors on
the hull, baking in summer and freezing in winter, about dis-
eases and accidents, about shipwrights doing 150 hours of overtime a month.

But in all these interventions by the workers there is a common thread, an egalitarian class feeling, fed by the resentment
against those who live on their surplus. The workers complain
about the maze of unequal bonuses favoring the management
and wonder whether "this can be called democracy." One delegate asks point blank: "What is the pattern of salaries for directors and ministers?" Another quotes the figure of 18,000 zlotys
(roughly eight times the average wage)[12] as the alleged monthly

income of the company chairperson and suggests that such fat salaries ought to be "slimmed" to improve workers' wages, because "some live in luxury, while others don't have enough for bread." No wonder, adds another speaker, that "among workers there is talk of classes in our society."

The workers complain about the parasitic burden resting on their backs. Some suggest they "get rid of excessive comforts in offices and the too many cars for officialdom." Many more talk about a drastic reduction of administrative staff, of the mass of supervisors, the vast army of security men. The party bureaucracy is not excluded from this list, the regional party secretary being mentioned specifically as "a budgetary figure, drawing profits which we have earned." There is a strong element of moral indignation in this resentment of "the arrogance among comrades who, thanks to our sweat, have gone to college." The myth of the workers' state is tackled head on by a delegate who dismisses the figure of seventeen dead in Szczecin as ridiculously low, but will not quarrel over figures: "when bullets are flying, men are falling. Yet what is really painful is that we have bought with our hard-won money these bullets against ourselves. How can it be that the working class should turn against the working class? How can we shoot at ourselves?"

The contradiction was tackled; it was not solved. The shipyard workers were well aware of the need to extend their legal rights and freedoms: "In our country," they pointed out, "there is no law authorizing a strike. Why not? All over the world they have it and we don't." They also gave many proofs of fighting solidarity, illustrated during the meeting by the unusual proposal that payment for the strike should only be made to those who took an active part in it. The strikers were dimly aware of their newly won power, but they also felt trapped. Without organized solidarity on a national scale, without any counter project, any economic or political alternative, they were at one and the same time the protagonists of the class struggle and prisoners of the myth that the government was somehow theirs. Thus they were half-resigned from the very start to surrender without achieving their objectives and clung desperately to the hope that this time they would not be cheated. Give the man a break, give the government a year or two to prove its good will—this was a recurring refrain in most workers' interventions.

It was not a blank check or an enthusiastic endorsement. One delegate reminded the audience quite plainly why once bitten, twice shy: "We have given our confidence to comrade Gomulka. People were shouting hurray and handing over their golden rings [to help the government]. And we were let down!" This time they were only to give Gierek the benefit of the doubt, lending an undertone of wistful resignation as the debate drew to its inevitable conclusion. "We don't know how to strike," said Baluka in his summing up, trying to give the most favorable, that is, broadest, interpretation to Gierek's half-promises. And the delegate from a department which had voted against a return to work sounded even sadder: "We haven't been convinced. We give up the strike not out of conviction but because everybody gives up. That's all." As the assembly was going to disperse, an anonymous voice from the hall stopped it in its tracks: "Just a word about those who will not come back among us." The dignitaries, the delegates, and the mass of workers in the yards then stood for a minute in silence, commemorating the victims.

Walking out into the night, or rather into the early morning, Gierek and his companions must have sighed with relief. They had gone through the dreaded baptism of fire. They knew that their democratic concessions did not really amount to much and on the rest they had yielded nothing. True, the day after, nay that very same day, they had to repeat their performance in Gdansk. But the outcome was now certain. Soon Gierek's "will you help?" and the workers' enthusiastic "yes, we shall!" would become the slogan of the new regime, the propaganda symbol of a new deal.

Yet if on the plane taking them back to the capital the rulers had the impression that they had won more than a battle, they were mistaken. This tale of three cities has a twist at the end, which occurred in a fourth. The shock reverberated through the whole country, across which sporadic strikes were taking place for higher wages or lower prices. In February the wave reached Lodz, the country's second largest town, the Polish Manchester, whose cotton mills had been built to supply the markets of tsarist Russia and whose striking traditions went back to the revolution of 1905 and beyond to the great strike of 1892. By February 13 seven textile mills were already on strike and the whole town was threatened with paralysis. A top delegation, headed this time by Premier Jaroszewicz, was rushed there at once. Only this time the greeting on the spot was not friendly. The story has it that when to make conversation the premier mentioned how hot it was in the mill, he was told by women operators in undiplomatic language to take his so and so evening dress off if he wanted to breathe. Worse still, there was no official committee with which to carry out negotiations. There was, probably, some secret caucus helping to coordinate the strike, but the women denied its very existence. The rulers thus were compelled to discuss with the workers en masse and the ladies of Lodz turned out to be neither polite nor cooperative. When Jaroszewicz tried on them the rhetorical "will you help?" the echo replied "not bloody likely until you bring the prices down."

Napoleon, it is said, feared nothing but hungry Paris. The equivalent nightmare for Polish bosses already before the war was the vision of the working women of Lodz laying down their tools and coming out into the streets. Panic can work miracles and turn into fact what yesterday was sworn as utterly impossible. In the evening of February 15 Warsaw radio announced that the price increase would be canceled from the start of the following month. Providential Soviet aid was magically produced to justify the about-face. But the authorities were still to have a moment of fright in an incident that tells a great deal about the collective memory of the labor movement. Asked to go back to work now that their demands had been met, the striking women of Lodz replied "not yet." Shift work is the rule in Polish textiles and it is an old custom that those who begin a strike are also the first to resume work. In waiting for their turn, the young women of Lodz were linking up with the prewar traditions of their class.

In exactly nine weeks things seemingly had gone a full circle. Prices were back to original levels; the workers were returning to work; the country seemed to be getting back to normal. Appearances, however, are often deceptive. In the interval, the fighting strikers of the Baltic and the stubborn women of Lodz had gained the right to challenge their government's economic policy. They had won for the working class the power to say no. Poland would never be quite the same.

The Workers' Veto

We once learned in textbooks about the *liberum veto* through which the Polish nobility, the *szlachta*, crippled the power of its elected kings. Future textbooks will tell us about another veto, probably more fateful for eastern Europe as a whole, the power of the Polish workers to paralyze the economic policy of their unelected rulers. But they will have to put this conquest in a proper perspective. The Polish workers proved in that memorable winter, as they were to confirm five years later, that they had the power to say no and the muscle for their opposition to count. They did not acquire any share in shaping of policy or any positive outlets outside party channels. The government had to accept as a fact of life the existence of an elemental force, spontaneous and unorganized, capable of suddenly bursting from below on the political stage. This resignation to a veto power should not be confused with the search for some kind of workers' democracy. To take even timid steps in that direction the regime would have to overhaul the whole system of representation, recognize the autonomy of the labor movement, and drop the fiction that the Communist Party is, by birthright and by definition, the representative of the working class—a fiction on which the Polish regime is not the only one to rest.

This is why Gierek's electoral concessions, seen by some as the main conquest of the strikers, could not really lead anywhere. The pledges were kept literally, and limited to Szczecin. New elections were held in the shipyards and the former members of the strike committee did not take full advantage of the circumstances. They did not stand on a common program or canvass together, and the bloc vote of the efficient party machine prevented some of them from being elected. Yet had they conducted a perfect campaign, the final outcome would not have been very different. The authorities were determined to nip the experience in the bud and by the summer of 1971 they felt strong enough to start removing from the shipyards the most active members of the strike committee. Some were fired, others were induced to change jobs, and still others became strangely accident prone, as if the Polish secret police were determined to prove they needed no lessons in cloak-and-dagger activity.[13] A year later Baluka himself, a prominent member of the workers' council, was "promoted" to secretary of the engineers union for the whole of the maritime region. Within weeks he lost his new job. He was not allowed to go back to the shipyards, but was finally authorized to resume work as a sailor and thus given an opportunity to emigrate.

If the experiment in tolerated democracy inevitably was ephemeral, the other conquest of the strikers—the price freeze—proved more lasting. It became a symbol, a taboo the government could transgress only at the risk of provoking the workers into action. Though this fundamental change in Poland's political equation was not perceived at the time by most observers, Gierek was well aware of his new dilemma, and to extricate himself he chose the flight forward. Whereas Gomulka had run the economy with deflationary caution, Gierek opted for all-out expansion, whatever the cost. Circumstances were favorable. The Soviet leaders, alarmed by the prospect of a contagious labor movement, were willing to help financially. The advanced capitalist countries were ready to lend, not only to get new outlets for their funds, but also glad to help a potentially awkward ally of the Soviet Union. Borrowing from East and West, benefiting from a short-term boom in coal, Poland's staple export, the new regime looked very successful for a time. Production was growing so fast as to strain resources well beyond planned calculations.

The first years of Gierek's regime were fat years. Between 1970 and 1975, according to official figures, nominal wages rose by 60 percent and real wages by 40 percent, that is, more than twice as fast as planned. A good share of this new purchasing power was spent on food, and with prices frozen for political reasons, the cost of food subsidies, growing fivefold within this short period, became prohibitive. The relative cheapness of food made it particularly attractive. Relying again on official figures, consumption of meat and meat products jumped within five years from 118 to 156 pounds per head. Polish agriculture, combining the disadvantages of state interference and private inefficiency, could not keep pace, and two bad harvests made matters worse. To satisfy demand Poland had to buy abroad. From a net exporter of food it became a net importer, as purchases of grain (essentially for fodder) climbed steadily to reach 7 million tons in 1975.

Poland, it was being said, is living and especially eating above its means. Such statements mean little unless one takes a country as an abstract entity (some people, after all, are eating better than others). Nor was Poland the only country in Europe at that time to have an external payments deficit. But it was in a worse position to bear it as the terms of trade turned against it. Gierek could no longer rely on external windfalls to boost his domestic position. The international economic crisis increased the cost of western imports, while rendering Polish exports less competitive. Debts were piling up. Things could clearly not go in this way for very long and since the government was unable to change radically its system of economic management and political rule, it was bound to cross the dangerous line and attack consumption through higher prices. Indeed, this shift of policy had been proclaimed for some time as inevitable. The price rise, therefore, did not come as a surprise. The surprise was that, oblivious of the past, the new rulers should have out-blundered their predecessors.

First as a tragedy, then as a tragic farce: the crisis of the summer of 1976 was an absurdly condensed remake of the 1970 drama, a grotesque version which revealed in full the still unapprehended meaning. On Thursday, June 24, Premier Jaroszewicz told the Polish parliament that "the time for decision had come" and the new prices would become operative the following Monday. Put off for so long, the increases were tremendous. Meat prices were to rise by an average of 69 percent, butter by more than half. Altogether, according to official calculations, the increased food bill would have added 16 percent to the cost of living index. The promised improvements in wages, salaries, and pensions were not taken by the mass of the people as sufficient compensation. The fact that these increases were proportionate, that is to say, unequal, added insult to injury. But the actual shape of the reform did not matter much. Within twenty-four hours Premier Jaroszewicz had to eat his words. He appeared on television on Friday evening, admitted that "many questions had been raised" in factories and that the bill, therefore, was withdrawn for further study "requiring at least several months." His performance was not even a face-saving device, since it fooled nobody.

The regime gave in because it had to. The morning after its announcement hell broke loose. This time the tractor workers of Ursus near Warsaw took the lead, storming out of the factory, occupying the railway line, and blocking trains, including the Paris-Moscow express. Throughout the day there was no fighting; only in the evening, when all was over, did the militia launch an offensive, beating everybody in its way. Next in the fray was Radom, an industrial city south of Warsaw where events followed almost literally the pattern set on the Baltic coast. There too, the workers from one big plant, the General Walter Armament Works, were the first to walk out, singing patriotic and revolutionary songs. They were joined by workers from other factories and by a big share of the town's population (160,000 inhabitants at the time). There too, they marched on the regional party headquarters, where the first secretary would not come out and his deputy, who did, would not negotiate with "the mob." As a result the plebian crowd got bad-tempered. A woman wanted to know the man's fat salary to contrast it with her own minimum wage. A man in worn overalls insisted on the price of the secretary's smart suit. Things got out of hand. Soon the party dignitary was stripped to his pants and the crowd stormed the building, throwing out stocks of luxurious food and drink amid cries of envious indignation. There was some looting, and fighting spread throughout the town, lasting well into the night. Strengthened by reinforcements sent from all over the country, the militia finally gained the upper hand and took its revenge, beating up and arresting whomever was out of doors.

Yet by the time the government won its military battles in

Ursus and Radom, the political battle was long lost. The rulers
had to surrender because the strike was spreading like lightning.
It reached Plock, a once sleepy town north of Warsaw turned
into a petrochemical center when it became the Polish terminal
of the Friendship Pipeline bringing in Soviet oil. The tide then
moved to Lodz, the proletarian fortress, to Poznan, where workers first rose twenty years earlier, to Gdansk, where the new
phase in the class struggle had begun. If the premier had not
rushed to the television studio to announce the official retreat,
Poland would have been paralyzed by a general strike.

Why did the new regime so misjudge the mood of the country?
Unlike the secluded Gomulka, Edward Gierek and his colleagues
traveled around the country, talked to people, and tried to sell
their policy. In establishing special links between 164 selected
big plants and the party's central committee they even thought
they had developed consultations to a fine art. Yet when it came
to a serious test, the whole mechanism failed dismally. The
technocrats did their sums, the party talked to itself, and . . .
got the wrong answer. The leaders naturally expected some
resistance from the workers, but they were taken aback by the
sweep of the revolt. However, it would be wrong to put the
blame solely on Gierek's lack of flair or the inefficiency of
his public relations. The reason for the misunderstanding goes
much deeper. Whatever its gimmicks, the new regime did not
change in any fundamental way its relationship with the working class, nor could it do so. To shift from ventriloquism,
however sophisticated, to a dialogue would have required allowing the workers to choose their own delegates, thus admitting
that the existing trade union and party channels are unrepre-
sentative, alien bodies parading as the expression of the working
class. It is doubtful whether Mr. Gierek ever contemplated such
political suicide.

The second crisis thus confirmed the lesson of the first, underlying its importance and stressing its limitations. The veto power
of the workers was now so clear that even skeptics had to admit its
existence. It had just shown itself in its spontaneous splendor. The
rise in prices had served as a symbolic signal. For this tocsin calling
the workers to strike to be heard throughout the country, it had to

be relayed by such spectacular acts as the blocking of the railways or the burning of party headquarters. The workers still had
no means for organizing, no channels for communication on a
national scale. In the series of strikes, or rather stoppages, which
once again followed this rediscovery of their power, the workers
had neither platform, nor organization to express or defend their
interests. In most cases plant managers were told, presumably
by a general instruction, to yield or half-yield when faced with
such an outburst of long-contained discontent. Then, the incident over and the passion spent, the most active participants, the
alleged "ringleaders" would be quietly removed, usually without collective resistance.[14] Gierek's incapacity to sense the mood
of the workers and their own inability to organize the defense of
their interests are two sides of the same coin. This stalemate is
also the sign of a transitional period, in which the labor movement is already sufficiently powerful to paralyze but not yet
strong enough to bargain, to impose policies, to reshape the
institutions—a provisional situation that, unfortunately, can last.

While spelling the complex message of its predecessor, the
second crisis also produced a lesson of its own, relevant to
eastern Europe as a whole, because it suggested a possible linkage
between workers and dissident intellectuals. In the winter of
1970 the rulers had sent the tanks first and surrendered only
afterward. In the summer of 1976 they surrendered almost at
once and struck surrepticiously afterward. The party was determined to reassert its authority. The humiliated security services were spoiling for revenge and they were given a free hand.
The two quick trials in Radom and Ursus were only the visible
side of a vast purge involving arrests, beatings, and mass reprisals
in factories throughout the country—the firing of thousands
who, branded as rebels, could not find other jobs. But the van-
quished wishing to teach a lesson to their victors found they
were unable to do their dirty work in the dark: the workers were
no longer alone.

In the spring of 1968, readers may recall, students were clubbed
and intellectuals purged amid the deadly silence of the workers.
In the winter of 1970 it was the turn of the workers to fight on
their own, their isolation symbolically illustrated by the refusal

of the Gdansk students to join the strikers on the march. Five years later, the dissident intelligentsia did not repeat its mistake.[15]

Individual protests against the repression were expressed at once in open letters to the authorities, which inevitably found no space in the official press. By September 1976 this movement discovered its forms of organization. The beginning was modest and crucial. A celebrated writer, Jerzy Andrzejewski, a veteran socialist economist, Edward Lipinski, a popular actress, Halina Mikolajska, and the coauthor of the already mentioned *An Open Letter to the Party Leaders*, Jacek Kuron, together with six other protesters set up the Committee for the Defense of the Workers, known by its Polish initials as KOR.[16] Its purpose was to provide financial, legal, and any other assistance to the victims and the largest possible publicity to the acts of repression. The government did not know how to handle this unprecedented situation. Its temptation was to break those who dared to oppose it openly, but it had to reckon with world opinion and, above all, with the possible reaction of the workers. The authorities therefore opted for harassment, arresting some members of the committee then releasing them, intimidating supporters, throwing people out of jobs. They tried to play cat-and-mouse, only the mouse refused to run and grew in size. By February 1977 Gierek half-yielded, announcing a partial amnesty. KOR replied that the amnesty must be total and unconditional, while all those involved in the repression should be brought to trial. Angered by this defiance and worried by the KOR's progress among students, the government reverted to rough tactics for a time, then gave up the battle. In July, all persons still in jail in connection with the previous year's events were released.

One battle over, the conflict went on. KOR extended its name, adding KSS, Committee of Social Self-Defense, thus showing its ambition to represent civil society in its struggle with the state. It also extended its membership and gradually the scope of its action. It helped to create a Polish *samizdat*, publishing reviews and even books that would not get past the censor. It was involved in the launching of a "flying university," enabling students to follow lectures in private apartments on subjects not included in the official curriculum. Sticking to its original conception, KOR has also sponsored a bi-monthly journal *Robotnik* (Worker), a tightly typed single page distributed in factories, which combines news about labor conflicts and conditions in Poland with relevant background information from abroad (e.g., about the development of the Spanish Workers' Commission under Franco). Boldly and publicly defying the authorities, KOR opened a breach through which other, more narrowly nationalist and conservative groupings have advanced also.

It would be inaccurate to draw from all this the conclusion that the Polish government is being challenged by a vast and openly organized opposition fighting on almost equal terms. The movement, however potentially crucial, is still marginal. Its failure to spread is partly due to internal weaknesses, to ideological disarray, to the understandable difficulty of forging a project after years and years spent without genuine debate. Some critics even argue that whereas in the 1960s Kuron and Modzelewski seemed to be ahead of their times in writing the open letter, today political expression lags well behind the social movement. Yet in passing judgment outsiders should keep in mind the odds against which the political dissidents are laboring. Finding paper, stencils, a typewriter, let alone a photostat machine, is a perilous exercise.[17] Each meeting or lecture can be broken up at any time by police thugs and activists live under permanent threat of arrest. If the key Warsaw members of KOR have hitherto been spared long-term jail sentences, because of their prominence, distributors and readers of *Robotnik* in the provinces always run the risk of police provocation, a beating, or the loss of their jobs, of any jobs.

The government does not tolerate an opposition; it has to put up with it. To break the still fragile links between workers and the intelligentsia is already a dangerous venture, rendered particularly perilous by the general state of social tension, fueled by economic discontent. The early fat years of the Gierek regime have been followed by a long sequence of very lean ones. Debts contracted in capitalist countries piled up to reach an accumulated total estimated at over $17 billion at the end of 1979: the servicing of this debt will absorb a good share of the Polish exports in the 1980s. The rising cost of oil and gas has contributed to the worsening of the external accounts. The planners had to scale down their grandiose targets, cut down and shift investments, and generally lower their sights. Shortages have become the rule and lining up in front of a food shop a habit to which one cannot get accustomed, keeping the nerves of the unprivileged permanently on edge.

Despite the setbacks, failures, and dangers, Edward Gierek almost miraculously soldiers on. In February 1980 the eighth congress of the United Polish Workers' Party gave him yet another mandate to rule. Recalling his pronouncements nine years earlier in front of the Szczecin workers, about his reluctance to take on the job, his wish to retire, and the urgent need to devise a method of regular succession no longer relying on a bloody crisis, this continuity is rather ironical. On paper, however, it looks very solid. Having got rid of his rivals, he has packed the politburo and the government with his nominees. But his obedient servants are of little use in solving his basic dilemma. He can no longer promise the Polish people an important improvement in their living standards in the foreseeable future. Neither can he buy their patience by political concessions, by granting them elements of positive as opposed to merely veto power. In the tenth year of his rule, frank admissions of difficulties or Churchillian accents about "blood and tears" are no longer enough. Mr. Gierek may look comfortably seated at the top, but he is sitting on a powder keg. The smallest incident could lead to a conflagration, a fire which might not be extinguished without Soviet intervention.

Does Poland Show The Way?

I will not attempt to forecast the timing, shape, or likely consequences of the next Polish explosion, and not only because crystal-gazing is a gratuitous exercise. From the very start I have tried to raise quite a different question. My purpose was to determine whether Poland is an exception to the rule of the Soviet bloc or a pioneer, whether the dramatic Polish events—the sudden reentry of the workers on the political stage—are a historical peculiarity or whether they set the pattern of things to come well beyond Poland's frontiers, signaling the revival of a labor movement throughout eastern Europe. Naturally, in a narrow sense, each event is specific. Yet before tackling this broader question of common trends we must first look at the two main features which seem to set Poland apart from the other members of the Soviet bloc: private farming and the mighty Catholic church.

Over three-quarters of the arable land in Poland—76 percent to be precise—is still in the hands of peasant smallholders. The collectivization drive never went as far as in the rest of eastern Europe and after the dismantlement authorized by Gomulka the state and collective sectors combined have remained marginal in Polish farming.[18] Polish farming, as was mentioned earlier, tends to get the worst of both worlds, since it does not benefit from the advantages of scale and the facilities to extract surpluses that the Soviet model provides, but on the other hand, comprises farm units that are too small to produce and prosper like their counterparts in the capitalist half of Europe. According to the 1970 census, only 14 percent of all private farms had more than 10 hectares and they accounted for 36 percent of all privately owned land. Next came farms ranging from 5 to 10 hectares; they represented 29 percent of the households and 39 percent of the land. Beyond that we find the "peasant-workers" and the "worker-peasants," to borrow the colorful distinction of the Polish sociologists. The former—32 percent of the households and 20 percent of the land—derive their income partly from farms ranging between 2 and 5 hectares and partly from other work. For the latter their small lots of less than 2 hectares are a subsidiary source of subsistence; they nevertheless still represented one-quarter of the peasant households, while owning 5 percent of the land.[19]

Though this structure of property looks eminently transitional, it has altered very little in the last twenty years.[20] The economic drawbacks of this hybrid system are obvious: with 30 percent of total labor power still employed on the land, Poland is a net importer of food. Politically, too, this state of things is a major obstacle for the country's rulers. The planners must allow for the reaction of the peasants as well as the vagaries of nature. The party leadership must reckon with the fact that it is running a country in which over one-quarter of the population are private property owners. In fairness, it must be added that this unresolved state of Polish agriculture should set a problem for the socialist opposition as well. If in a moment of heady optimism one envisages the prospect of the socialist transformation of the whole European continent, the "peasant question" figures more prominently for Poland than for most countries of eastern or western (though not southern) Europe. The Polish movement will have to elaborate its own agrarian program if it wants to advance from critical dissent to the role of a purposeful opposition with an alternative project.

More striking still is the second Polish anomaly, the spiritual hold and political power of the Catholic church. When the Polish Pope, John Paul II, revisited his homeland in 1979, gathering huge and enthusiastic crowds, dominating the political stage, speaking like the spiritual master of the land, his apotheosis could be interpreted as the condemnation of the regime in the thirty-fifth year of its existence. His triumph was the certificate of ideological and political bankruptcy for an allegedly communist regime. The judgment may sound harsh; after all, Poland was a devout Catholic country before the war too. Admittedly. But at the time there was also an anticlerical trend among socialists, communists, and a progressive intelligentsia which all opposed the church as an institution backing the landowners, blessing the capitalist, flirting with anti-Semitism and living in sin with Pilsudski and his colonels. The power of the church then rested on the backwardness of a nation kept in darkness and on the support of the mighty. Even immediately after the war the Catholic church still looked and acted as the upholder of property and privilege against any progressive reform. Afterward, if I may say so, the regime succeeded in bestowing upon it a new virginity.

It did so, to cut a long story short, by failing to provide an alternative and by tarnishing through its bastard and oppressive regime the very name of socialism. Unable to establish its ideological hegemony, to win the battle for the minds of the people, the regime assumed it could cut the influence of religion down to size by coercion, by forbidding the building of churches, for example; it merely endowed the Catholic hierarchy with the halo of martyrdom. As from failure to failure the rule from above became more distant, more alien, more oppressive, the Catholic church appeared as the main force of resistance and the regime, unwittingly, did everything possible to embellish its image. In 1968 the "communist" party, under the thinnest "anti-Zionist" disguise, carried out an anti-Semitic purge, eliminating the remnants of a people. The church expressed its sympathy for the victims. In 1970, when the "workers' state" was shooting the workers, bishops spoke of "the rightful struggle of the Polish workers" and Cardinal Wyszynski, quoting the Gospel, could talk about "the defense of the working man against exploitation." In 1976, when workers and intellectuals were being arrested, the church pleaded for their liberation. Deprived of its prewar allies, it adroitly switched its slogans from the rights of property to the rights of man.

John Paul II preaching against woman's right to dispose of her body may be taken by us for what he is, the charismatic and conservative head of a vast international institution which, whatever the feelings and actions of individual members and even sections, stands as an institution on the side of the established order of exploitation and inequality. For millions of Poles, on the other hand, he looks like the Redeemer, not just a spiritual shepherd, but the champion of national and social resistance. It is the party which now stands as the symbol of power and privilege.

This spiritual hold on the nation gives the church temporal power which the party cannot ignore. When attempting to woo the people, the leadership makes concessions to the church as an institution. When Gomulka returned to power, he granted to the ecclesiastical authorities, admittedly only for a time, the right to provide religious instruction during school hours. (Thus, in "socialist" Poland the church enjoyed a privilege unthinkable in lay France ever since the separation of church and state.) One of Gierek's first moves was to give legal status to property the Catholic church hitherto held de facto in the former German territories. Even the Pope's own visit could be taken as a tactical

gamble, a concession made by a regime to ease tensions following
the economic strains linked with the terrible winter of 1978–1979

In the short or even in the medium run, the parallel power of
the Catholic church makes things easier for the dissidents and
increases their room for maneuver. Many members of KOR
would claim they owe their freedom to the pressure or the direct
intervention of the church. Yet leftwing dissidents are mistaken
if they confuse this tactical coincidence of interests with a strate
gic alliance. They run the risk of being sacrificed as pawns in the
complex game played between the two international churches
And in the long run, the ideological hegemony of the Catholic
church casts a shadow over Poland's evolution in a progressive
direction. But this line of thought would divert us to another
major interrogation over the chances of rehabilitating the idea of
socialism in eastern Europe after decades of its unfortunate
identification with the powers that be.

Meanwhile, the Polish situation appears as a Greek drama of
impending doom, despite the intentions of all the main actors.
The church, perfectly poised, trying to consolidate its position
and benefiting from the weaknesses of the regime, has no stake
in another upheaval. The party leaders have no wish to return to
Warsaw aboard Soviet tanks; others would then be picked to
take over their jobs. The dissidents have appealed to the government time and again to make concessions, to change the atmosphere in the country so as to avoid a national tragedy.[21] As for the
Russians, they too have no interest in a confrontation. To invade
and then hold down pugnacious Poland, which with over 35
million inhabitants is by far the second biggest member of the
bloc, could not be described as an enviable task. Yet whatever
the wishes of all the protagonists, the tensions are such that
nobody in Warsaw asks whether everything will blow up once
again, but when it will happen. The crucial question is whether
the explosion can be put off sufficiently to allow for the emergence
of a political movement, resting on real social forces, strong enough
to move beyond veto power to impose changes in policies and
institutions, but also cohesive enough and sufficiently in charge
of the situation to dissuade the Russians from taking the plunge.
It is difficult to be very optimistic about this race against the clock.

This rather gloomy digression has taken us away from the heart of the matter. So Poland, with its peasant smallholders and its dominating church, is peculiar. But so in their own way are all the countries of the Soviet bloc. Each has to be analyzed and studied carefully in its specificity. In the Polish case, for instance, one would also have to take into account, among many other factors, deep-seated nationalism, strengthened if not bred by the conspicuous absence of sovereignty, and finding a natural outlet in anti-Russian feeling. Historical traditions, social changes, even the cleverness or blunders of the leadership all have their place in the complex political equation. But the relevant question is whether some common trends and general tendencies can be distinguished, transcending the differences and cutting across national frontiers, whether in somewhat different surroundings the same causes are likely to produce similar effects.

The Polish workers were driven into the streets in the winter of 1970 by a direct challenge to their living standards. They struck again, less than six years later, when this attack was openly, almost ostentatiously, repeated. Both events may have been precipitated partly by technocratic miscalculation and the blunders of the apparatchiks. But the policy which they were trying to apply was inspired by the logic of the system, and within its limits was dictated by economic necessity. Similar economic difficulties are likely to drive other east European countries in the same direction. The early seventies were relatively fat years, with concessions to the consumer, foreign borrowing, and loose accounting. The future looks leaner, with prospects of stiffer controls and belt-tightening. For a series of reasons, the new decade is bound to be one of retrenchment throughout the bloc.

Having lived on credit, many eastern European countries must now service the accumulated debts. In a climate of capitalist crisis the hopes of paying back through industrial exports have vanished, while shipments of Soviet oil cannot be extended at will. Indeed, except for the USSR, all members of the bloc have been badly affected by the fast-rising cost of fuel, a burden which inevitably will increase. Yet all the external factors merely aggravate the fundamental domestic predicament: the countries of eastern Europe are no longer able to rely on untapped sources of labor to boost industrial output. Having for some time preached the passage from extensive to more intensive forms of production, they will now have to carry the principle into practice through sheer necessity. However reluctantly, they will have to more than tinker with their methods of management, in spite of the political risks involved. Each will do it in its own fashion, allowing for its special circumstances, but all will be threatened with the spread of the "Polish disease."

Poland, having shown the way, need not necessarily remain in the lead. Each country and each movement have their handicaps and their assets. East Germany, burdened with Prussian discipline, has also a true Marxist tradition, illustrated by people like Rudolf Bahro. Czechoslovakia, while strangled by the most repressive system, has not only its Chartists; it also has the collective memory of the Prague spring and the admittedly ambiguous feeling that a popular movement might have changed the shape of the future. In Hungary, nearly a quarter of a century after the event, the bloody invasion still preys on the national unconscious. On the other hand, it is in Hungary that the economic experiment has gone furthest and may soon begin to loosen the social fabric. Finally, the Soviet Union itself combines the most ruthless and rigid mechanisms of power with a very acute economic dilemma and, possibly, the most explosive potential.

I do not have the foolish ambition of drawing up a sort of league table, with an order of precedence or a chart of future explosions and advances of the working class. Even after the closest and most detailed analysis, this would be a futile, pseudoscientific exercise. But I am ready, metaphorically, to stick my neck out and venture that here, there, and possibly everywhere, the eighties will witness the build-up of a labor movement, the growing intervention of the workers as a class in the politics of eastern Europe, an intervention likely to change the concept and the very nature of dissidence throughout the area.

When, at the end of the millenium, historians with a perspective reconstruct the full story of this crucial revival, they will devote much space to the Polish events, sketched out here in their barest outlines. The battling workers of the Baltic and the striking women of Lodz will figure prominently in this story as pioneers. Hopefully, the writers may also describe this period as marking a turning point in the dissident movement, the intellectuals finally grasping the point that they must forge links with popular forces if they wish to play a historical and not merely a heroic part. Hopefully, because this is the only way to break the deadlock. United action between young workers and students, between the evolving proletariat and other, even faster changing sections of the labor force is a nightmare haunting the ruling establishments in Moscow and Warsaw as well as in Paris or Rome.

Conclusion

Ex Occidente Lux?

Despite its rhetorical flourish the conclusion may well be read as rather gloomy. If the labor movement in eastern Europe is in its pioneering stage, the analogy is with the French silk workers, the *Canuts* of Lyons, or at best with the English Chartists, and emancipation looms distant on the horizon. The sobering effect of this historical analogy is not necessarily harmful. Too often we have been victims of the lyrical illusion of a mythical proletariat fully clad in class consciousness seizing power in order to establish a classless and stateless society, only to discover that power was in the hands of a self-appointed "vanguard" and society was heading in a very different direction. Too many people have approached socialism as a religion and when their god failed, instead of recovering their bearings after a healthy bout of iconoclasm, they knelt in front of other deities, including the golden calf, or they simply contracted out of politics. Throughout the western world we are now in the throes of one of these periodic rituals of great disenchantment.

On reflection, however, the prospect is not quite as dark as might be suggested by the analogy. It is true that the workers in eastern Europe still have to conquer the most elementary rights of organization and self-expression, but they are waging their struggle at an incomparably higher stage of economic development. The rapid industrialization of the Soviet bloc and the resulting changes in the social structure of the population have narrowed the gap between the two halves of Europe. If the political demands of the East European labor movement take us back to the nineteenth century, its economic horizon belongs very much to the end of the twentieth and in many respects is not

197

very different from our own. Thus the prospect for a speedy growth of that movement does not rest only on the abstract concept of an acceleration of history. The striking contrast between the level of development of the productive forces and of the social and political relations opens up enormous vistas. Admittedly, it also sets very serious problems.

One logical consequence of this contrast is the inevitable emphasis on political freedoms in the East European contest. If these pages do not seem infected by the latest French flu, the fashionable reduction of all conflicts to the ahistorical confrontation between the human rights and the totalitarian state, this does not mean that I am unaware of the political dimension. To clear up all possible misunderstandings, let me repeat here my basic assumptions. Socialism conceived as "the free association of all the producers" always necessarily implied such an expansion of all freedoms and such a degree of collective control over our social environment that our painfully gained political rights in the capitalist West appeared by comparison for what they are, the rudimentary elements of a future democracy. Furthermore, if this association is seen not as a gift from heaven, a strange present from above, but as a patient conquest from below, its very possibility is inseparable from the continued extension of the political consciousness of the mass of the people, itself unthinkable without experiments, debates, and a permanent confrontation of ideas. My objection to the existing platforms of human rights in eastern Europe was not that the dissidents were too bold in asking for elementary civil rights. It was that leaving out any social content they would not be able to attract mass support and therefore would not achieve these minimal aims.

The Soviet bloc will not be the exception to the general rule. However righteous the trumpets of Jericho, in real life they do not bring down the walls of the solidly entrenched Bastilles. All our rights, most abstract-sounding on the statute books, are the result of concrete, protracted class struggles, the outcome, often already out-dated, of past social battles involving masses of people. If the East European dissidents fail to translate such general principles as equality, the rule of law, the freedom of speech, or the right of assembly into concrete terms of wages and salaries, conditions of work and leisure, effects on the hierarchical structure and on everyday life, they will not involve millions in their dangerous struggle and will remain an easy prey for their ruthless rulers. The Polish intellectuals were helpless standing alone in 1968. Eight years later, though only a handful to start with, they began to matter when they had the historical sense to side with the striking workers.

The other consequence of the advanced state of economic development in the Soviet bloc is to render plausible an extension of the common struggle to the whole of Europe, in spite of the enormous political differences. Undoubtedly, this common front will not spring up overnight. The dissident movements of eastern Europe still have to grow within their national boundaries. The contacts across frontiers between the Polish KOR and the Czech Chartists are only the difficult beginnings of an indispensable alliance if the challenge from the satellite countries is to be sufficiently serious to force the Kremlin to ponder over the risks of an invasion. Ultimately, the dissidents of eastern Europe will have to join hands with their Soviet comrades to consolidate their position and ensure the radical transformation of the bloc as a whole. Yet this internationalism within the frontiers of the Soviet empire, as vital as it is difficult to build, does not preclude an effective collaboration transcending the divide between the two blocs. And I do not mean here the expression of western sympathy for, or solidarity with, the victims of repression, but the elaboration of common strategies leading finally to joint action.

Is it not Utopian to imagine common preoccupations shared by movements operating in such different political frameworks? Nationalization, the ownership of the means of production, on the surface an issue dividing the "socialist" East from the capitalist West, furnishes the elements of an interesting answer to this question. On paper, the producers of eastern Europe are the masters of their means. In practice, they remain the alienated servants of the machine. Indeed, their long experience has tragically confirmed what should have been obvious to a Marxist (though visibly was not): unaccompanied by radical changes in social relations, in the structure of power on the shop floor, and in the methods of organization and planning on the national scale, nationalization of production leads nowhere or, more accurately, it contains no guarantee of an advance in the direction of socialism.

But this bitter experience weighs as heavily on the collective mind of the western labor movement. French or Italian workers no longer greet the platform of nationalization with the same enthusiasm as they did in the past. To some extent this is due to the illusory nature of partial nationalization, to the so-called problem of effective control over the "commanding heights" of the economy. To an even larger extent this mood is the result of the patent Soviet failure. In which way will the legal transfer of ownership, even if it reaches the point of no return, alter fundamentally my fate? To this relevant question there is as yet no valid answer. Any breakthrough toward genuine workers' control combined with democratic planning, any proof that workers' collective mastery over their work and their environment is not a dream will find a tremendous echo on both sides of the great divide. *Pace* Pascal, truth on this side of the Elbe does not become an untruth on the other.

As soon as the issue of cooperation with dissidents from eastern Europe is raised, one meets within the western Left two conflicting reactions, which might be summarized as the twin sins of phony purity and unnecessary identification. Asked to protest against the deportation of Sakharov from Moscow to Gorky, for instance, the purists take out their magnifying glasses to study the *Weltanschauung* of the victim. They thus confuse the difference between fighting with and fighting for. As we argued earlier in these pages, we have the duty to defend not only a Sakharov but a Solzhenitsyn as well. Freedom, to quote Rosa Luxemburg's truism, is freedom of expression for those who think differently. Even from a purely tactical viewpoint the purists are wrong. To leave to our hypocritical establishment and to its faithful servants the monopoly of protest against repression in eastern Europe is to facilitate the task of their propaganda purporting that socialism can bring nothing else but "empty soviets and the electrification of barbed wire."

More understandable is the reluctance of the purists to join protests with very strange bedfellows. The hypocrisy of scribblers who approved the bombing of Vietnam and now cry over the intervention in Afghanistan, who love strikers in Poland and hate them at home, who shed crocodile tears over dissidents in eastern Europe while turning a blind eye on repression in Chile or Argentina is certainly nauseating. But it is not surprising, nor does it represent an insuperable difficulty. To get rid of such unpalatable companions it is enough to spell clearly the principles on which the protest is based. Add a reference to Pinochet or Videla, to imperialism and its crimes, to the exploitation of man by man, and these honorable men will run away, to borrow their metaphor, like the Devil sprinkled with holy water.

Completely opposite and yet springing from the same misconception is the tendency to idealize the East European opposition and to identify with all its facets. For a good section of the western Left, one is tempted to write former Left: the dissidents are the redeemers, their words are gospel truth and by definition they can do no wrong. This attitude is not only absurd, it does a disservice to the very movement it pretends to encourage. Undoubtedly, the rising voice of dissent is a challenge to the western Left. Even for us who did not suddenly discover the existence of the concentration camp universe with the gulag fashion of the seventies, their testimony is vital. It compels us to re-examine critically all our assumptions. But the reverse is as true. The dissidents are only opening their eyes. Their ignorance of the outside world, of their own society, and of its past is perfectly comprehensible. So are their prejudices. The retrospective idealization of tsarist Russia, with its stench, its serfdom, and its knout, or of Pilsudski's Poland, is understandable and tells us a great deal about present strains and stresses, but it remains reactionary nevertheless. What the dissidents need, beyond the natural solidarity, is sympathetic criticism rather than blind adoration. In any case, as the movement grows and reveals its differentiation, as the collaboration shifts from the level of solidarity to that of common action, the phony postures will vanish on their own. Gradually, each group in the West will have to choose its own natural allies.

But can western socialists find partners in the East? Is not the very idea of class struggle breaking across frontiers one more of the nineteenth-century illusions collapsing against the rugged reality of our times? In 1979, as the echo of the armed clash between Chinese and Vietnamese troops sounded from a distance as the lugubrious requiem for proletarian internationalism, the skeptics had reasons to wonder and the cynics to gloat. The publication at that time of Rudolf Bahro's *The Alternative for Eastern Europe* was like an antidote to despair, a justification for cautious optimism, because here was an East German author who was fully aware of the differences between blocs yet was raising in his context our major problems. The relevant point was not whether one agreed entirely with Bahro's analyses and proposals. The extraordinary thing was the extent to which, talking about his own world, he was dealing with ours. Thus his book was not only an invitation to a dialogue. It was a call to common struggle, first on the European and then on a world scale.

Admittedly, one swallow does not make a spring, but it is a sign. Bahro's book was neither a borrowing from the West nor an artificial creation. For all the originality of the author's vision, it was a product of eastern Europe, a symptom of the ripening of its development. If there are no more Bahros there as yet it is not because Marxist tools are unsuitable when restored to their original critical function, or because, more generally, socialist analyses and solutions are inadequate. The reason is simply that this is not where most critics are seeking their inspiration. For an east European thinker a great deal of courage and foresight is required to disentangle the subversive hard core of Marxism from the apologetic official doctrine of "really existing socialism."

In this wretched confusion lies the main obstacle to the spread of a socialist opposition in the Soviet bloc and therefore to common strategies on both sides of the great divide. The identification of socialism with the regimes ruling there hangs like a curse on the nascent labor movement in eastern Europe. *Panzersozialismus* (socialism of the tank) is not a metaphor for people living there. To the East German it conjures up the concrete vision of Soviet tanks quelling the Berlin workers' rising in 1953; to the Hungarian it recalls the bloody crushing of the national insurrection of 1956; to the Czech it means the tragic ending of the Prague spring twelve years later; and to the Pole it means the permanent threat on the frontier acting as a warning against reforms. Nor is socialism just associated with foreign imposition. In the Soviet Union and all the other countries of the bloc the lack of freedom, the permanent lie, the repression, the social injustices and inequalities are taken as an inherent, integral part of the system. If that is socialism, no wonder they are seeking some other solution, often irrationally. Outsiders may talk wisely about growing pains, lapses, or deviations. In the seventh decade after the October Revolution and the fourth after the extension of the Soviet empire such talk will not do within its frontiers. The least the western Left should do is to drop the shibboleth and stop talking about "really existing socialism" without contemptuous quotation marks. The most that it could do, at least in principle, is to show by example what socialism really is.

Ex Oriente Lux, wrote Stalin at the height of the civil war,[1] when the Bolsheviks were still pinning their hopes on the spread of the revolution westward. But the proletariat of the advanced capitalist countries did not come to the rescue of backward Mother Russia. This failure not only had tragic consequences for the grandiose attempt by the workers to conquer state power, it also rendered relevant Stalin's slogan. For a good quarter of a century millions of people throughout the world fought the exploiters, resisted the oppressors, driven along by the conviction that the Soviet Union was showing the way of the future. Even when the illusions about the Soviet paradise were deflated, the eastern wind was still prevailing for those who perceived in Mao's China, particularly during the Cultural Revolution, a potential alternative. It is only in the very recent period that people in the western world have ceased to seek salvation in the East.

Marx's ideas unquestionably have exercised an extraordinary influence on the course of world events, and yet his predictions so far have been curiously reversed. Revolutions did break out in countries where the productive forces clearly had not reached the end of the tether, bringing about the strangest results. On the other hand, the advanced capitalist countries, for which his analysis had been designed, have shown an unexpected capacity for adaptation and survival. But is this a temporary aberration or a permanent flaw in the theory?

Paradoxically, the Soviet Union is as much in need of a western rescue operation as it was sixty years ago, though in a very different way. Then, the Bolsheviks were looking to a victorious western proletariat for material aid, technology, and organization so as to ease their immense task of "primitive accumulation" and to render it politically bearable. Today the Soviet Union is itself an industrial power and can purchase advanced technology in the capitalist world. What it now requires from the West is an example, an inspiration capable of resurrecting the ideals for which the October Revolution was originally fought. Let us imagine a West European attempt, starting perhaps in France or Italy, to change the foundations of society from below, to alter radically the social division of labor, tackle all inequalities (including such millenial oppressions as that of woman by man), and attack the omnipotent state not merely through vituperation as is now the fashion but by trying to eliminate its social roots. By its very nature, such an effort would not take the dramatic form of the seizure of the Winter Palace. It would require time to reshape more than the institutions and space beyond national frontiers for survival. But whatever its chance of final success, the very attempt would prove contagious and modify the political climate not only in western Europe but in Prague or Warsaw and in Kiev or Moscow as well. The ruling apparatchiks would tremble with reason, though they would not be the only ones to shiver. Solzhenitsyn would curse, the Pope cast anathemas, and the pied pipers of the Pentagon would forget their love for the contaminated Soviet dissidents.

Let us not get carried away. Merely to suggest such a dazzling prospect is to invite derision in our times of contempt and despair. In 1968, when French students and workers were paralyzing their country while the Czechs were venturing on an unchartered road, the ghost of revolution was haunting Europe once again. Today it is the specter of reaction that apparently reigns supreme throughout the continent and beyond. In the meantime, Czechoslovakia has been "normalized," the shaken power of the Soviet apparatchiks restored, and the Brezhnev doctrine of limited sovereignty extended to Kabul. In western Europe the potentially revolutionary movement was led through electoral channels to political defeat. The forces struggling against established rule did not vanish; they were even reinforced by such newcomers as women's liberation or the ecological movement. Yet dispersed, with no coherent prospect, and lacking new forms of organization to coordinate their action, they proved unable to more than threaten the ruling class. Having recovered its poise, the establishment also recovered its domination over ideology and used it to prevent the main danger, that of a frontal attack. With the gulag as a bogey, it managed to impose throughout society the idea that to rebel individually, locally, over a single issue might sometimes be right, but to try to turn this rebellion into a global revolutionary project is sheer folly, leading inevitably to the concentration camp.

And so order, or rather the established disorder, reigns once again in Paris and Prague, in Rome or Warsaw, in the Soviet Union as well as in the United States. Strangely, all over the place this order now rests on less solid economic foundations than when it was under open attack. When the May movement swept through France or when Italy was crippled by its "hot autumn," the international capitalist machine, advancing at a fair speed, was still giving the impression of ticking nicely. Today the advanced capitalist West, with its 18 million unemployed, stagnating production, galloping inflation, and a symptomatic monetary disorder, is in incomparably worse shape. Not surprisingly, the economic crisis threw the labor movement onto the defensive, the traditional struggle over pay and security of employment replacing the more advanced demands clashing with the logic of the capitalist system. But this retreat need not last. The illusions of consensus and reformist dreams are vanishing together with the legend of a capitalist cure for crises. The provisional way out for the ruling classes lies in higher exploitation at home and abroad as well as in increasingly authoritarian rule.

In the Soviet bloc the consequences of the deepening economic crisis are not exactly parallel. At the time of the invasion of Czechoslovakia, the slowdown in production, though already worrying, had not yet reached the present alarming proportions. The instinctive reaction of the leaders in the Kremlin was to tighten the screws, reinforce repression, and block still further the channels for the expression of discontent. Yet, unable to restore the full terror of the Stalinist regime and therefore to carry on with zero growth, they will be driven to introduce economic reforms which they had resisted up to now as politically too dangerous. Thus in both East and West the future of the ruling establishments is not as safe as their present ascendancy would suggest.

Paradoxically, in their resistance to internal pressure both can rely on each other in a strange form of conflicting complicity. Western propaganda had seized the gulag adroitly as an effective weapon to demoralize its young rebels. It will now draw the picture of a monolithic monster armed to the teeth with nuclear weapons in order to preach throughout the western world the sermon of national unity, that is to say, of social submission. Such Soviet ventures as that in Afghanistan can only help the masterminds of this mobilization and "moral rearmament." The reverse, however, is equally true. The "yellow peril" may be used to appeal to the irrational instincts of the Soviet population but it cannot be seriously presented as an immediate mortal danger. The American giant reawakening from the slumber induced by Vietnam followed by Watergate and reemerging as the international gendarme is much more credible. It is a realistic villain for new vigilance campaigns.

Will a new polarization drive us back to the dilemmas of the cold war, to the inevitable choice of a lesser evil, if we want to avoid marginal impotence? Not necessarily. Stalinism may be very far from buried, but Stalin is dead and some of the Manichean divisions of his time have disappeared too. Gone are the days when you were either for Stalin's Soviet Union which could do no wrong or you were against it and often did not care about the company. Strange as it may seem, there was relatively little room in between. Now there is apparently more scope for maneuver, for proclaiming a plague on both their houses while trying to exploit both their contradictions and their conflicts.

Amid political poison and social putrefaction an era is coming to an end. On the western soil littered with broken hopes, shattered illusions, and imported ready-made models, space reappears for a socialist revival, though not from scratch. The socialist movement has its heritage with its glorious memories but also with crimes perpetrated in its name. The latter, from the deviations and treasons of the Second International through Stalin's atrocities down to the latest Cambodian horror story, will have to be studied most carefully, not out of masochism, but in order to learn the reasons why, so as to avoid tragic repetitions.

Learning from past mistakes is not sufficient for a revival, especially since in the last half century things have changed in some respects beyond recognition. Productive forces have grown so far in both East and West as to put old problems in an entirely new setting. The nature and purposes of industrial growth, productivism itself, the patterns of consumption, labor and leisure, and the meaning of their relationship—all such issues have to be seen in an altered context both in eastern and western Europe. The proletariat, while not vanishing in an imaginary postindustrial society, has a different composition and possibly an altered part to play. Peasants have been largely replaced in numbers by the newly alienated salary earners. New groups are beginning to claim their rightful roles on the social stage. Last but not least, new political actors have appeared in the third world, a crucial factor I can only mention in these conspicuously Euro-centered pages.

Taking it all into account, the balance sheet of the last half-century, though belying Marxist predictions, may not be as negative as the current mood suggests, and the prospects therefore also may be brighter. For the old seekers after God, the searchers of artificial paradises, or those amid the more recent generations who wanted everything here and now, the search for a socialist revival will inevitably look like a Sisyphean task. For others, whether more patient or more stubborn, it looks both urgent and indispensable. Urgent since, with the nuclear arms piling up, the alternative is no longer barbarism but doomsday. And indispensable because as societies decay, irrational forces will tend to fill the vacuum. They already do. The victory of Khomeini, the success of Solzhenitsyn, the popularity of Wojtyla, all in their way illustrate the temporary failure of socialism to answer the questions of the day.

The main message of these pages is that in this socialist quest we can count on potential partners in the other half of Europe. The mole did not stop digging on reaching the Elbe, and the monster is not as monolithic as it is being painted. Social differentiation inaugurated by Stalin has continued to deepen under his successors, although the new social figures are still rather inarticulate throughout the bloc. They will awaken and speak up when their vital interests are at stake, as they are likely to be if fear of economic stagnation drives the Kremlin onto the road of reform.

This is not a triumphant message. It promises no certain victory. It does not even ensure that when things begin moving they will necessarily and at once move in a progressive direction. On the other hand, after a period when history had horrible hiccups and then gave the impression of standing hopelessly still, it is quite encouraging to be able to assert this inevitability of change, to proclaim *Eppur si muove*, adding, with the modesty imposed by our past failures and current disarray, that we have a part to play in this common movement.

Postscript

Third Act in Poland

"Be realistic, ask for the impossible."
French slogan, May 1968

I have not enough space to thank all those who rendered my last Polish journey so precious, but I can mention here at least some of the people who helped me particularly to understand the events and to revive them: notably Bogdan Lis, Alina Pienkowska, Josef Przybylski, Anna Walentynowicz, and Lech Walesa, all members of the Gdansk presidium; Stanislaw Daniel and Czeslaw Niezgoda, heads of the strike committees in Lublin at the FSC truck factory and the railways, respectively; Jan Nakonieczyny of Solidarity in Pulawy; Jan Litynski in Walbrzych; Jacek Kuron and Adam Michnik of KOR, and the "experts" Bronislaw Geremek, Tadeusz Kowalik, and Tadeusz Mazowiecki in Warsaw, as well as Karol Modzelewski in Wroclaw. They have provided some of the facts. I alone am responsible for their interpretation.

It looked like the signing of a peace treaty between two sovereign powers. The time was about five o'clock in the evening on that memorable Sunday when the two protagonists, their brief speeches over, signed the twenty-one-point protocol amid flashes of cameras and the noise of tape recorders. The setting admittedly was far from typical for a diplomatic function. The ceremony was being held in the Lenin Shipyards and broadcast through loudspeakers to thousands of workers standing outside the red brick conference hall. Nor was the signed document a traditional peace treaty. Rather, it was a truce in Poland's class struggle. Mieczyslaw Jagielski, a deputy prime minister, signed on behalf of the ruling establishment and Lech Walesa signed for the MKS, the interfactory strike committee from the Gdansk region, standing on this solemn occasion for the Polish working class. The date was August 31, 1980, a date to remember.

The compromise reached at that juncture can be described as genuinely historical. Each of the contracting parties had to admit the limits of its power, at least for the time being. The workers, recognizing the political imperatives of geography, accepted the prevailing regime, acknowledged the preponderance of the party and the inevitability of existing international alliances. The government, grasping at last the full might of the labor movement, had to grant something unprecedented in the Soviet bloc: not just the right to strike but the freedom to set up independent labor unions.

Following the usual pattern, the Polish social contract, too, had its ambiguities. The two partners barely concealed their unspoken reservations. The workers assumed that their unexpected victory was only the beginning; having advanced so far, they were ready to pause for a while in order to consolidate, then to venture further on the uncharted road. The rulers, on the contrary, signed hoping that what had to be conceded in haste in the hour of danger would be recovered, or at least neutralized, at leisure. Yet before one begins pondering whether these two contradictory powers (one flowing from above, the other from below) are provisionally compatible, assessing thereby the prospects of this historical compromise, it is first necessary to recall how the compromise was achieved. For this we must revive the crucial third act in the Polish drama, the sixty days that reached their climax in Gdansk.

Whatever God may do with the minds of those he has designed to ruin, an outgoing ruling class always looks strangely bewildered when faced with a rising and massive social movement. The two Edwards—Gierek the party boss and Babiuch his prime minister since February—were thus following illustrious precedents in the summer of 1980. Like actors in an old-fashioned comedy, the Polish leaders throughout the crisis were either running in the wrong direction or always missing the bus.

On paper, their design was clever and their reasoning crafty: if you can't beat them, cheat them. Unable to defeat the working class in direct confrontation, the regime planned to by-pass the immovable object. Instead of announcing frankly and openly a sharp rise in food prices, it intended to reach the same objective surreptitiously. And indeed, the decree providing for an increase of meat prices from July 1, 1980, was not proclaimed amid a brass of trumpets by one of the country's rulers. A minor functionary, the deputy head of the cooperative *spolem*, appeared on television the day after to mumble a few confused explanations, leaving the public in doubt as to whether the decree was for Poland as a whole, and whether it fully applied to factory canteens where workers buy part of their meat. The confusion was intentional.

It would not be quite accurate to describe the 1980 crisis as a direct response to a rise in food prices, as was true of its two predecessors. The government had learned from its previous blunders and had managed to put up prices without provoking a riot. It had done so thanks to a Polish tautology—"commercial shops." Outwardly these shops are like any other. Only their prices are higher and over time they have absorbed an increasing proportion of decent quality goods. Together with that other "socialist" invention, the *pewex* shop or outlet for "internal export" (that is, a place where privileged natives can buy provided they have foreign currency), the commercial shops were signs of growing social differentiation. They were also a camouflage for inflation. The decree of July 1 was merely an extension of this disguise: it transferred many better cuts of meat to "commercial" prices. Indeed, contemptuous officials dismissed the first stoppages as "strikes for bacon," since the most painful was the increase in the bacon price, from 27 to 45 zlotys a kilogram. They would have been wiser to perceive that higher prices had merely precipitated a much deeper revolt, due to utter exasperation and hurt human dignity. The claim that the decision had been taken after proper consultation was really the last straw. "So they want to screw us once again," one heard throughout the country, "but this time it won't work." The message most often was put in cruder terms.

The response of the workers was immediate. At Ursus, the

tractor factory which had exploded in 1976, workers in three departments downed their tools on July 1. The three departments got a raise the day after. Stoppages then inevitably spread from shop to shop and were brought to an end only by wage increases ranging from 10 to 15 percent. The following week, several plants were affected in the Warsaw region alone, including the Zeran motorworks of 1956 fame. Productive norms, family allowances, and food supplies were involved in some of these conflicts, but everywhere the strikers rapidly were back to work with higher paychecks. Unwittingly, the state was acting as a sponsor of the strike.

These flexible official tactics might have worked if the Polish labor movement had not gained experience and had not forged internal links in the preceding period. By this time it had both experience and a network of contacts. In this connection the part played by the Committee for Social Self-Defense (the old KOR) and its subsidiaries—such as *Robotnik* (Worker) edited by Jan Litynski—cannot be overestimated. Until his arrest in the second half of August the small apartment of KOR leader Jacek Kuron was a network hub; it served as a clearing house for strikers and for quite a time it was the only source of information both for Poland and the outside world.[1] Failure to keep concessions in the dark meant that the whole operation had exactly the opposite effect. Warsaw wits, with their knack for paraphrase, put it in a nutshell: Lenin, they argued, got it wrong when he claimed "those who do not work do not eat"; Poland has reached a higher stage: here "those who do not strike do not eat meat." Such was the July message.

The Polish strike was national without being truly general, according to the traditional revolutionary pattern. There was no violent tide sweeping key industrial centers first and then continuing the invasion until the whole country was brought to a standstill. Instead the movement was spotty and sporadic, affecting one factory in a town, one shop in a plant, coming to an end in one place then resuming next door or in the same place upon news that much more had been obtained by neighbors. Even the KOR, which tried to monitor all stoppages, could not keep track. This was not only because those reporting for KOR were being arrested or beaten up by the security police; the size of the movement could not be measured properly because of its very nature, since quite often a warning strike or even the threat of one was enough for the management to yield.

As the resistance of the workers stiffened, the establishment was forced to make even more concessions. On July 11 managers of important plants were flown to Warsaw and told by the central committee to buy "social peace"—cheaply if possible, at any price if need be. By then the authorities had also the strangest of strategic reserves: refrigerators on wheels, full of meat and sausage, ready to come to the rescue wherever a serious strike was threatened. The whole strategy, if rather costly and politically not very bold, had the advantage of preventing the movement from gathering momentum, from uniting and thus putting the question of power on the agenda. Until mid-August, Gierek and his colleagues, however uneasy they were, felt politically safe. They might have been less assured had they studied more carefully the one exception to the July message, the commune of Lublin, a forerunner of Gdansk.

Lublin lies about 200 km to the southeast of Warsaw. Its region belongs to the so-called B-Poland, B standing here for rural and backward. The city itself, with its castle and its old town, has a history going back to the tenth century. Socially, the town is very clearly divided into two parts. There is the old, elegant Lublin of the apparatchiks, the professional people, the intelligentsia (this is an important academic town, including a famous Catholic university) and the Lublin of the workers, or rather, the new proletarians. With close to 300,000 inhabitants, the city's population has nearly trebled compared with prewar days and the town now stretches well beyond the historic center, with blocks and blocks of apartment buildings. Lublin's roots are still in the countryside: the region remains 60 percent rural. The proletariat is thus largely made up of peasant-workers and peasants turned workers. Local sociologists admitted to me after the event that they had been convinced that these newcomers into the working class, impressed by their new status, would be the last to enter the fray. In fact, they took the lead in this summer of discontent.

The movement actually began on July 9 next door in Swidnik, a new town of about 40,000 people, at the WSK plant, a firm producing transport equipment, including helicopters. About this Swidnik episode a story circulates around Poland that is too good to be true. When the WSK workers began their strike, the story runs, the authorities rushed food to the plant. The workers went proudly home with the meat; then having eaten it, they felt ashamed. "We were bought off with a bone, like dogs," they concluded angrily and resumed their strike with a vengeance. Checked on the spot, the version is only half accurate. The part about food supplies is true. Local people had not seen such veal, such sausages, and such chocolates for years. But they resumed their strike, somewhat later, because the management had not kept its pledges (they also struck twice more out of solidarity). And yet there is something in this partly apocryphal story. In Swidnik, in Pulawy, in Lublin itself, throughout the area, participants in the conflict told me about two phases in the strikes—a first when workers, surprised by their success, grabbed anything that was offered, and a second when feeling they had sold their rights "for twenty groshy," for a dime, they became politically more conscious and more ambitious.

Whatever the case may be, by Friday July 11, when the Swidnik workers first went back to work, the strike had spread to Lublin, not far from the castle, to the FSC truck factory, employing 10,000 people. Here action was precipitated by a combination of higher meat prices and stiffer production norms. Too much was too much. The workers downed their tools spontaneously and marched to meet the management. At first they did not dare to speak up, but courage came together with collective organization. Remembering the bloody precedent of neighboring Radom in 1976, the workers insisted on discipline and on a refusal to march out of the factory. Drinking vodka was strictly forbidden. A strike committee of eighty was elected, which then picked twenty people to sort out the demands of the workers and negotiate on that basis.

"You didn't invent anything," the local strike leader, Stanislaw Daniel, was later to tell Walesa. He was exaggerating: the Lublin platform did not include an open demand for free trade unions.

But it provided an egalitarian proposal for wage increases (higher percentages for the lower paid); it attacked the social privileges of the police and the army (their higher family allowances and pensions); it called for the abolition of "commercial" prices and *pewex* shops; it demanded freedom of the press. The thirty-five articles of the Lublin platform thus foreshadowed the twenty-one points of the Gdansk Charter.[2]

Admittedly, there was another difference. Four days after they struck, the truck factory workers settled for less than half the loaf. By Wednesday, July 16, the lead in Lublin was taken over by the railway workers, and their intervention caught the attention of the whole country. It did so partly because theirs was the first railway strike in Poland since the war, and largely because Lublin was an important link with the Soviet Union; the Poles were convinced all their missing food had traveled to Moscow for the Olympic games and the stoppage looked like thumbing their noses at the mighty neighbor. The authorities tried unsuccessfully to break the strike by all sorts of means, including the use of scabs from other regions. The railway workers, once the aristocracy of labor, as their leader put it to me, felt they were the most degraded section of the working class. They were in a fighting mood and struck in a most disciplined fashion. They asked for higher wages, better food supplies, family allowances on par with the police and the army, and free Saturdays. They also fought for unions "that would not take orders from above." They refused to take part in the usual comedy of reelection and instead put up their own candidates. This is how Czeslaw Niezgoda, the head of the strike committee, the following month became the elected head of the official workers' council.[3]

The railway workers called off their strike on the evening of Saturday, July 19, bringing to an end a momentous week which saw virtually the whole of Lublin paralyzed. Municipal transportation did not run nor did the buses linking Lublin with other areas. Most of the city's workers, employed in chemical, engineering, or building industries as well as in the local production cooperatives, were idle. Mechanized bakeries stood still and even in hospitals only emergency services were functioning. During the week the bulk of the population seemed both proud and perturbed. Clearly, people had sympathy for the strikers: there was no grumbling at the railway station despite the fact that this was the holiday period. But the same people were worried, frightened of shortages, of the militia that had vanished, frightened, too, of Big Brother and of the unknown.

In many ways Lublin was a dress rehearsal. It revealed the depth of popular discontent, the new self-discipline and maturity of the workers, who stayed within the gates of their factories. It also showed potential elements of parallel power, as the ban on alcohol, for instance, was extended from the factory to the town as a whole. It also showed the egalitarianism and the obviously political nature of the movement, or the way in which individual fears can grow into collective courage. Yet Lublin was also only a dress rehearsal. It had a general strike but no joint strike committee. It had political ambitions but no conviction that its demands could be carried through. It lacked tradition, economic weight, and symbolic political attraction to act as a focus for the country as a whole. Lublin merely outlined what was going to happen elsewhere.

One link with the future was personal. The man who came at the height of the strike to buy peace through concessions was none other than Mieczyslaw Jagielski, the deputy prime minister, whom we shall meet again in the second phase of the Gdansk negotiations. It was in Lublin that he earned his first laurels as peacemaker. His fellows from the establishment were grateful even if the cost was fairly high. By then it was no longer relevant to measure the situation in economic terms. Financially, the whole operation of raising meat prices was an obvious failure. The cost was to rise still further in late July and early August as peace and quiet had to be purchased again and again in new plants, new branches, and new towns. But the rulers could still use the printing presses to save their political necks.

The movement was beginning to get too close even for their political comfort. In Warsaw, after the workers from the big plants voiced their demands, other sections began to stake their claims. Drivers distributing newspapers struck one evening and got their raises the morning after. Garbage collectors had to hold out longer for their reward. On August 11 it was the turn of municipal transportation, in a strike involving almost all the buses and about half the depots of tramways. Late the next evening, a Tuesday, a group of young men provoked a big traffic jam, stopping the remaining trams and other vehicles. The KOR at once issued a statement, as it had done when there was talk of an open mass meeting in Lublin, warning against moves likely to give hardliners an opportunity to intervene. But there was no time to determine whether the young people in Warsaw had acted out of innocent zeal or on orders from above. The limelight shifted brutally to the Lenin Shipyards in Gdansk, where ten years earlier it had all begun.

Anna Walentynowicz, first a welder, then a crane operator, is a veteran at the Lenin Shipyards. When you see how the workers look up to and talk to *pani Anya* (Mrs. Anya), as she is called affectionately, there can be no doubt that she is a sort of mother figure for the young crew. Fiftyish, small, with a nice smile, she is kindness personified to her friends. But she can also be tough and stubborn. She does not suffer bullies gladly nor will she take no for an answer when she feels she is in the right.

Anna Walentynowicz had belonged to the 1970 strike committee and was also a founder member of the Committee for the Free Trade Unions of the Coastal Region, a small group that was to play an important role throughout the crisis.[4] Because of her past, as well as her views and her activity, she was resented by the management, which chose to remove her from the Lenin Shipyards. Undaunted, she took her case to court and surprisingly won. Less surprisingly, the management calmly refused to reinstate her. There followed a tug of war. Coming to work, Walentynowicz would find her clothing and equipment locked up—or even herself taken and locked up. One day plainclothesmen grabbed her and hustled her into a car. As she was screaming, the car rushed off and in the hurry ran over a cyclist. Quite obviously, Walentynowicz was a pain in the neck to a management too stupid to grasp that times had changed.

On August 14, a Thursday, Anna Walentynowicz was at the shipyards hospital as an out-patient. But she knew through her free trade union friends that this was D-day. At four in the morning they were already outside the shipyards with 10,000 leaflets. By six, when the first shift was supposed to start, in the two hull sections and the engine department, small groups had gathered behind banners demanding the reinstatement of Walentynowicz and a raise in wages. The crowd swayed for a moment, as the most faithful supervisors and party cardholders tried to keep the labor force at work.[5] Then a small procession moved on, swelling its ranks on the way. It stopped near the gate where the first strikers had been shot ten years earlier, moved on to a square close to the management building, and improvised a mass meeting, using an excavator as the platform. The general manager was told to climb on. It was about nine when a new actor entered the stage. Having climbed over the barrier, he went straight up to the manager.

"Do you know me?" he asked. "You should—you sacked me. But I've worked here for years and I got my mandate from the crew." Then, turning his back to the manager, he addressed the crowd, now several thousand strong: "I proclaim a sit-in strike. . . ." The newcomer with a moustache and a twinkle in his eye was Lech Walesa.[6]

The strike was on. As if to add insult to injury, the management was forced to send a car for Walentynowicz; she was to join the improvised strike committee headed by Walesa that was designed to prepare the platform for negotiations. Unlike in 1970, the management had instructions from above and was ready for concessions. Three rounds of talk were held the very first day and three of the workers' demands were granted: the reinstatement of victims of political repression, guarantees for strikers, and last but not least, the promise to build a monument for the dead of 1970. Still on the agenda were family allowances on a par with those of the police and a monthly pay raise of 2000 zlotys for everyone.

Friday was a day of expectation, for strikers and leaders both. The strike spread to other yards and other branches: to the Northern Shipyards and the Repairs Shipyard in Gdansk, to the Paris Commune Shipyards in neighboring Gdynia, to enterprises working for the shipyards and to workers in the harbor. Warsaw also realized at once it faced an entirely new challenge. Gierek rushed back from his holiday in the Soviet Union and Premier Babiuch addressed the nation. Though he admitted publicly the existence of labor troubles, his speech was insignificant except for the following passage: "Our faithful friends believe that we shall be able to cope and wish it with all their hearts." The implication was obvious: if we can't, they will. Hypothetical Soviet tanks had thus made their official entry. They were to figure throughout the crisis as a political weapon to soften the strikers. But the Gdansk workers, while showing exemplary restraint, refused to be frightened into surrendering.

Saturday was crucial and might have proved a turning point. By two in the afternoon the negotiations were over. Prodded by Tadeusz Fiszbach, the "reformist" regional party secretary, the shipyards manager granted the workers an across the board raise of 1500 zlotys, quite a lot of money on paper.[7] A rather reluctant Walesa had to follow the views of his committee, accept the terms, and proclaim the end of the strike. But as soon as he reached the crowd near the gate, he sensed that for once he had misjudged the mood of the rank and file.[8] "You can't betray us, Leszek!" "How shall we look people in the face?" questioned another, while a tram conductor put it plainly: "They settle with you, but won't even talk to us." Walesa immediately changed his mind and opted for a solidarity strike. But the internal radio system was cut off after the management's announcement of the end of the strike and of penalties for those who stayed in the shipyards beyond six o'clock.

It was imperative to keep a number of workers inside in order to preserve the shipyards as a base. For this, in the absence of a broadcasting system, it was necessary to appeal to the workers as they were leaving through the gates. Here Alina Pienkowska, a nurse at the shipyards hospital and a very youthful widow, was to play a leading part. This young woman had been so timid that at school she would ask her neighbor to put the question to the teacher. Here she had to brave a tough, mainly male crowd, with hostile questioners planted within it by the management and the party. The occasion clearly makes the woman and not only the man. Pienkowska and her comrades managed to keep enough workers inside the shipyards to keep the strike going.

Not everybody was aware of the latest twist. Andrzej Gwiazda, a graduate engineer, and Bogdan Lis, a worker, who were to be among the most active and influential members of the strike committee, both thought it was all over at the Lenin Shipyards. They went back next door to their own base, Elmor, a plant producing electrical equipment, checked that the boys wanted to carry on, jumped into a "tiny one," as the Poles call their little Fiats, and went on a round of striking plants to decide on possible joint action. They invited representatives to their own place, where they were in for a pleasant surprise. They could move next door: the Lenin Shipyards were still the fortress of the strikers.

That very Saturday night the MKS, Polish initials for the inter-factory strike committee, was duly organized and the whole structure was shaped. Individual plants could set up their own strike committees as they wished; usually it was one delegate for each shop. But they were entitled to a specific number of representatives on the joint committee: three to start with; the figure dropped to one as the number of striking plants rose within a week to several hundred. The MKS immediately chose its presidium, headed again by Walesa and provisionally numbering fourteen members, with seats left vacant for the big enterprises still unrepresented. It also stated bluntly that only this joint committee was entitled to negotiate with the central authorities on key, common issues and to proclaim the end of the strike. By Sunday, the delegates had also produced their platform, the twenty-one-point charter. Its crucial first article provided for "free trade unions independent of party and employers"; the second demanded the right to strike. The lines of battle were drawn.

The other side, too, grasped that the real trial of strength was on. On Monday, August 18, Gierek himself addressed the nation. While his speech—with hints of danger and the offer of new elections to the old unions—fell flat, it was revealing. It confirmed a determination not to negotiate with the joint committee, with the organized representatives of the working class. In order to divide the strikers, a governmental commission headed by Tadeusz Pyka was sent to Gdansk with powers to bribe individual plants away. Pyka could claim some initial success, notably with the Northern and the Repairs Shipyards, but when it came to putting his promises on paper, he asked for a break to consult Warsaw. He came back with watered down proposals, provoking the delegates, who were in any case under pressure from the rank and file not to go it alone, to break off the talks; they swore they would never be led up the garden path in this way again.

Had the wave of strikes receded, Gierek would have been in the clear. But it did not. The rising membership of the Gdansk MKS read like a death warrant for the official schemes: 21 on Sunday, more than 250 two days later, it was to top 700. This explains why each plant was reduced to a single delegate: more could not be packed into the conference hall of the Lenin Shipyards. And as it grew in numbers, the MKS grew in confidence. By Tuesday, public utilities, the food manufacturers, and the health services were functioning by the express permission of the MKS and the sale of alcohol was banned throughout the Gdansk area, on its advice, by the *voivoda* (analogous to the French regional prefect). The interfactory committee acted and appeared as an organ of parallel power.

The MKS was also gaining outside support. On Tuesday, August 19, the day after Gierek's intervention, the other big Polish harbor, Szczecin, was brought to a standstill. An MKS set up at the Warski Shipyards elaborated a thirty-five-point platform, preparing itself for negotiations. With the whole maritime coast paralyzed by strikes, this was a repetition of the 1970 events, only on a different scale and in another atmosphere. This time, there was no shooting, no skirmishes, no street demonstrations. Calm, confident, determined, the workers stayed in their plants as if these were impregnable fortresses.

Messages of sympathy were reaching the Gdansk shipyards from factories all over the country. And not only from factories: an expression of solidarity of the progressive intelligentsia with the workers "who are fighting for their and our right to a better life" was issued on Wednesday, August 20. Inspired originally by teachers at the "flying university," the idea at first was of a few glorious names appealing to both sides to avoid a conflict.

The teachers then changed their minds and within twenty-four hours collected sixty-four signatures of prominent intellectuals—hence the name "the appeal of the sixty-four"—and by the end of the week the number of signatories had quadrupled, including names which had never previously appeared under a dissident text.

Two of the organizers—Tadeusz Mazowiecki, editor of the leftish Catholic publication *Wiez* (Link) and Bronislaw Geremek, a medieval historian of international repute—traveled with the appeal, changing cars, covering up their tracks until they reached what seemed to them as the really free town of Gdansk. There Walesa greeted them warmly with frank common sense: "The appeal is fine, but . . . we're getting ready for negotiations . . . we workers know what we want but they are better at putting it into words. . . ." The intellectuals were asked to perform their function as "experts." The two organizers rang up their friends in the capital while the MKS got in touch with the Gdansk prefect, who then asked for six seats to be reserved on the next morning's plane. Though there was still a hitch at the Warsaw airport, the people finally arrived and at the opening of the following week the workers had their own official commission experts, made up roughly half and half of leftwing Catholics and independents with a Marxist background.[9]

In their recollections of the first contact with the movement all experts stress the same, highly instructive, aspect. Let us remember that we are dealing with people who were bright, brave, and committed: they had not come as peacemakers, but as advisers for one of the sides. Nevertheless, since they were supposed to help in the negotiations they asked about acceptable compromises and possible fallback positions, particularly on free trade unions, which from Warsaw (or outside) seemed a rather far-fetched goal. They were all taken aback by the answer. From the first worker they talked to in the shipyards to the presidium which was unanimous on this issue, they were told that on this there was no question of budging—the free unions were not negotiable. Walesa summed it up in his colorful fashion: "If I gave in on this, I could not go to the gate. . . . I would be swept away. . . ."

The unanimous determination shows how quickly political consciousness develops in the heat of battle. At the beginning of the conflict the young "veterans" from the Committee for Free Trade Unions had to explain to their comrades that unless they had an instrument to defend their rights, the 2000 zlotys, or whatever they got, would rapidly be reduced to peanuts. A week later the rank and file had absorbed and integrated the lesson so well that if the leaders had wished to go back on the trade union issue—which they clearly did not—they would have been overthrown. Yet this also meant something else. When at the conference table the workers' delegates repeatedly told the other side that the first point was crucial, that once this was granted everything else was negotiable, they meant it, they were dead serious. Thus from the very start the negotiations were for the highest stakes. The party had to admit not only that its unions were phony; it had to accept the terrible prospect of workers having their own, genuine, independent representation.

But we are running ahead. We had not yet reached the point of negotiation. Gierek was a reluctant learner, advancing when he really had to, then dragging his feet again. The unsuccessful Pyka was recalled on Wednesday, August 20, and two other deputy prime ministers were sent instead to the maritime provinces. Kazimierz Barcikowski, in Szczecin, was allowed to embark on direct negotiations with the strikers almost at once. In Gdansk, where it mattered more because the eyes of the whole country were focused on the Lenin Shipyards, Mieczyslaw Jagielski was told to keep on trying. He attempted to carry on branch negotiations with big plants, by-passing the MKS. Indeed, judging by the recollections of the participants, that middle of the week was probably the moment of highest tension and apprehension in the shipyards. The MKS, with eyes and ears everywhere, knew the authorities were preparing a coup. Reinforcements of riot police had been sent up, headed by a general, and an operation codenamed "Little Evening" planned. This involved a helicopter raid, the seizure of the presidium at its Gdansk headquarters, and the destruction of the printing presses in the Gdynia Paris Commune Shipyards, on which the strikers were soon to print their counter-propaganda sheet, called, like the future union, *Solidarity*.

Finally, nothing came of the coup plans because the rulers realized that the inevitable reply to their move would have been a general strike crippling the whole country. Gierek did not want to stay in office propped up directly by Russian tanks. And so Jagielski had to resign himself to the inevitable. On Friday evening he told three emissaries from the shipyards that preliminary talks would begin the day after.

The main gate to the Lenin Shipyards looked throughout the second half of August like a cross between a flower show and a Catholic patriotic shrine, with posters of the Pope and national flags. In front of the gate it was half Hyde Park and half an open-air temple, as crowds thronged for political meetings or Sunday mass. From this main gate to the conference hall there were no more than about 300 meters. For representatives of the establishment, having to walk between two ranks of young, tough, hooting shipwrights, it must have felt like miles and miles. On Saturday, at about two in the afternoon, prefect Jerzy Kolodziejski was the first to run the metaphorical gauntlet. Though preceded by stewards, he looked as pale as death. A worker talking to a neighbor expressed the mood of the moment: "Look at him! The son of a bitch is more frightened than we are. . . ."

The prefect was there to discuss procedure. Officialdom wanted debates behind closed doors while the workers wanted an open treaty openly arrived at. The workers carried the day. The conference building had a small room at the back for meetings between delegations, while plenary sessions took place in the big hall, into which more than a thousand were packed. Talks from the small room were relayed to the big hall, while proceedings in the latter were beamed by loudspeakers throughout the shipyards and beyond. Only later, once agreement had been reached over respective experts, were two working parties set up, one generally political, the second economic.

Meanwhile, six hours after the prefect, Jagielski arrived at the gate in a minibus with his party. This time Walesa had great pains to contain a crowd yelling, "On your knees!" "Ask forgiveness!" and less polite epithets revealing the Slavonic wealth of swear words. The ordeal must have been nerve-racking, since one of Jagielski's followers, a party secretary, was heard muttering on reaching the small conference room: "Savages . . . animals . . . the wild East. . . ." The strenuous arrival did not prevent good manners, however. Jagielski, the official representative of the "workers' state," addressed the workers' chosen speaker as "Mr. President," causing Walesa, unused to such titles, to turn around and look behind, wondering to whom he was talking. But these formal concessions were the only one the deputy prime minister made on this first occasion. Otherwise he was not giving anything away. In principle, he agreed with all the twenty-one points. In practice, he rejected them one by one, starting with the first. He did not even yield on the strikers' precondition, the resumption of telephone links between Gdansk and the rest of the country. Jagielski was clearly playing for time. He was flying back to Warsaw to report to a crucial central committee session that had to decide how to handle this open rising of the Polish working class.

On Sunday, August 24, the tenth day of their strike, the workers of Gdansk brought down the government. That evening Gierek reappeared on television after a tense session of the central committee and in a twenty-minute broadcast announced a major reshuffle of the leadership, admitted past mistakes, and promised economic reforms for the future. Since this was no gift horse, the workers looked into its mouth; as they had a memory, they were not overimpressed.

Changes at the top were undoubtedly substantial. Six out of the eighteen members of the politburo were kicked out, as were Premier Babiuch and several of his ministers. But ten years earlier an equal number had been thrown overboard after the workers' rising, including the top leader, Gomulka. And now as then, those taking over the jobs—Jozef Pinkowski, the new premier, or Stefan Olszowski, the pragmatic climber returning to the politburo—were products of the same party machine. This perhaps was inevitable, but so was the skepticism. While pleased with the disgrace of some of the hardliners, such as the trade union boss Jan Szydlak or Jerzy Lukasiewicz, responsible for propaganda, the strikers saw no guarantee in these personal permutations. As to promises of economic reform, the Polish road to near bankruptcy is littered with such pledges.

Why should the strikers have trusted a leadership, however reshuffled, which was holding Kuron, Michnik, and their other friends from the KOR in prison? Jailed on August 20 as soon as the situation got serious, they had been unashamedly released and then rearrested every forty-eight hours ever since so as to avoid the bother of putting up charges against them. Why should they have believed in the good intentions of a partner who had cut off the maritime provinces from the rest of the country and Gdansk from Szczecin? In the eighth week of labor unrest and the second of their own stoppage, the pressure on the Gdansk strikers to yield, to be "reasonable," was piling up. *Pravda* and *Tass* were multiplying stories about "anti-socialist elements" in Poland. The Polish press, the radio, and television were full of not-so-gentle hints about the country's past, its partition, the tsarist occupation. Even the Catholic church was mobilized for the purpose, with Cardinal Wyszynski suddenly shown at length on television, preaching prudence and responsibility.[10] The Gdansk MKS, both flexible in manner and firm on principles, refused to resume talks until communications were restored and the Warsaw bullies were forced to give in.

When the negotiations resumed (or rather, started in earnest) on Tuesday, August 26, they went straight to the heart of the matter. The problem of free trade unions dominated the agenda in the political commission as well as in plenary sessions. At first Jagielski argued as if he too were for a complete overhaul. The unions, he admitted, had failed in their task, they represented nobody and had to be entirely renewed. He really meant reelected in the same framework. From the very start, as one of the participants was to put it, the question was whether one opted for the reorganization of the old unions or the creation of entirely new ones. The strikers had no intention of pouring their new, heady wine into the old, dirty, and detested bottles.

However, they were ready for verbal and more than verbal concessions. On the advice of their experts, they dropped the adjective "free" because of its special, pro-western connotations ("free world," "free Europe," etc.), and proposed "independent and self-governing" instead. One might argue, rightly, that the second term really contains the first. The workers' delegates were also aware of this: they simply produced two adjectives so as to have one to drop in the bargaining. Since the other side made no objection, however, the two stuck and the budding union was christened by its Polish initials, NSZZ *Solidarnosc*, standing for the independent, self-governing trade union, Solidarity.

The name was fine, though not its content. The government was being asked to accept something staggering, to admit that the workers required their own organization to defend themselves against the party and the employers, lumped here significantly together. To get this swallowed in Warsaw first, in Moscow after, required quite a lot of political dressing. After a first consultation with the capital the government delegation rejected the draft, citing unspecified preconditions to fulfill. The workers then offered their own views on the means of production: we are not against collective property, they argued, neither are we against socialism; the new unions accept these principles. That was fine, but lent itself to many interpretations. It was necessary to include the passage about the Communist Party "playing a leading role in the state" and about "not undermining the established system of international alliances" for the official delegation finally to decide that the package could be sold to the central committee and to Poland's neighbors. And the first point settled, the next twenty presented no unsurmountable obstacles.

With a peaceful compromise in sight, the temperature, strangely enough, rose suddenly within Polish society. Friday was a day of panic in Warsaw and as the news from there spread, of anxiety throughout the world. It was taken for granted in the Polish capital that the central committee convened for the next day would reject the Gdansk agreement and remove Gierek as too soft. It was not quite clear whether the diehards seizing power would take the labor movement on their own or would call the Russians to the rescue. On the other hand, the proclamation of the state of siege was such a certainty that many people did not sleep at home that night, only to find out in the morning that the Szczecin agreement had already been signed, while the Gdansk Charter was to be blessed that very day and signed on the next.

Had it all been imagined? There are still rumors in Warsaw that Kirilenko and Suslov had been in Poland, at Bialowieza, on August 28, and that they told their Polish comrades, "We know there are no anti-Soviet demonstrations and we shall not intervene; you must manage on your own." Future historians will disentangle fact from fancy. But already it can be shown that pressure on Gierek was strong to avoid confrontation. In the last week of the conflict the Polish labor movement was literally rallying around Gdansk. On Tuesday, August 26, it was Wroclaw, headed by its transportation workers, which set up an MKS and proclaimed a solidarity strike. The day after, it was the turn of neighboring Walbrzych. By Friday the mines around Jastrzebie and the steel mills of Katowice were paralyzed, and the government's last island—upper Silesia—was flooded by the strikes. Gierek, it must be granted, never tried to shoot his way out of trouble, and even the Russians were probably reluctant to face the Polish working class in so open a confrontation. The odds favored a compromise.

It was then, on Saturday, with victory almost within their grasp, that a certain malaise appeared among the Gdansk strikers. It was not just the apprehension of a return to the dreary routine of everyday work after the exciting fraternity of common struggle. The strikers were somewhat bewildered. Whether "within the state" or within society, the "leading role" of the Communist Party struck them as a dangerous reminder of the past; for once, not enough explaining had been done about the necessary balancing act. Equally, everything was now being hurried through. The authorities having cut contacts on Friday, the Szczecin strikers did not know their Gdansk comrades had won the day over the first article and signed a less favorable agreement, with the result that pressure was being put on Gdansk to follow suit. Jagielski and his colleagues were also reversing the argument about the crucial nature of that first point and asking for compensation. In the ensuing rush, mistakes were apparently made over wages in the economic commission.

Wages as an issue illustrate the quick maturing of the movement. On the third day of their stoppage the strikers could have obtained a raise of 1500 zlotys. After two weeks, having learned about the importance of their organization and the unimportance of printed paper, they were willing to settle provisionally for the leveling raise of 1000 zlotys for the lowest paid and 500 zlotys for those in the higher income bracket. But in the rush to get the document through, the government side was allowed to leave the 2000 zlotys as the long-term end and branch negotiations as the ill-defined means. The mistake was to cause trouble later. In the meantime, the true cause of the malaise was solidarity and the real trouble was over the fourth point, dealing with political prisoners: more precisely, over the members of KOR, arrested without trial and unmentioned in the text.

Obviously, the striking workers could not let their old friends down. With Jagielski waffling about the independence of the judiciary, the question was whether one trusted his promise or one refused to sign the agreement. Differences on this issue, and even more the gossip surrounding it, were to hurt and leave wounds that are still unhealed. The confusion is best illustrated by Walesa himself, who on the last Sunday first threatened an ultimatum—it's either/or—and then came back ten minutes later to proclaim: "We won't let these people down. We shall sign the agreements and if they are not freed, we shall strike." His contradictory propositions were as thunderously applauded and unanimously approved by the MKS in session. Maybe the strikers were by then aware, deep in their hearts, that the government was bound to free the prisoners and maybe Walesa, with his uncanny flair, did express the mood of the shipyards when he drew the following balance sheet: "Have we got it all? No. But we have a great deal, all that was possible in the present situation. And the rest we can win together because we have our trade union."

The other points were signed one after another in an atmosphere of growing enthusiasm.[11] Thus the stage was set for the ceremony described at the beginning of this postscript.

The Polish workers did obtain "a great deal" and the ceremony was more important than a mere peace treaty. History has its ironic coincidences. The Comintern was launched by the Bolsheviks with twenty-one conditions. The labor movement in Poland, and therefore in eastern Europe, was now formally revived with twenty-one points.[12] The first point of the Gdansk Charter destroyed the myth of the workers' state, the legend of the Communist Party as the incarnation of the higher interests of the proletariat. It openly proclaimed the need for the workers, there as everywhere, to take their destiny into their own hands. As such, and whatever may yet happen, August 31 marks the opening of an era.

However wisely they might have moved, the authorities could not have turned this defeat into victory. But they were in a position to learn from the defeat and even to take advantage of it, harnessing Solidarity to joint action on a national scale against an economic prospect that was bleak in the best of cases. Once again, they chose instead to be too clever by half. It was not specified in the agreement whether the main provision—the right to set up independent unions—applied only locally or for the whole of Poland. The price paid for this intentional ambiguity was three weeks of stoppages as region after region struck, combining its own specific grievances with the demand for the Gdansk Charter. Admittedly, this was no longer a dangerous tide threatening the regime, though this tail end of the general strike proved sufficient to engulf Edward Gierek.

In the changed political climate surprises were many. On September 5, for instance, the Polish parliament reverberated with really critical speeches, as if this rubber-stamp institution wished to compete with Westminster. Observers, however, were even more struck by a conspicuous absence, that of the party's first secretary. The reason was revealed late that night, at the end of a special session of the central committee: Gierek had had a stroke and was removed from both politburo and secretariat. While the heart trouble was genuine, the excuse for his dismissal was not; leaderships in eastern Europe are full of worse invalids.

Ten years earlier Gierek had told the shipyard workers of Szczecin that something would have to be done to ensure a system of succession so that leaders "would not have to be swept away by a wave." But he did nothing, and was now himself cast aside by the biggest tide of the postwar period. His place was taken over by fifty-three-year-old Stanislaw Kania, a stodgy apparatchik of peasant origin. The fact that Kania used to be in charge of the army and the police in the party secretariat is not the most disturbing; it is also known that during the Gdansk crisis he pleaded for compromise, not out of liberalism, but as a result of a sober assessment of the balance of forces. The question mark hanging over Kania and the whole new leadership is different: Will it have the stature to match this unprecedented situation and the imagination to face the unknown?

Imperceptibly, we have moved from the third act, describing the spectacular conquest by the working class of the right to organize, to the fourth, barely begun and of uncertain duration, which should show how the system adapts itself to an entirely new deal. But before moving from history, however instant, into crystal gazing, let us stop for a moment to record some of the main features of the Polish movement.

The focus throughout the world had been on Gdansk, which made sense. In the western media the accent was often on the religious fervor of the workers, which was also to a certain extent understandable. After all, one is not accustomed, particularly in the western half of the continent of Europe, to see strikers celebrating mass or a leader seeking God's blessing for his daily round in the class struggle. Yet this emphasis on an admittedly important aspect should not distort the image of the new labor movement maturing at an unexpected pace.[13]

The most striking contrast with the past was the calm assertion of their power by the workers. This time they did not need a tocsin—the stoppage of a train, the burning of party headquarters—as a call to national action. Obsessed by the experiences of 1970 and 1976, they would not march out into the streets, avoiding anything that could lead to a provocation. In Poland, where drunkenness is a major social evil, the word "strike" was synonymous with sobriety. But there was an even more eloquent example of self-discipline. In a country where anti-Russian feeling is now visceral, where you tell a passer-by, "Lousy day," and get the reply "It will be better when we've got rid of the Russkies," not a single public anti-Soviet pronouncement was recorded throughout the crisis.

Another sign of maturity was the shedding of illusions. The

ideas of workers' councils and self-government, which flourished for a spell in 1956 as Gomulka returned to power, were still based on the assumption that in a "socialist Poland" the workers were somehow the masters of their factories. By 1970 this rosy vision was well shaken. Ten years later the Polish strikers, acting very much as a "class against," were talking in classical Marxist terms of "them" and "us": they were insisting on independent trade unions as a guarantee of some sort of workers' power in the struggle with the omnipresent employer, the state.[14] (This more lucid outlook, we shall see, presents its own problems.)

The movement was also more openly political. Its egalitarianism was plain to see: all wage demands were equal, not proportionate, and all infringements of this rule were in favor of the lowest paid. The profound solidarity found an expression, for instance, in the Gdansk Charter, the shipyard workers including in their platform the many demands of the nurses, who do not have the same bargaining strength.[15] But the most significant change was the new capacity of the workers' movement to rise above their immediate material preoccupations, to express political demands, to act as a voice for the society as a whole.

This description of the working class as able to lead other sections and to enforce its own fundamental interests as "the revolutionary interests of society itself" sounds as if it were lifted straight from the pages of Marx. Let me hasten to add that this is my own assessment of a movement which was neither headed by convinced Marxists nor probably interpreted in this fashion by the participants.[16] Despite its practical wisdom and self-discipline, the Polish labor movement has not yet found its bearings. It is still groping toward a project and searching for an ideology. Unfortunately, though understandably after thirty-five years of deceit and exploitation, it does not seek inspiration in what it still views as the creed of its (class) enemy. The gap between what the movement does and what it says, between its performance and its perception of this performance, adds to the general confusion.

Western observers were bewitched and bewildered by the glorious Polish summer: not only the establishment voices, who love strikes only when they are staged on the other side of the

Elbe, but the western Left, which has some excuses for its per-
plexity. What do you do with a movement which starts, as the
Gdansk strike did, by singing the International and the religious-
patriotic hymn to "God who has protected Poland over centuries"? Lenin, whose statue in the big conference hall was
unmolested but also totally ignored, may have been puzzled by
the praying strikers, though with his well-known shrewdness,
he certainly would have perceived the hard core of class struggle
beneath the religious veneer.

That sounds too easy. Let us leave Lenin out of it and avoid
facile exits through inaccurate metaphors. The religious element, as was shown earlier in this book, is no veneer. It is too
heavy a layer for my liking. My undisguised sympathy for the
movement is not a form of blindness prompted by wishful thinking. To put it plainly, if the Polish workers must carry posters of
a compatriot, I would have been happier had they picked Rosa
Luxemburg rather than Pope John Paul II. Or, to take another
example, I too was perturbed on seeing the first picture of a
Walesa interview, not so much by the crucifix as by the portrait
of Pilsudski in the background (even if my Polish friends tried
to explain to me that this was not Pilsudski the marshal with
his colonels, but the earlier social democrat and fighter for
national independence).

Faced by such objections over the nature of the movement, I
can only answer with the argument that runs throughout this
book. When the events and heroes of current history fail to
conform exactly to the desired or expected pattern, the only wise
solution is to seek the reason why and try if possible to influence
the shape of things. Getting cross with history and withdrawing
cursing under the tent will lead us nowhere. I say this more
easily now that the Polish summer justifies reasoned hope rather
than sulking. The red mole may weave unexpected patterns and
assume strange disguises; it is digging, digging fast, and moving
in roughly the right direction.

But how far will it be allowed to dig? To answer this question,
which takes us into the future and raises the shadow of the
Soviet tank, I shall have to use shorthand, relying on notes jotted

down during the journey through Poland immediately after the storm. Things read differently from a distance. "How long can the Russians put up with this state of things?"—the question seen quite often in the western press sounds in Warsaw almost obscene. There it looks like an invitation to invade, as if the authors did not care how many Polish corpses were required to confirm their Manichean version of "socialism" as wicked and unchangeable.

Not that the Poles themselves ignore the risk of invasion. In the Gdansk negotiations, as one of the "experts" put it to me, it figured on two levels. On the higher "eschatological" plane, it was very present in the workers' minds, and it explains the acceptance of "party preponderance" or the "established system of alliances." On the level of day-to-day negotiations, on the other hand, they refused to take it into account, because this would have led them to surrender.

Similarly today, the Polish opposition wants to avoid the contrasting errors of blissful ignorance and metaphysical gloom. That the Kremlin hates what is happening in Poland stands to reason. Not for nothing did the Russians resume radio jamming as the Polish strike spread, while the East Germans and the Czechs subsequently set up a *cordon sanitaire* to prevent the extension of Polish flu. Distaste, however, does not necessarily imply the extreme response, and invasion is not written inexorably into this script like doom into a Greek tragedy.

To put it differently, it is true that a system based on the Soviet model of rule from above is historically incompatible with a counter-power flowing from below. But this incompatibility only becomes explosive in the long run if we assume that the Soviet system is immutable, frozen forever. This is an absurd assumption. After all, who would have guessed in July, nay, in mid-August, that the Polish workers would win, peacefully and so soon, the right to strike and to organize as a class?

If the Russians did not intervene at the time, it was not out of generosity. They, too, must calculate. Their troops are bogged down in Afghanistan. To take on an almost united Poland, with its 35 million inhabitants, is no joke on its own. What impact would such a venture have on detente, on the arms race, on the

Soviet bloc's trade with the West? These are only some of the factors that Moscow must take into account. Still, seen in this way from Warsaw, the invasion ceases to be an inevitable curse and becomes a calculated risk. Even if the Poles cannot claim control over all the elements in the equation, they have power over many. If the regime were to collapse, for instance, the Russians would not hesitate to invade. While the Polish workers can carry their fight far, they cannot take it to its logical conclusion, the seizure of power. They have the complicated task of winning concessions from the authorities while simultaneously propping them up.

Much will thus depend on the capacity of the Polish Communist Party to measure up to this situation. I do not share the view of some members of the Polish opposition who think that only Moscow matters, as in Warsaw there is a political void. The party apparatus and the security services, though shaken and torn apart by the events, are still very much there. On the other hand, it is true that the leadership (and the apparatus) have lost their hold over the 3 million Communist Party members, many of whom, as we saw, were active in the strikes. In the effort to reassert its power and also to regain some control over the labor movement, the leadership may blunder dangerously.

The peril for the leadership is increased by a predicament of its own making—the campaign against corruption. On the day after its defeat in Gdansk, the government played the classic game for diverting attention from the fundamental flaws of the system: it put the blame on a few individuals (getting rid, incidentally, of some of Gierek's followers). The case of Maciej Szczepanski, the former head of television, with his villas, his pornographic films, and his two mulatto mistresses, did catch the imagination of the Poles. The snag is that corruption in Poland does not belong to the realm of fancy. Gierek told the Poles to "enrich themselves," and during the ten years of his reign many party dignitaries took him at his word. Launching a campaign against corruption, the authorities thus opened Pandora's box. While I was in Walbrzych, for example, the regional party boss was being accused openly in a public meeting of using public funds to build a private villa costing over 7 million zlotys, the equivalent of roughly 150 years' worth of average wages. And his case was only one of many. The potential victims might conclude that Soviet tanks are preferable to a Polish jail, and they might get an opportunity to act on their conclusions because of the divisions at the top. Stanislaw Kania is not yet fully in the saddle. Several competitors are ostensibly jockeying for position and this competition takes place at a time when a united and determined leadership is required to reach agreement with the unions. The absence of cohesion is the more perturbing since the government is not confronting a well-oiled labor machine easily maneuvered by its own establishment.

Potentially, Solidarity is mighty. It is already several million strong and it will soon count within its ranks the bulk of Poland's blue- and white-collar workers. In this respect the triumph is undeniable. But this mighty labor federation is still run on a shoestring. Its leaders have hardly slept or eaten in the last three months, have lost weight, and are living on their nerves. The clerical and other technical work is done by volunteers: students, or women who have come out of early retirement or are working for the movement on unpaid leave. The whole organization has barely had time to deal with its own affairs. On September 17, spurred by its Wroclaw branch, it opted for a degree of centralism.[17] In order to face the state and its institutions, the regional bodies decided not to go it alone but to register as part of one single organization.

Logically, this preliminary debate should have been followed by a fundamental one about the very nature and purpose of Solidarity. How far should the unions collaborate with the management and the authorities at local, regional, and national levels? If they do, they run the risk of being integrated, corrupted, and swallowed. If they do not, how will they perform their self-chosen task of participating in the shaping of the country's economic policy? Confusion and ambiguity were in fact written into the Gdansk compromise. On the one hand, the labor unions promised not to play a political role. On the other, they are supposed to influence such highly "nonpolitical" decisions as the distribution of the national income between consumption and accumulation, the use of the social consumption fund, the wage policy, and so on. But instead of seeking solutions for their key problems, the unions were wasting their time in permanent skirmishes on the local level and on the national level in the big battle with the state over registration, the promised right to strike, and the unfulfilled pledges over wages.

Time is thus being wasted when the economic situation should have driven the government to seek a "social contract" at almost any cost. After the excitement of the summer comes the autumn with its unpaid bills. Lines are lengthening for meat, beginning to form for sugar and bread. The harvest is again poor and the prospects for food supplies bad. If nothing is done to consolidate the Polish foreign debt, its servicing will absorb almost the whole revenue from Poland's exports to the West. Even if everybody proves very generous, the economic situation of the country will be very difficult in the next few years. The collaboration of the labor movement is indispensable to get through this lean period, to initiate the necessary monetary and managerial reforms, to boost productivity.

Poland's workers have shown, notably in Gdansk, that they can tighten their belts if needed and are able to look beyond their narrow, immediate interests. But they will do so only for political reward and when they feel that their economic sacrifices will not be wasted once again through a combination of mismanagement and injustice. Had the government decided to actively anger the workers at the local level, it would not have acted otherwise. First they threatened the workers with the loss of all sorts of social benefits if they joined Solidarity. Then local party and old union bosses tried all possible tricks to make it more difficult for them to organize. Finally came the national trouble over registration. The rank and file are losing their tempers and Walesa together with his colleagues may find it increasingly difficult to contain the movement.

Judging by his performance during the first two months in office, Stanislaw Kania does not look like a man who has opted for confrontation, knowing full well that the risks of intervention would now be high. Watched by the Russians and by his domestic rivals, he gives the impression of trying to please the former, outmaneuver the latter, and consolidate his position by strengthening the party. In attempting to do it all at once, he glides perilously from blunder to blunder. A Soviet invasion is not inevitable, but Poland may drift into disaster. In the next few months the main threat hanging over Poland will not come from inexorable fate but from the antics of the sorcerer's apprentices.

The fourth act has scarcely begun. At best it will be a cliff-hanger, with periods of respite between long bouts of brinkman-ship. Its span is uncertain. It may end abruptly for reasons stretching beyond Poland to Soviet in-fighting or the balance of power in the world. It may also endure. Indeed, the longer it lasts the better, since the fourth act can only end successfully if it merges into a fifth, played on the international stage and including the Soviet Union.

Whatever the fourth act may hold, the third is already un-forgettable. The sixty days culminating in the Gdansk agree-ment not only shook Poland beyond recognition. By showing that the apparently impossible can be achieved, they have opened new ways for the labor movement throughout eastern Europe and, as such, have found their place in our common history.

Poland-Paris, October-November 1980

Notes

Introduction: Stalin Is Dead

1. Not that I consider the determination of the nature of a social formation unimportant; quite the contrary. But too often in debates over the Soviet Union the formula, instead of springing from a thorough analysis of the formation, replaces that analysis.
2. This is not the only criterion by which to compare the two systems. We know that ours has more subtle ways to preserve its ideological domination. Besides, my case cannot be taken as a rule. The comparison would be different with the United States in the McCarthy period and certainly with, say, most countries of Latin America today. Admittedly, these countries do not pretend to be socialist, but this is an argument for us, not for advocates of the capitalist system.
3. The so-called crisis of Marxism may well be an awakening, the growing awareness of the progress and adaptation required after fifty years when the only living thought was heretical.

Solzhenitsyn: The Witness and the Prophet

1. The word "zek" is Soviet slang for prisoner.
2. Subsequent events, while not justifying Solzhenitsyn, go some way to explain the current disarray on the Left.
3. See the tale of the smiling Buddha in *The First Circle* (London: Fontana, 1970). Published in the United States by Harper & Row, 1968.
4. A. Solzhenitsyn, *The Oak and the Calf* (New York: Harper & Row, 1980), pp. 112, 119.
5. Ibid., p. 112.
6. A. Solzhenitsyn, *Letter to the Soviet Leaders* (New York: Harper & Row, 1976).
7. *The Oak and the Calf*, p. 119.

8. A. Solzhenitsyn et al., *From Under the Rubble* (London: Collins and Harvill Press, 1975), p. 22.

9. Ibid., p. 24.

10. This phrase comes from Nikolai Chernyshevsky.

11. "They even experienced that 'happiness' we are forever hearing about, which was sometimes called pastoral or patriarchal (and it is not a literary invention)." And immediately following: "and for ten centuries millions of our peasant forebears died feeling that their lives had not been too unbearable." *From Under the Rubble*, p. 23.

12. *Letter to the Soviet Leaders.*

13. *From Under the Rubble*, p. 271.

14. Ibid., p. 122.

15. A. Solzhenitsyn et al., *Iz Pod Glyb* (Paris: YMCA Press, 1974) p. 10.

16 *The Oak and the Calf*, pp. 255–56.

17. This term refers to the terrible Article 58 of the Penal Code. Its fourteen paragraphs covered the whole possible range of "anti-Soviet" activities.

18. "Unable to make two steps forward in abstraction; from now on to stick to the concrete." *The Oak and the Calf*, p. 13.

19. Here, e.g., is his quip about Trotsky: "There is no basis for assuming that if Trotsky had fallen into their jaws, he would have conducted himself with any less debasement or that his resistance would have proved stronger than theirs." *The Gulag Archipelago*, Vol. I (London: Fontana, 1974), p. 410. Published in the United States by Harper & Row, 1973. Trotsky, like Solzhenitsyn deported from Russia, was not greeted in the West with comparable enthusiasm. He found a "planet without a visa." And his fate was also to be different not only because times have changed. The KGB could still find a Mornand-Jackson and a killer's axe. Did it ever cross Solzhenitsyn's mind that the "abject" Trotsky was taken by the masters in the Kremlin as an incomparably greater potential threat than his would-be censor. Probably not, since modesty is not one of Solzhenitsyn's vices.

20. *The Gulag Archipelago*, Vol. I, p. 130.

21. *The Gulag Archipelago*, Vol. II (London: Fontana, 1976), pp. 373–74; cf. 303–7. Published in the United States by Harper & Row, 1975.

22. Ibid., p. 585.

23. Ibid., p. 42.

24. *The Gulag Archipelago*, Vol. I, p. 266.

25. Following are a few examples; the attentive reader will find plenty more throughout *The Gulag Archipelago*. "How many years it would take to reveal, direct and confirm the necessary line, until the defense would stand as one with the prosecution and the court, and the accused would be in agreement with them too, and all the resolutions of the workers as well!" Ibid., p. 305; cf. pp. 310–11; cf. also Vol. II, pp. 110, 141, 622, and 642.

26. *The Gulag Archipelago*, Vol. I, p. 341.

27. David Burg and George Feifer, *Solzhenitsyn* (New York: Stein and Day, 1973).

28. *The Gulag Archipelago*, Vol. I, p. 164.
29. See "An Incident at Krechetovka Station," in A. Solzhenitsyn, *Stories and Prose Poems* (Harmondsworth: Penguin Books, 1973).
30. *The First Circle*, p. 245.
31. Ibid., p. 683.
32. *The Gulag Archipelago*, Vol. I, p. 613.
33. Ibid., Vol. II, p. 594–98.
34. *The Oak and the Calf*, p. 4.
35. *The First Circle*, p. 159.
36. Ibid., pp. 281–82.
37. Ibid., pp. 375–76.
38. Ibid., p. 422.
39. Ibid., p. 447.
40. *Cancer Ward* (Harmondsworth: Penguin Books, 1971), pp. 438–40. Published in the United States by Farrar, Straus & Giroux, and Bantam Books, 1969.
41. Georg Lukács, *Solzhenitsyn* (London: Merlin Press, 1970), p. 66.
42. *The Oak and the Calf*, p. 89.
43. *The Gulag Archipelago*, Vol. II, p. 354.
44. *The Oak and the Calf*, p. 14.
45. Ibid., p. 150. Personally I doubt whether a lasting reconciliation between Solzhenitsyn and the regime was ever in the cards. Not that he was not ready for some concessions, while narrow nationalism provided some common ground. But Solzhenitsyn proudly views himself as the spokesman for the dead, bound to carry out the last will of the victims of the gulag. He could not yield on this issue, whereas the public denunciation not just of Stalin's direct accomplices, but of all the helpers and informers is bound to shake the structure of power in the Soviet Union.
46. F. L. Tvardovskaya, the daughter of the poet, makes the point about his one-sidedness, but since she does not answer any of his charges, she in no way restores the balance. See her letter in *Unita* (Rome), June 24, 1975.
47. *The Oak and the Calf*, p. 85.
48. Ibid., pp. 254–55.
49. The text, incidentally, was not published, and we thus learn that the *samizdat*, too, exercises its own censorship.
50. *The Oak and the Calf*, p. 284.
51. Ibid.
52. The Russians have a saying for this kind of debate: "I give you a quotation and you answer with a footnote." Only the word *ssylka* has a double meaning: footnote and deportation.
53. This is Innokenty's saying in *The First Circle*, p. 436, and Solzhenitsyn says it in *The Oak and the Calf*, p. 296.
54. *From Under the Rubble*, p. 261.
55. *The Oak and the Calf*, p. 327.
56. When Solzhenitsyn describes the Constitutional Democrats or Cadets as

forming "the most dangerous ranks of the revolution" under tsardom, for example, he merely shows his own bias in reaction to official Soviet versions. But when he describes 1933 as one of the years of most active propaganda in favor of equality, he reveals his own ignorance. Two years earlier, in a famous speech, Stalin had insisted on the need for a highly differentiated scale of wages. From then on attacks against egalitarianism gathered strength to reach a climax at the party's seventeenth congress in 1934. See I. Deutscher, *Stalin* (London: Oxford University Press, 1967), pp. 338–40.

57. Egalitarianism, in my opinion, will now become an increasingly vital ingredient in all radical movements of social transformation, both in the East and in the West.

58. *The Oak and the Calf*, p. 68.

59. *The Gulag Archipelago*, pp. 390–91.

60. *From Under the Rubble*, p. 18.

61. For an analysis of its evolution and some examples of its prose see Alexander Yanov, *the Russian New Right* (Berkeley: University of California Press, 1978).

62. Roy Medvedev, *Kniga o sotsialisticheskoy demokratii* (Amsterdam: 1972).

63. For concrete examples see Yanov, *The Russian New Right*, ch. 3.

The Soviet Union: Seeds of Change

1. See Y. Yevtushenko, *A Precocious Autobiography* (London: Collins and Harvill Press, 1963).

2. The most prominent and original among them was undoubtedly Isaac Deutscher. I had the privilege of being his friend and have never concealed my intellectual debt. But neither the friendship nor elements contained in his public and private pronouncements give me the right to claim how his views would have evolved with changing circumstances. I can only remind the reader that even at his most optimistic, Deutscher had an open mind about the possibility of gradual change. See, for example, *The Prophet Outcast* (London and New York: Oxford University Press, 1963), p. 313: "Only experience, in which there may be more surprises than are dreamt of in any philosophy, can provide the answer. At any rate, the present writer prefers to leave the final judgment on Trotsky's idea of a political revolution to a historian of the next generation."

3. A sample of Khrushchev's own contribution can be seen in *Pravda*, January 31, 1937: "Stalin is hope; he is expectation; he is the beacon that guides all progressive mankind. Stalin is our banner! Stalin is our will! Stalin is our victory."

4. Bulganin, Kaganovich, Malenkov, Molotov, Pervukhin, Saburov, and Voroshilov voted against him. Kosygin, Mikoyan, and Suslov probably sided with him.

5. This case, which led to the execution of many Leningraders, headed by politburo member N. Voznesensky, is still shrouded in mystery.

6. At least one-quarter of the members of the all-union central committee and presidium, one-third of the members of central committees of republics and committees of subdivisions of republics (*krays* and *oblasts*), and one-half of the members below that level were to be renewed at each election. This specific provision in the 1961 party statutes (article 25) disappears from party rules at the twenty-third congress in 1966.

7. This is compared with 12.5 percent of total investment between 1918 and 1941; cf. N. Lagutin, *Ekonomicheskaya Gazeta* 50 (December 1977).

8. For an excellent summary and analysis of this debate see Moshe Lewin, *Political Undercurrents in Soviet Economic Debates* (Princeton, N.J.: Princeton University Press, 1974).

9. To stick to the Moldavian connection, Konstantin Chernenko, now a full member of the politburo, was in charge of *agitprop* in Kishinev under Brezhnev; Sergiey Trapeznikov, later chief of the science and education department of the central committee, was head of the party academy there, while Nikolay Shchelokov, future Soviet minister of internal affairs, was deputy prime minister in Moldavia.

10. On his death in April 1976, the ministry was taken over by Dmitri Ustinov who, despite his title of marshal, is a party man, more accurately, the representative of the military-technocratic complex. Born in 1908, Ustinov graduated from Leningrad's Military Engineering Institute. Having worked as an engineer, he was commissar and then minister of the arms industry and subsequently minister of the defense industry. Then for six years he was deputy prime minister and for a couple of years first deputy prime minister dealing with the economy. From 1965 till his appointment as minister of defense he was a member of the party secretariat.

11. See Marx's 1869 introduction to the second German edition of the *18th Brumaire*: "I, on the contrary, demonstrate how the *class struggle* in France created circumstances and relationships that made it possible for a grotesque mediocrity to play a hero's part." In Marx and Engels, *Selected Works*, Vol. I (Moscow: Foreign Languages Publishing House, 1955), p. 244.

12. Data for January 17, 1979, from preliminary population census figures published by the Central Stastistical Office, in *Pravda*, April 22, 1979. Earlier figures from respective yearbooks *Narodnoye Khozyaystvo SSSR* (hereafter *Nar. Khoz.* plus the year).

13. Altogether 42 million hectares of land were reclaimed, of which over 25 million hectares were in Kazakhstan. In that republic production of grain rose about fivefold within a quarter of a century, reaching 28 million tons in 1978. See *Ekonomicheskaya Gazeta* 15 (April, 1979).

14. In 1978 the average *kolkhoz* had 3,700 hectares of land under cultivation; it owned 1,788 heads of cattle; 1,078 pigs; and 1,832 sheep and goats. It averaged 42 tractors; 11 harvesters; and 19 lorries. The comparable figure for a *sovkhoz* were 5,500 hectares; 1,905 cattle; 1,112 pigs; 3,318 sheep and goats; 59 tractors; 18 harvester; and 27 lorries. *Nar. Khoz.*, 1978.

15. See A. Kochetkov, *Sotsialno-ekonomicheskyie aspekty gradostroitelsva* (Socialeconomic Aspects of Townbuilding), in *Voprosy Ekonomiki* 10 (1975).

16. "Allow me to congratulate you on being the vanguard of a non-existing class," Shlyapnikov retorted sarcastically to Lenin at the eleventh party congress in 1922, the latter having accused the Workers' Opposition of speaking in the name of an imaginary, nonexisting proletariat.

17. "According to sociological surveys carried out during the ninth Five-Year Plan (1970–1975), in Chelyabinsk, Ufa, and Moscow, 55 to 60 percent of newcomers into the working class is recruited from working-class families." M. Rutkevich, *Dvizhenye sovietskovo naroda k sotsialnoy odnorodnosti* (The Rise of the Soviet People to Social Homogeneity), *Kommunist* 7 (May 1977).

18. The following data is taken from *Nar. Khoz.*, 1978 and relevant years.

19. P. D. Pavlenok, *Formirovanye i razvitye sotsialno-klasovoy struktury sotsialisticheskovo obshchestva* (Formation and Development of the Social Class Structure in a Socialist Society), Moscow University, 1978.

20. For a good summary and analysis of Soviet writing on the subject see Murray Yanovitch, *Social and Economic Inequality in the Soviet Union* (White Plains, N.Y.: M. E. Sharpe, 1977).

21. In the statistical yearbook 1977 compare employment in industry (p. 129) and number of specialists by branch (p. 394).

22. V. S. Semenov in F. V. Konstantinov, ed., *Stroitelstvo kommunizma i razvitye obshchestvennykh otnoshenii* (Moscow, 1966); quoted in M. Matthews, *Class and Society in Soviet Russia* (London: Allen Lane, 1972). For figures from population census see *Nar. Khoz.*, 1960, or *Pravda*, February 4, 1960.

23. M. Rutkevich, *Sotsialnaya struktura razvitovo sotsialisticheskovo obshchestva* (Social Structure of a Developed Socialist Society), *Kommunist* 2 (January 1974).

24. This idea is developed by Istvan Meszaros in *Il Manifesto: Power and Opposition in Post-Revolutionary Societies* (London: Ink Links, 1979).

25. E. Kapustin, *Ekonomicheski aspekt sotsialisticheskovo obraza zhizni* (The Economic Aspect of the Socialist Image of Life), *Voprosy Ekonomiki* 6 (1975).

26. Naturally I am not suggesting that Trotsky ignored the difference between nationalized and socialized property or that latter-day Trotskyists are backing Stalinist diehards.

27. F. A. Vodolazsky, *Vysshyi princip partiinovo rukovodstva* (The Higher Principle of Party Leadership), *Kommunist* 12 (August 1979).

28. For Zinoviev see particularly *The Yawning Heights* (New York: Random House, 1979). See also G. Konrad and I. Szelenyi, *The Road of the Intellectuals to Class Power* (New York: Harcourt, Brace, Jovanovich, 1979); Rudolf Bahro, *The Alternative in Eastern Europe* (London: New Left Books, 1978).

29. He was released in 1979 and at once expelled to the Federal Republic of Germany.

30. Admittedly there are graduates and graduates and some party bosses obtain their degrees in peculiar fashion.

31. The Academy of Social Sciences and the Party Higher School run by the party's central committee in Moscow and similar institutions at the level of the republics.

32. Lewin, *Political Undercurrents in Soviet Economic Debates*.

33. For the text of the measures, see *Ekonomicheskaya Gazeta* 32 (August 1979).

34. "One of the reasons for the high proportion of manual work is that about half the people freed in an enterprise through mechanization do not leave that enterprise, but move to another shop, to auxiliary work, etc." P. Khromov, *Zakon rosta proizvoditelnosti truda v uslovyakh razvitovo sotsialisma*, *Voprosy Ekonomiki* 7 (1975), hereafter *Vop. Ek.* On hoarding of labor, high share of manual work and effect on productivity see also D. Karpuhkin, *Istochnik obshchestvennovo bogatstva*, *Vop. Ek.* 2 (1979) and V. Moskvich and V. Ananyev, *Professionalno-kvalfikatsyonnaya struktura rabochykh*, *Vop Ek.* 6 (1979).

35. A host of younger economists followed in the footsteps of such better known figures as V. Nemchinov, V. Novozhilov, or L. Kantorovich.

36. It is claimed that between 1960 and 1975 national income rose by 160 percent and Soviet exports by 380 percent. See Yu. Vorobiev, T. Checheleva, *Ekonomika SSSR—yedynyi narodno-khozyastviennyi kompleks*, *Vop. Ek.* 3 (1979).

37. Here and in what follows the trade figures for 1979 are taken from *Ekonomicheskaya Gazeta* 13 (March 1980).

38. For petroleum and petroleum products the reference period has since been shortened.

39. Preliminary report on January 1979 census is in *Pravda*, April 22, 1979.

40. To take the most striking example, already in 1959, according to census data, Russians accounted for 43.1 percent of the population of the Kazakh SSR and Kazakhs for only 29.6 percent. See *Pravda*, February 4, 1960.

41. If between 1959 and 1970 rural population declined by 3 percent, over the same period the number of people aged 20–24 living in the countryside dropped by 45 percent; aged 25–29 by 43 percent; aged 30–34 by 11 percent. See V. N. Yakimov, *Tekhnicheski progress i vosproizvodstvo rabochey sily v kolkhozakh*, *Ekonomika*, 1976.

42. Quoted in L. Sytova, *Istochniki rabochey sily*, *Vop. Ek.* 6 (1978).

43. For background on free trade unions see the collection of documents edited by V. Haynes and O. Semyonova, *Syndicalisme et liberté en Union Soviétique* (Paris: Maspero, 1979).

44. Rosa Luxemburg, *The Russian Revolution* (Ann Arbor: University of Michigan, 1961).

45. For examples, see Alexander Yanov, *The Russian New Right* (Berkeley: University of California Press, 1978).

Poland: The Workers Enter the Stage

1. In the following section I have drawn on the recorded recollections of philosopher and historian Krzysztof Pomian, who was a youthful actor, then a witness and a victim of the events. I hope he will expand them to provide a valuable history of the period. I am the more grateful for his contribution since our ideological premises are now well apart. It goes without saying that he bears no responsibility whatsoever for the ideas contained in this book.

2. In so doing they very often abandoned their original ideals. Thus twenty years later one of the best known among them, Leszek Kolakowski, likened the very idea of nontotalitarian communism to "boiling ice." See his piece in P. Kende and K. Pomian, eds., *1956 Varsovie-Budapest* (Paris: Seuil, 1978).

3. Jacek Kuron and Karol Modzelewski, *An Open Letter to the Party Leaders* (London: Pluto Press, n.d.), published in the United States in the journal *New Politics* 5, nos. 2 and 3.

4. "In practice the workers' self-government council has very limited possibilities to control the manager, whereas he has every possibility to inspire the council and influence its decisions." H. Najduchowska, in Jan Szczepanski, *Przemysl i Spoleczenstwo w Polsce Ludowej* (Industry and Society in People's Poland) (Ossolineum: Polish Academy of Sciences, 1969).

5. Certainly the current leadership cannot, since it has promoted into the politburo Mr. Andrzej Werblan, one of the main preachers of ethnic purity at the time.

6. This is an allusion to a prewar Polish joke: "It's all the fault of the Jews and the cyclists. . . . Why the cyclists? Why the Jews?"

7. For the description of the events of that winter I have drawn on newspapers and journals published in Poland, particularly *Glos Wybrzeza*, December 18, 1970, and on two books of documents and commentaries published in Paris by the Institut Literacki: *Poznan 1956-Grudzien 1970* and *Rewolta Szczecinska i jej Znaczenie*, both issued in 1971.

8. Poland was then divided into seventeen regions or *voivodships*. This administrative division applied also to party institutions. The PCP thus had *voivodship* committees in such regional capitals as Gdansk or Szczecin. A reform in 1975 raised the number of regions from seventeen to forty-nine.

9. Gdansk with 376,000 inhabitants was sixth, while Gdynia had 195,000 and Sopot 47,000 people. The agglomeration thus had 618,000 inhabitants at the time of the events.

10. In addition to sources quoted, see B. Sulik, "The Workers," in the Paris

journal *Kultura* 10 (1976). Sulik is the author of "Three Days in Szczecin," a BBC film reconstructing the January 1971 strike.

11. In the pages that follow I am using the Polish transcript of the nine hours of tape published in *Rewolta Szczecinska* cited above. Extracts were published in English as a document in *New Left Review* 72 (March-April, 1972).

12. 1 zloty = $.03; there are about 30 zlotys in $1.00.

13. Bogdan Golaszewski, who had led the workers from the tube section out on strike, was found dead, gassed in his bachelor apartment on August 10, 1971. Some time later, Adam Ulfik, one of the leaders of the strike committee, was attacked at home by two strangers who opened the gas and left him chloroformed on the floor. He just managed to awaken in time. See Sulik, in *Kultura*.

14. See the example described in the Polish underground paper *Robotnik* included in a collection of documents prefaced by K. Pomian, *La renaissance du movement ouvrier* (Paris: International Committee Against the Repression, 1979).

15. The intelligentsia was already mobilized, in a sense, by the campaign launched the previous autumn against two articles of the proposed new Polish constitution, one stressing "the leading role of the Polish United Workers' Party" (i.e., the PCP) and the second providing, equally constitutionally, that Poland is a member of the "world socialist system" tied by "a fraternal and unbreakable link with the Soviet Union." Petitions protesting against such principles being written into the constitution were signed by tens of thousands.

16. KOR's membership subsequently grew. It can be roughly divided into an older generation of prewar socialists (mostly members of the Polish Socialist Party or PPS) and a new generation led by students active in the 1960s, like Adam Michnik. For the activity and translated texts of KOR see also an earlier publication of the International Committee Against the Repression, *Documents du Comité de Defense des Ouvriers de Pologne* (Paris, 1977).

17. The trial in June 1980 of Miroslaw Chojecki, head of the *samizdat* publication *Nova*, showed how difficult a task open, unofficial publishing is in Poland. But it also revealed that the authorities must now take precautions when dealing with fairly prominent dissidents.

18. In 1978 private farming accounted for 77 percent of global production and 76 percent of land utilization. See *Maly Rocznik Statystyczny*, 1979.

19. Quoted in the chapter on transformation of the peasants as a class in W. Wesolowski, ed., *Ksztalt Struktury Spolecznej* (Ossolineum: Polish Academy of Sciences, 1978).

20. The share of farms of more than 10 hectares went up from around 12 percent of the total in 1960 to less than 14 percent in 1977. Latest figures in *Maly Rocznik Statystyczny*, 1979.

21. This point is made in several texts by members of KOR and developed in an unpublished letter to Gierek by the former activist K. Modzelewski.

Conclusion: Ex Occidente Lux?

1. For Stalin's eastern leaning see I. Deutscher, *Stalin* (London and New York: Oxford University Press, 1966), pp. 206–10.

Postscript: Third Act in Poland

1. According to Kuron the government did not stop them earlier because (a) it knew it could not prevent them from spreading information altogether and thus (b) it was learning what was happening and what the strikers intended to do.

2. This platform included the following: "To abolish commercial prices; to unify prices for all social groups, including the state apparatus" (Article 1); "to raise family allowances to the level of the militia and the army" (Article 3); to inform sincerely and truly about the situation in our country . . . to guarantee the freedom of the press" (Article 13); "to abolish shops for privileged social groups" (Article 14); and "to enable the purchase in zlotys of goods hitherto available only in *pewex* shops" (Article 16).

3. In conversation with Czeslaw Niezgoda he talked of those practicing Catholics who did not belong to the party as second-rate citizens in Poland and clearly included himself among them. Stanislaw Daniel talked of the socialist regime for which "we or our fathers have fought" and sounded like a (former?) party member. Such views do not prevent them from collaborating as chairperson and deputy chairperson of the presidium of the founding committee of the Lublin regional union. Solidarity has members with all sorts of backgrounds.

4. The committee cannot be described as "underground," since it acted openly and published its paper, *The Worker of the Coast*. But it was continually persecuted. The Gwiazdas, Kolodziej, Pienkowska, Przybylski, Walentynowicz, Walesa—most of the leaders of the strike committee had a connection with the "free unions."

5. Many party members were active, even prominent, in the strike movement. Whereas in 1970 they had participated only in the first phase and dropped out when it became obvious that the movement clashed with the party, not merely with a given leadership, this time they stayed throughout. Some claim they no longer care about changing the party.

6. The KOR reported a case of repression that took place on July 31, in which the police arrested an electrician, ex-member of the Gdansk strike committee and member of the free unions. The security police picked him up as he was pushing his baby in a pram, leaving baby and pram in front of his apartment. Nobody was there as his wife was giving birth to a fifth child. The reader will have guessed that the unknown thirty-seven-year-old electrician

was Lech Walesa, whose face was soon to be splashed on the front page of newspapers throughout the world. As usual, the mass media magnified the leader so that the public did not know that Walesa was very much part of an efficient team. This does not alter the fact that he was also one of those born leaders, sensing the mood of the crowd and knowing how to express it, with an uncanny instinct for how far one can afford to go.

7. The average Polish wage at the time was around 4000 zlotys a month. Workers in the shipyards often earned more with overtime, but nurses got only about 2500 zlotys a month.

8. In private conversation Walesa claimed that he did it all consciously, as this was the only way to get rid of the original strike committee, in which the management had succeeded in planting its own people.

9. The chairperson, Mazowiecki, Bogdan Cywinski, and Andrzej Wielowieyski belong to the first category; Geremek, the economists Tadeusz Kowalik and Waldemar Kuczynski, as well as Jadwiga Staniszkis, the sociologist, to the second.

10. The Catholic church subsequently protested that the extracts from his sermon were chosen in a biased way, which is true, but the full text, published in *Slowo Powszechne* on August 29, 1980, was also pleading for compromise.

11. For a vivid description, see Bernard Guetta, *"J'accepte, je signe!"* in *Le Monde*, 2 September 1980.

12. The twenty-one points, in brief, are as follows. Point 1 sets up new, independent, self-governing trade unions which will be the representatives of the working class. Point 2 "guarantees the right to strike," while Point 3 provides for "the freedom of expression and publication." Point 4 ensures redress for victims of repression, while Point 5 insists the country must be informed fairly about the MKS and its demands. Point 6 states that the debate over economic reform should be general and public. Point 7 deals with strike pay, Point 8 with proposed increases in wages, and Point 9 with the establishment of a sliding scale for wages. Points 10, 11, and 12 set out provisions for improvement in food supplies, the abolition of commercial and *pewex* shops, and the provisional reintroduction of meat rationing. Point 13 tackles the privileges of the police and the apparatus. Points 14, 15, and 16 cover old-age pensions and the health services. Points 17 and 18 deal with kindergartens for working women and better paid maternity leave. Point 19, 20 and 21 deal with housing, work distant from home, and Saturday as a rest day.

13. The mass meetings during the Pope's visit, with the police out of the way, gave many Poles the feeling that they could run things on their own. The visit, I was told, thus helped precipitate events.

14. Another aspect of the movement which merits further analysis is its youth. Take the two vice-presidents of the Gdansk MKS: Bogdan Lis was twenty-eight, Andrzej Kolodziej, from the Paris Commune Shipyards, not quite twenty-one. During the first nights of the sit-in strike those who stayed on guard were almost exclusively the young, partly because they braved the cold, largely

because they were less frightened. Generally, the workers from this new generation have a secondary or technical education and cannot easily be distinguished from the technicians. Somebody should do a study of Poland's "new working class."

15. Actually the demands of the nurses look more impressive in the agreement than the rest. This is partly accidental. In the final rush to produce the document, the appendices to Point 16, concerned with the health services, were by mistake typed into the main text.

16. When Adam Michnik writes, "The workers fought for the rights and interests of the whole society" (*Biuletyn Informacyjny*, August-September 1980), I wonder whether he is echoing Marx consciously.

17. An influential role was played on this occasion by Karol Modzelewski, driven by recent events not to devote all his time to medieval history. But as he points out, his scheme can hardly be described as highly "centralistic" since the proposed national commission is a conciliatory body which cannot impose its will upon a reluctant minority. The real point debated was whether the union should be all-national.

Index